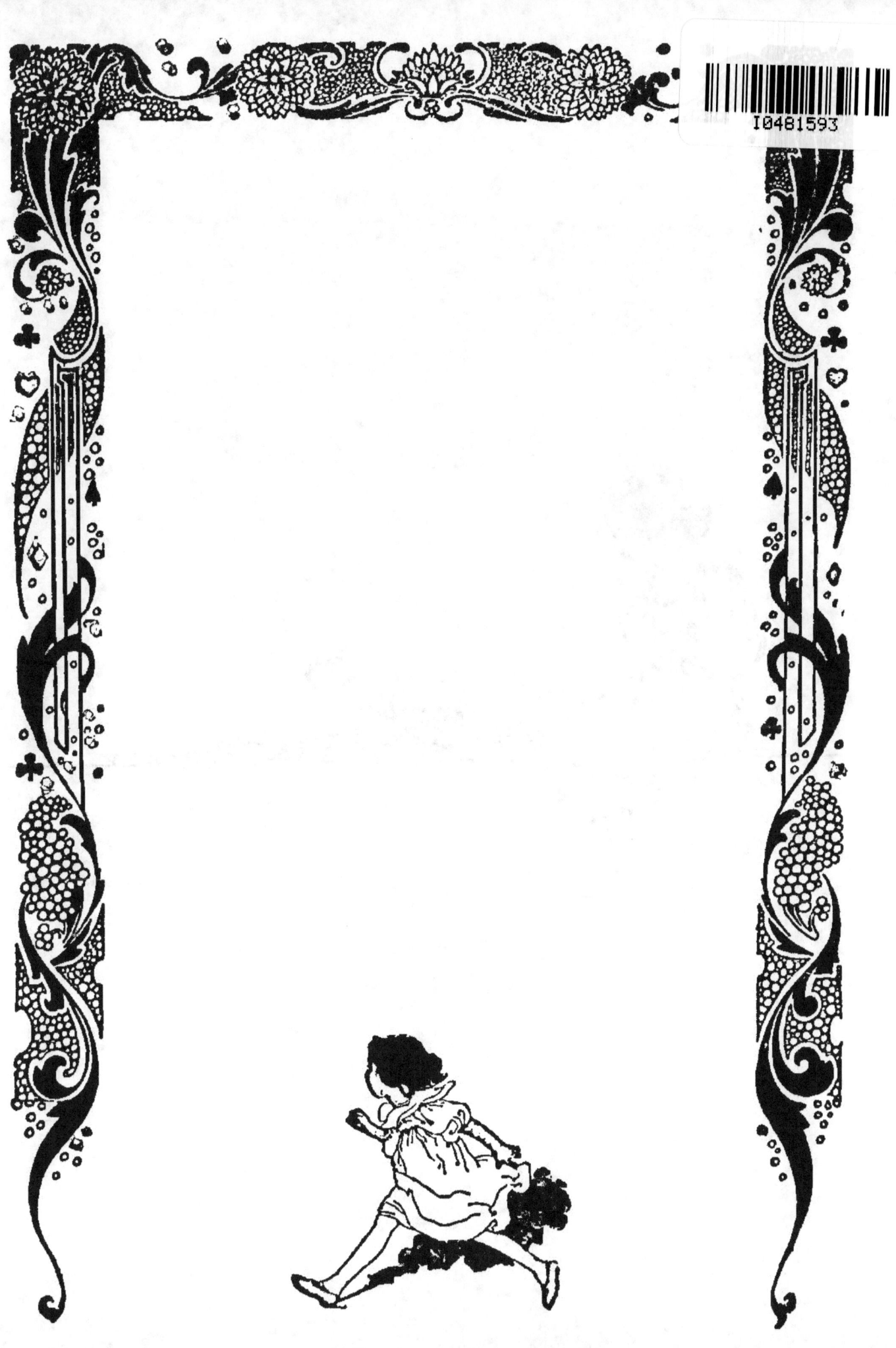

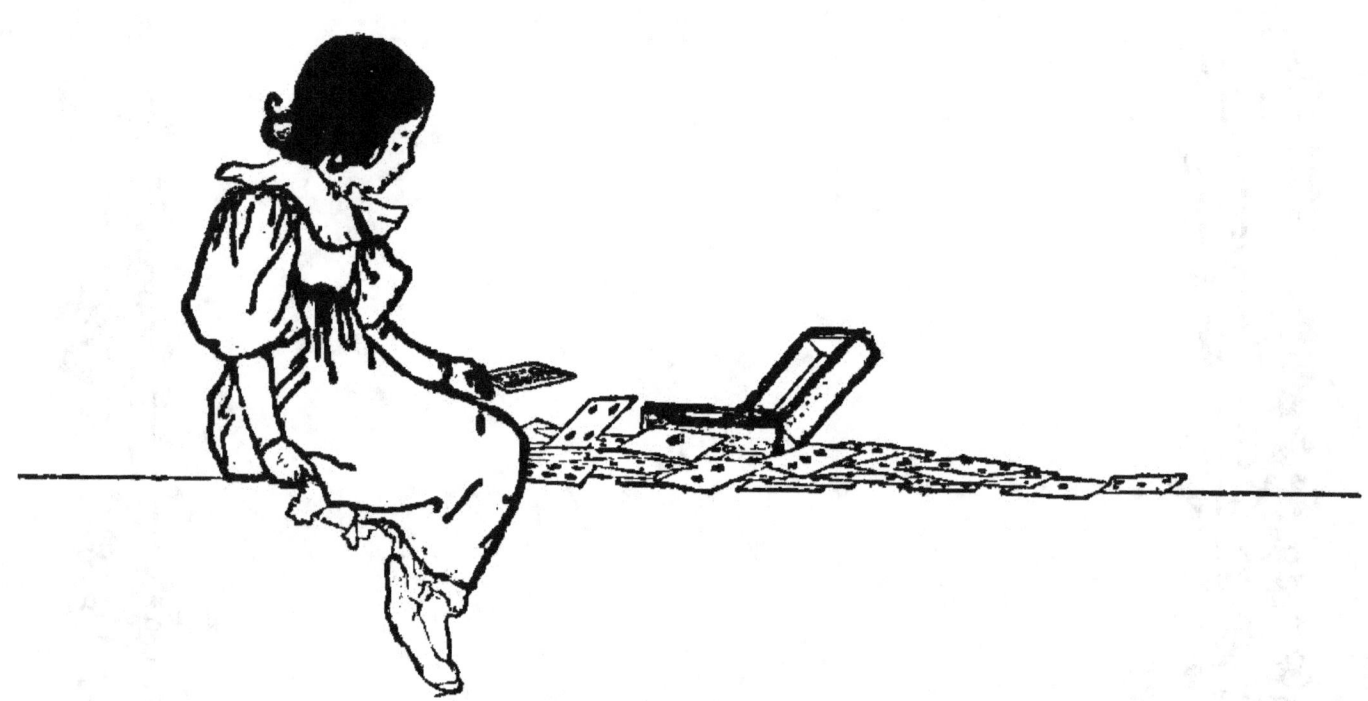

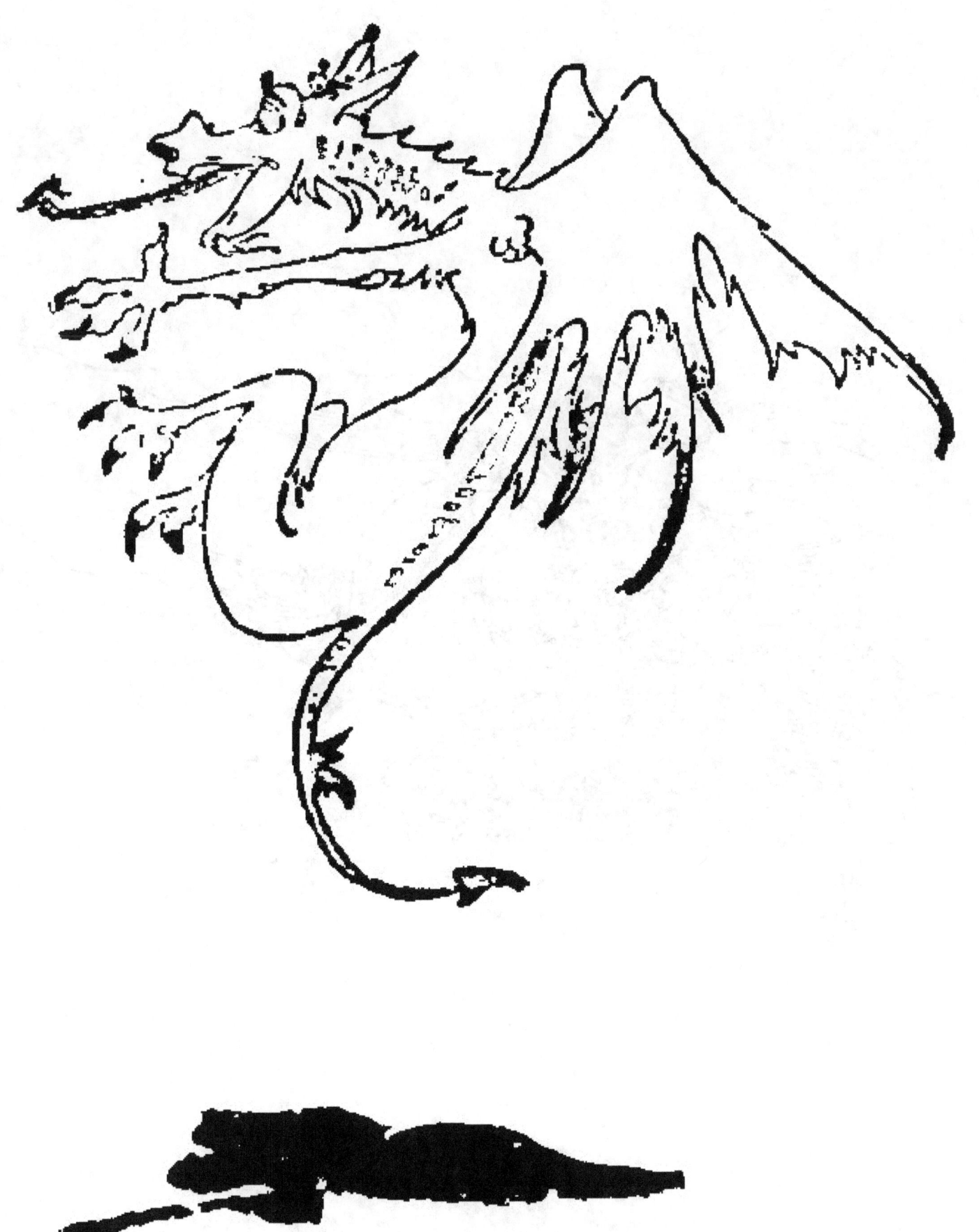

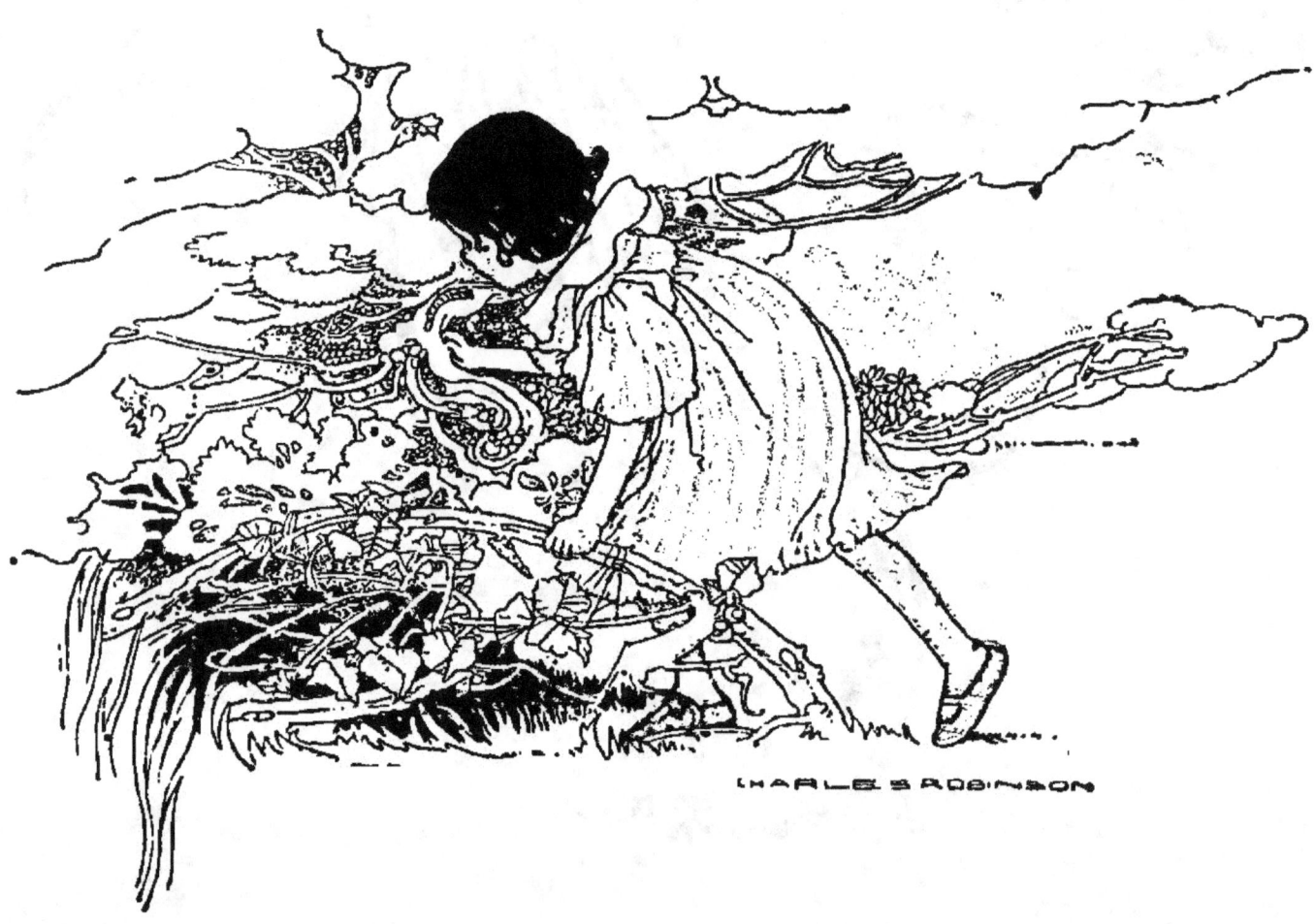

CHARLES ROBINSON

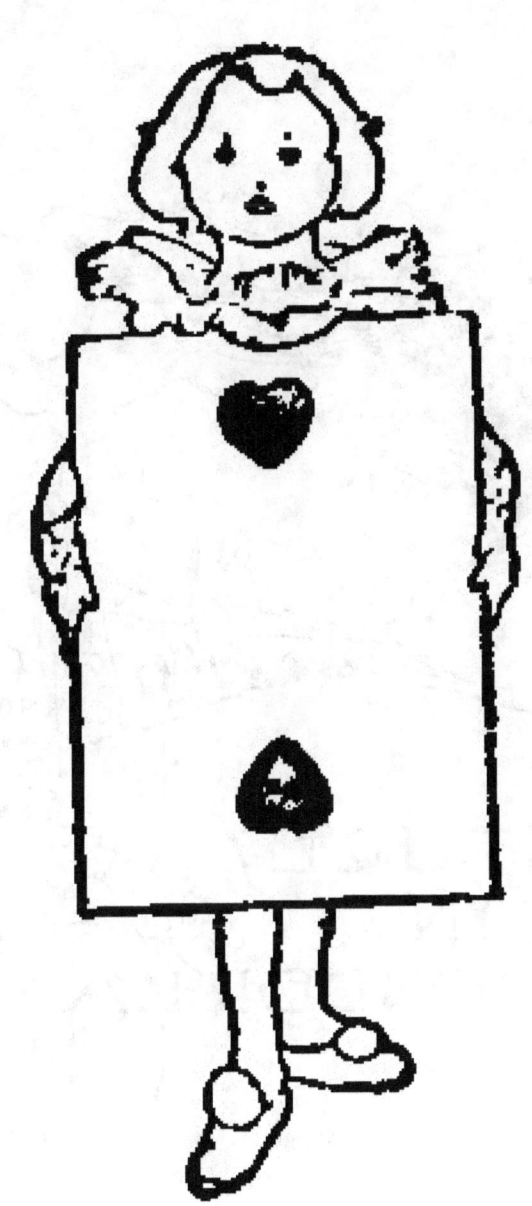

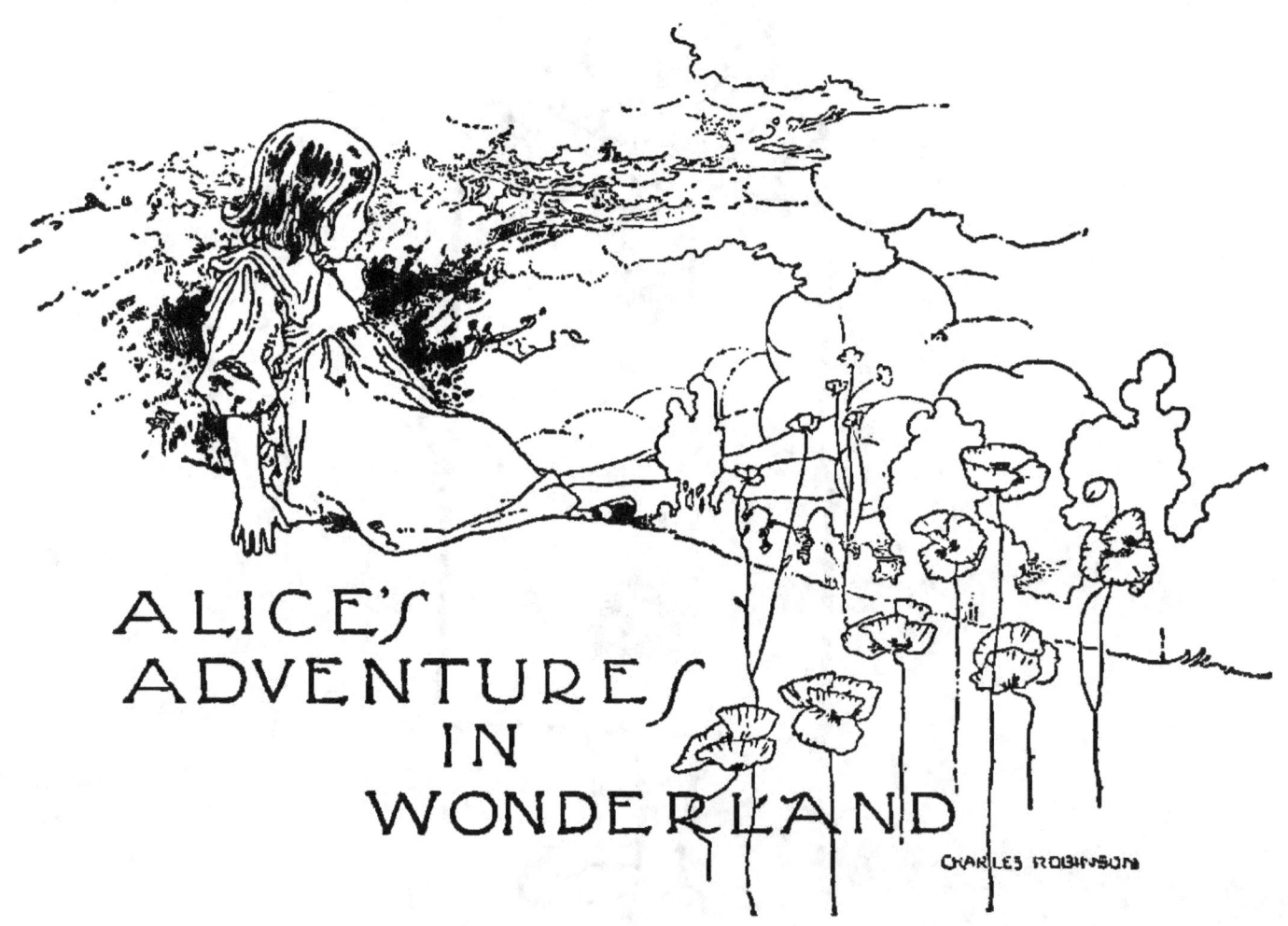

ALICE'S ADVENTURES IN WONDERLAND

CHARLES ROBINSON

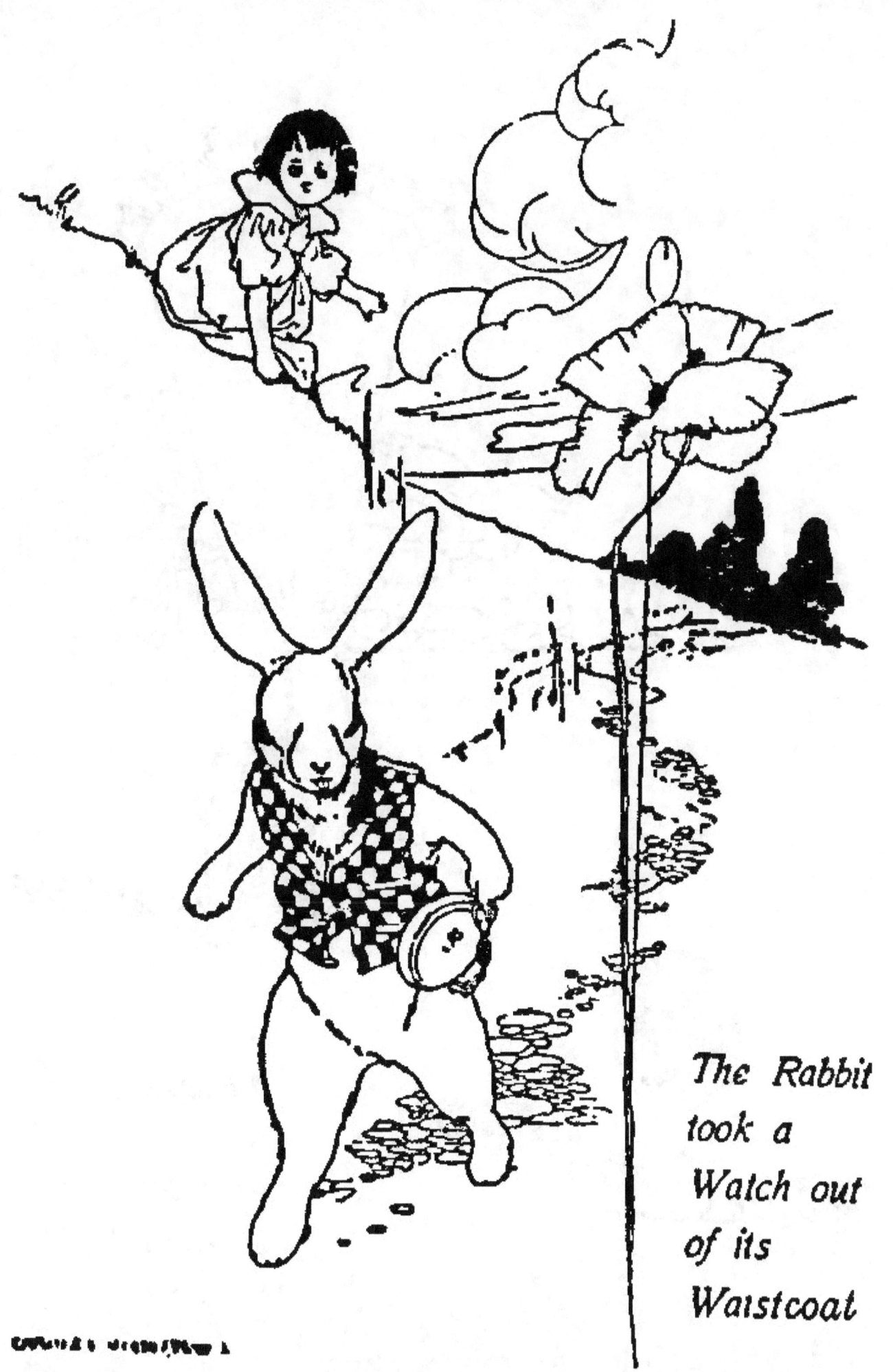

The Rabbit took a Watch out of its Waistcoat

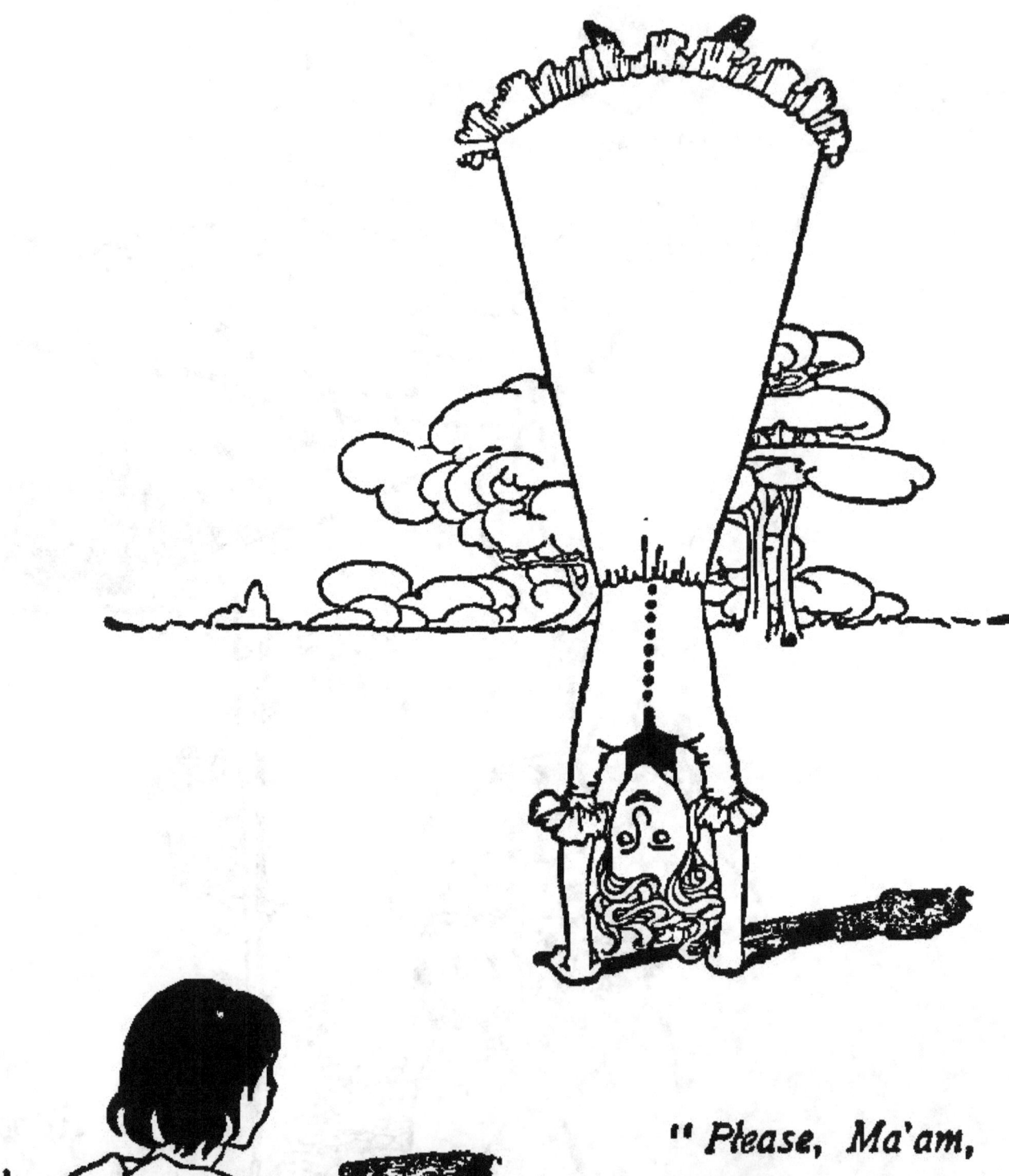

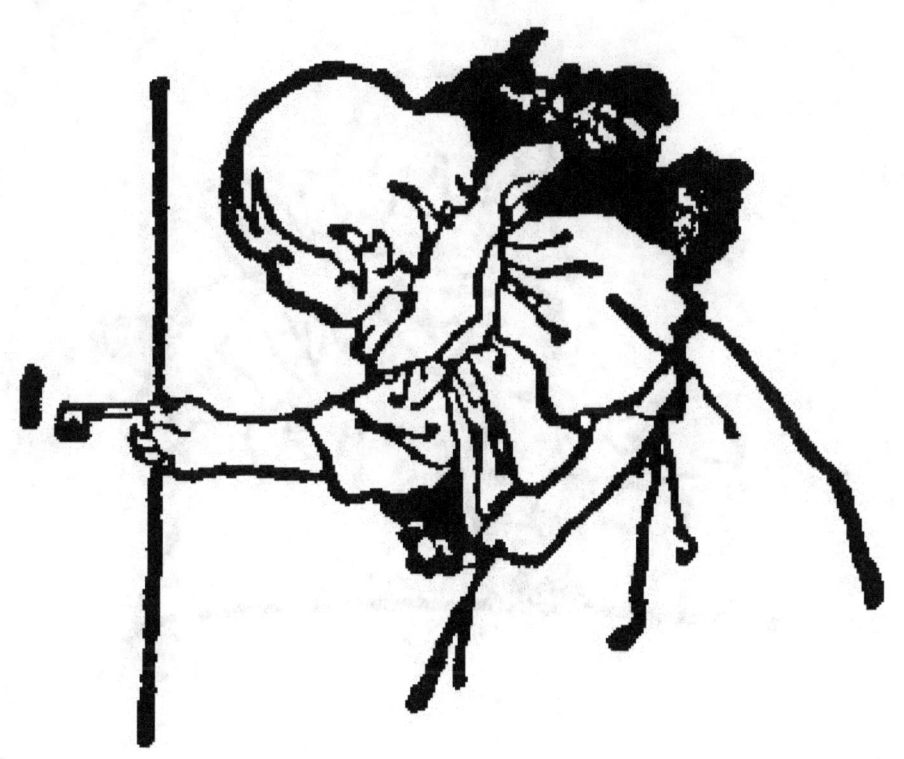

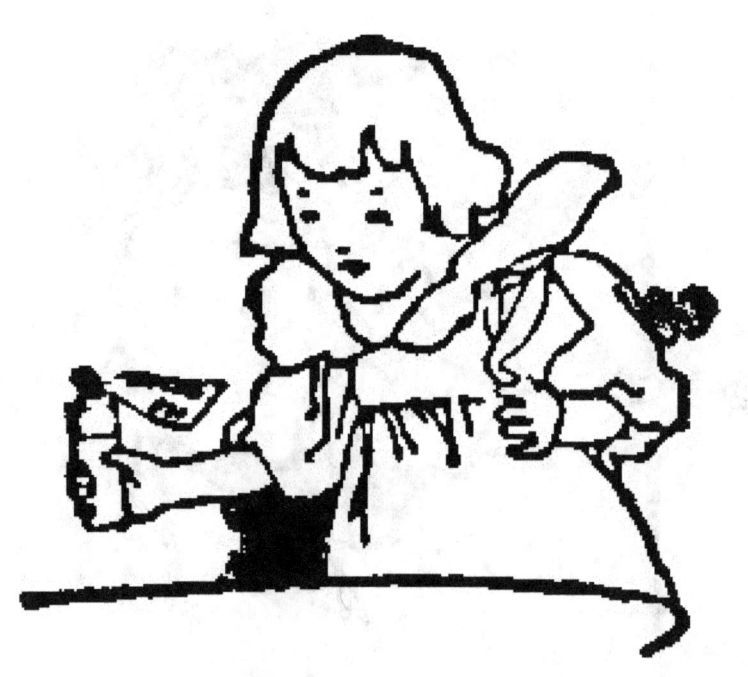

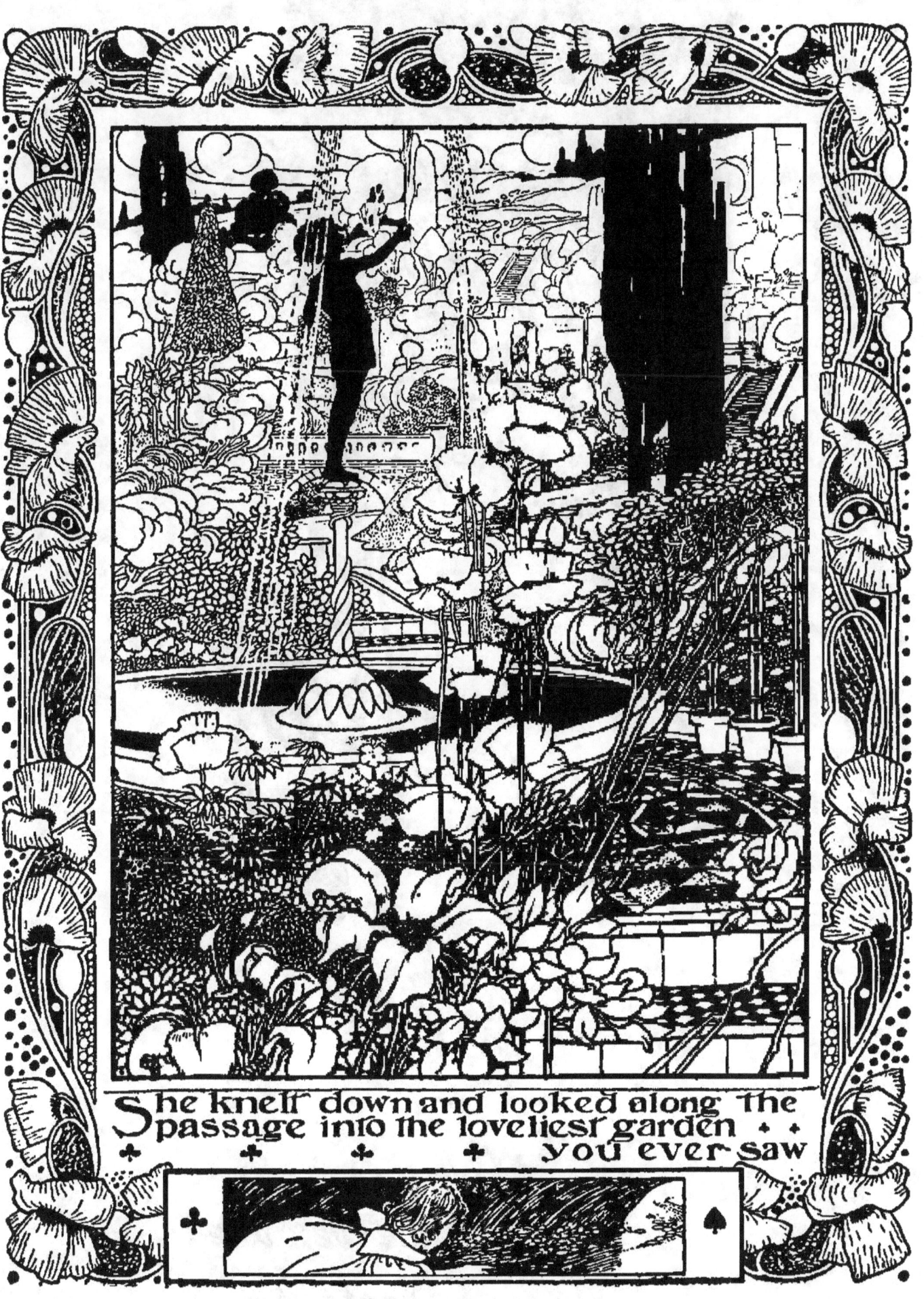

She knelt down and looked along the passage into the loveliest garden you ever saw

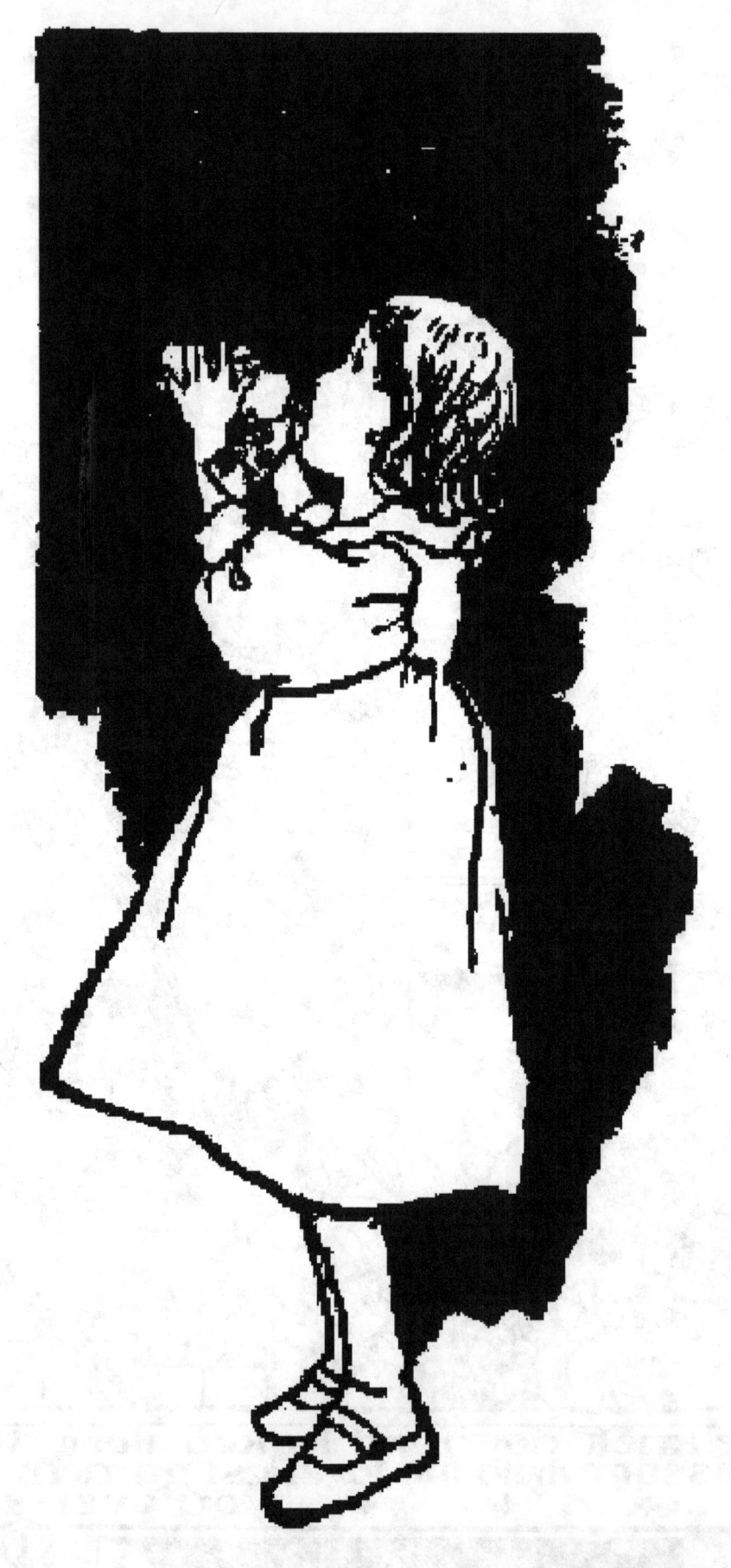

*Alice ventured
to taste it.*

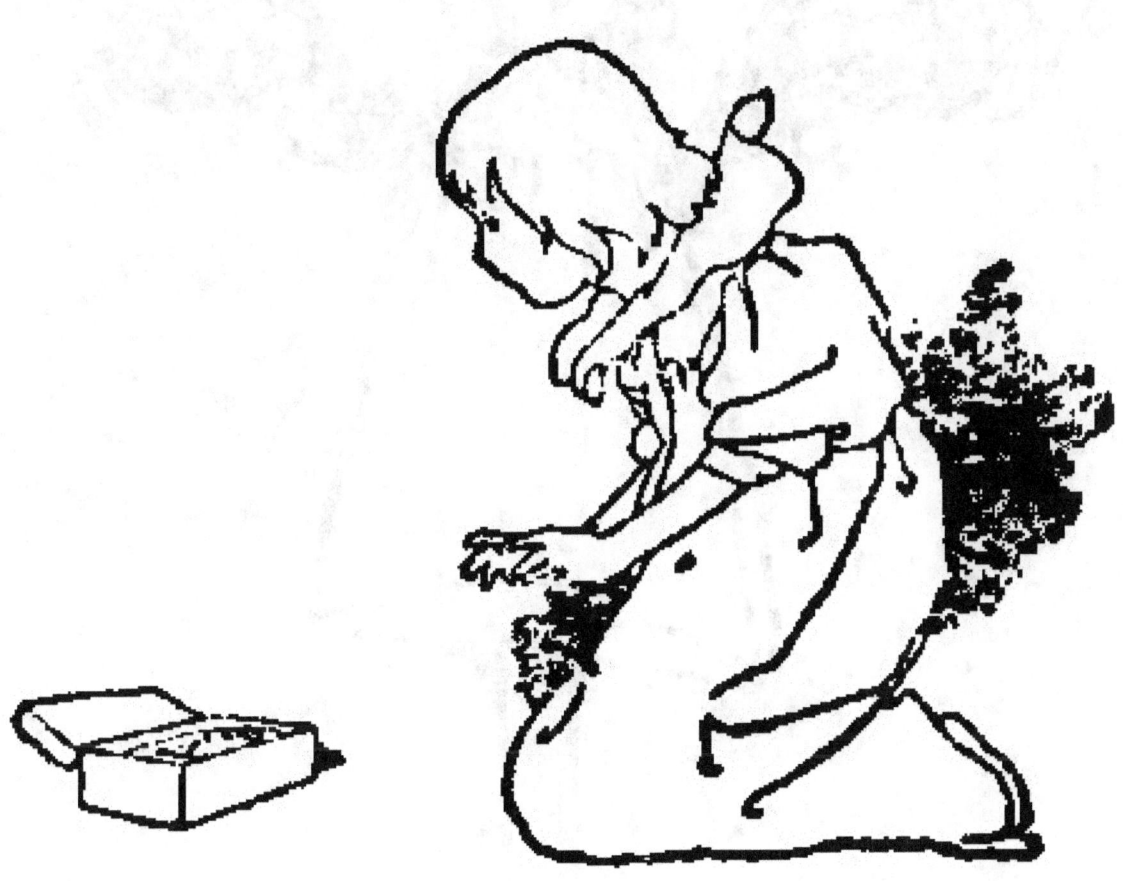

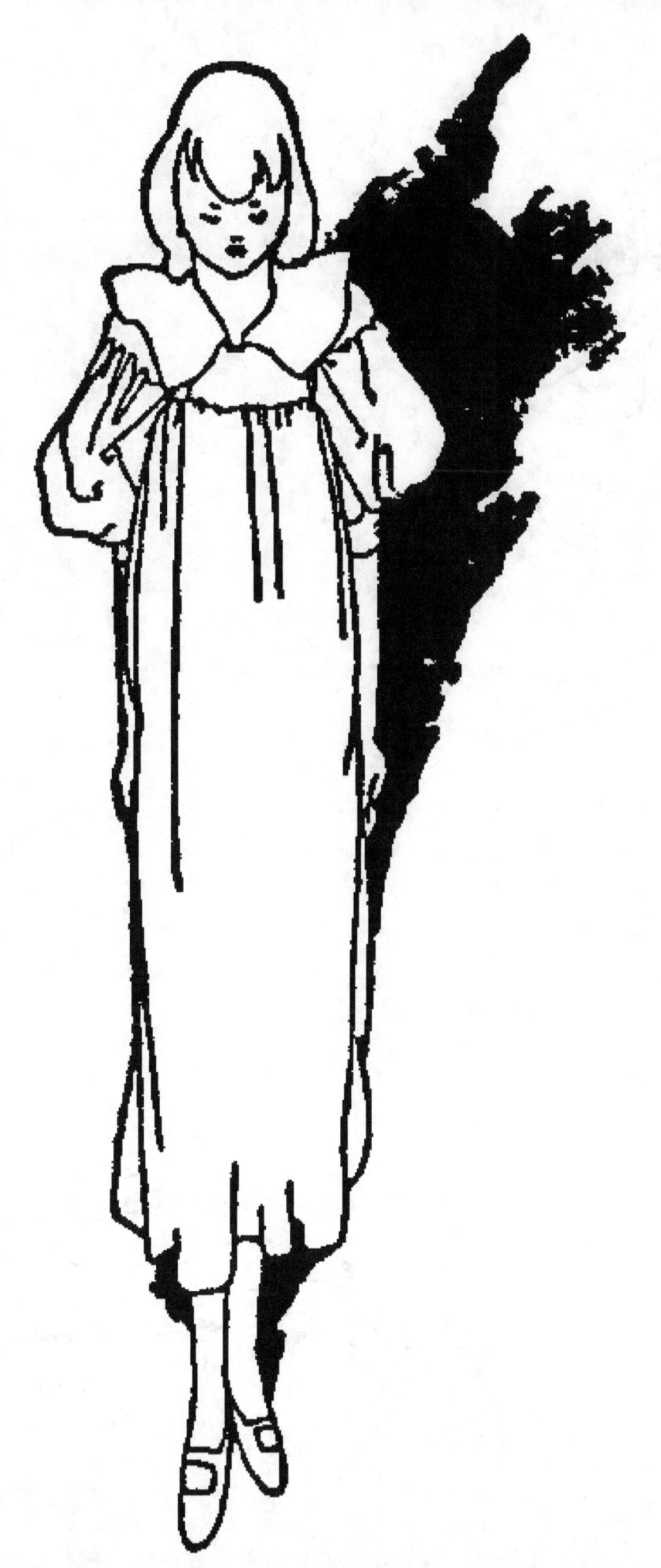

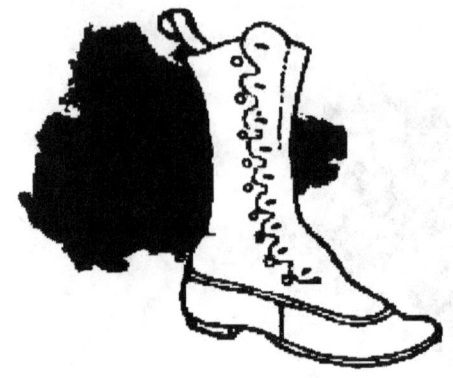

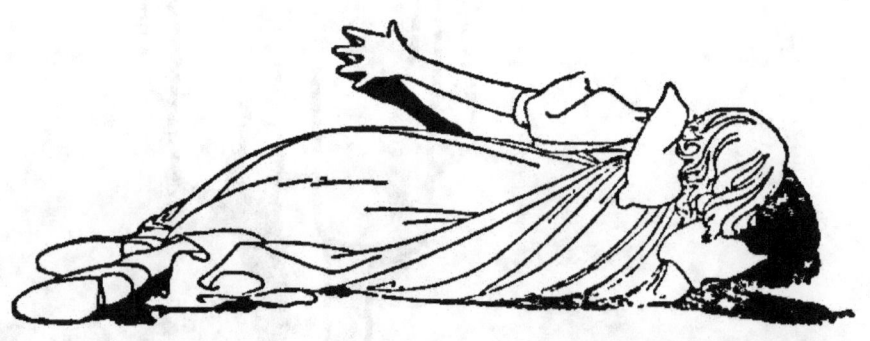

It was as much as she could do . . to look through.

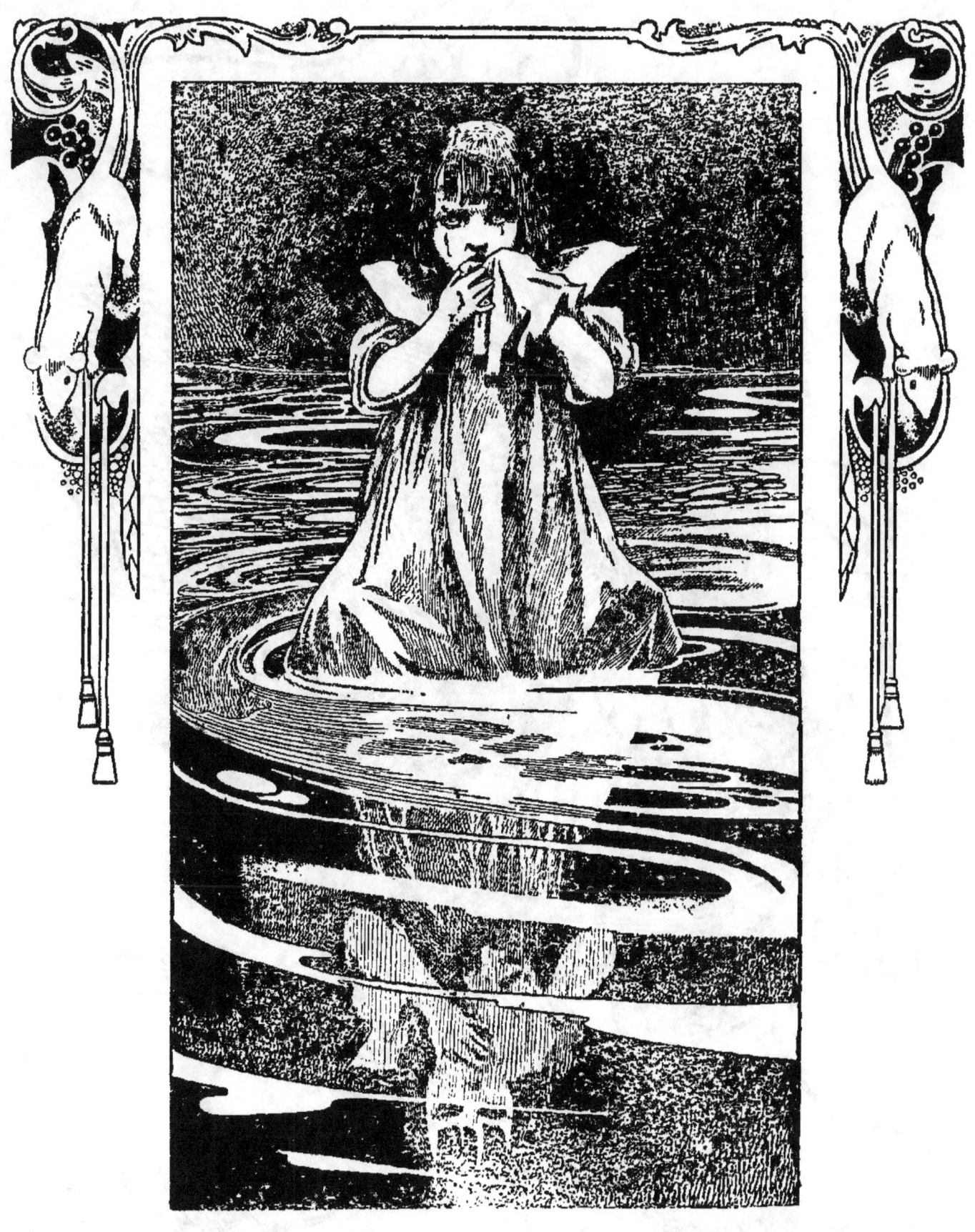

There was a large pool all around her about four inches deep and reaching half down the hall

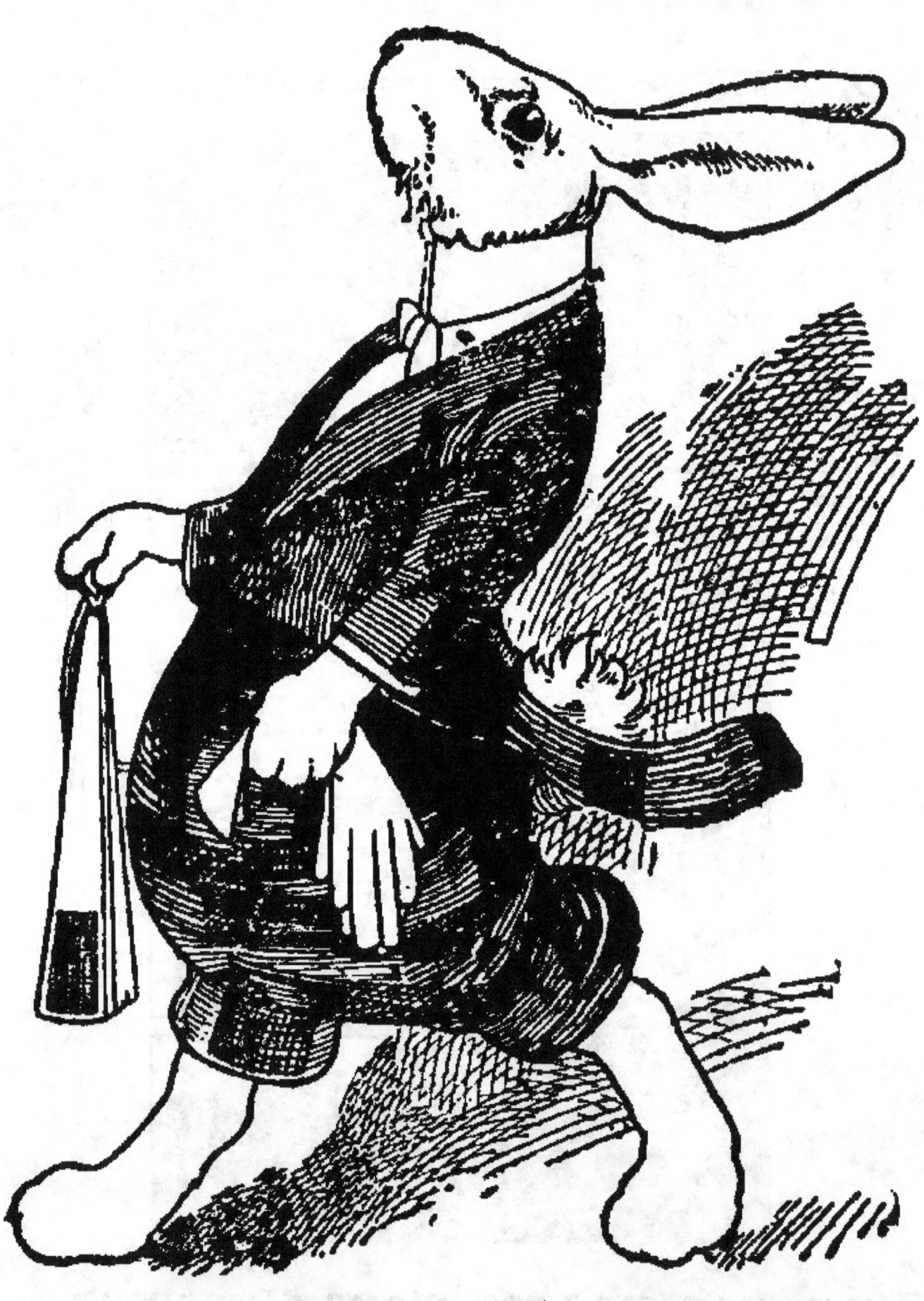

It was the White Rabbit returning splendidly dressed.

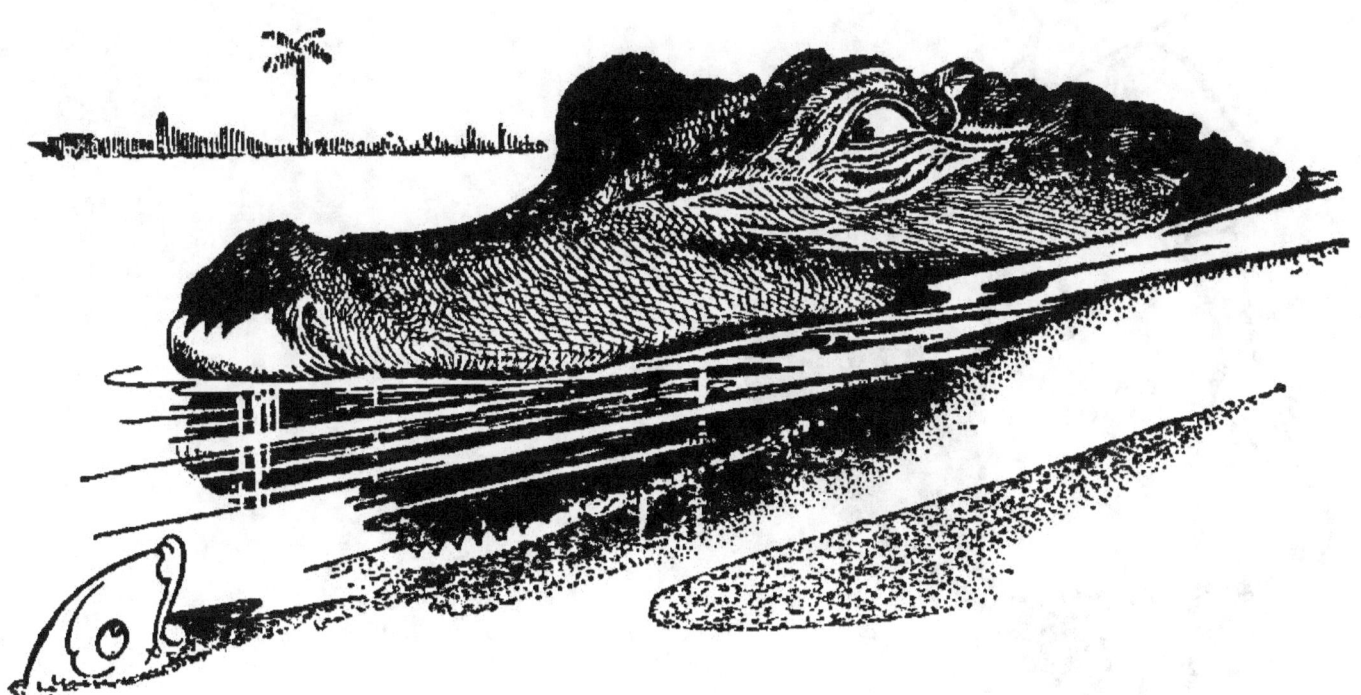

" And welcomes little fishes in,
    With gently smiling jaws!"

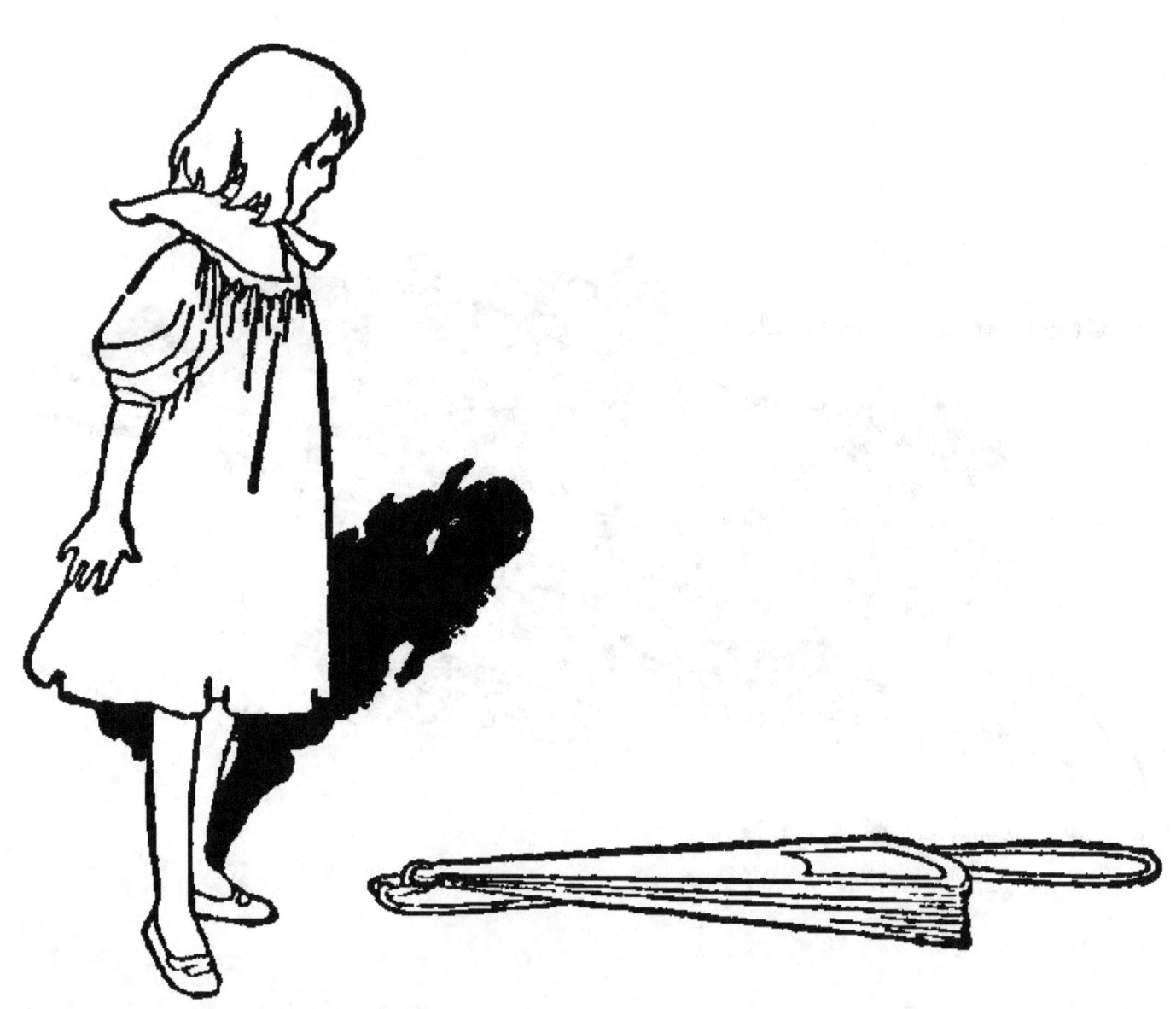

She dropped it hastily.

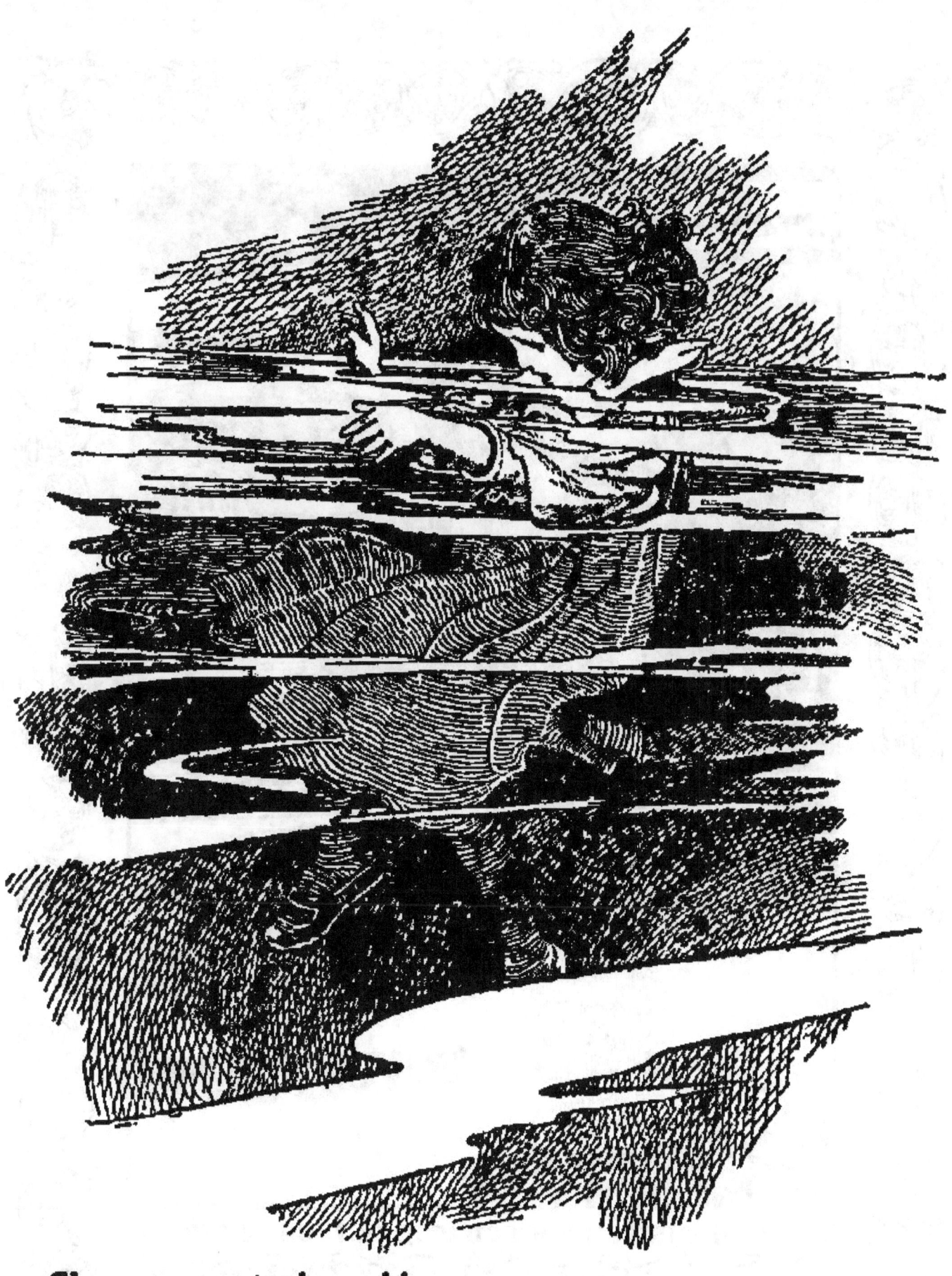

She was up to her chin in salt water.

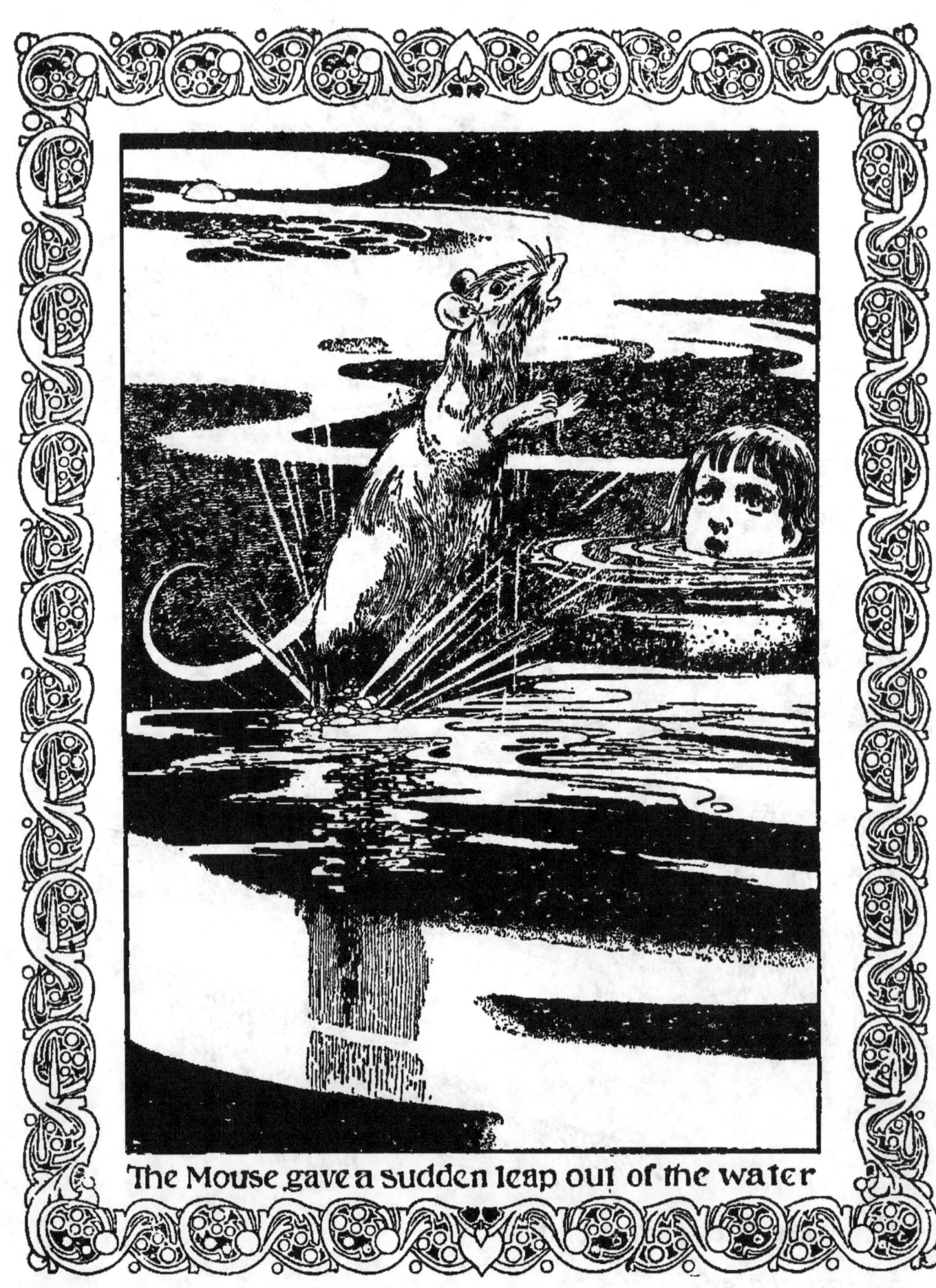

The Mouse gave a sudden leap out of the water

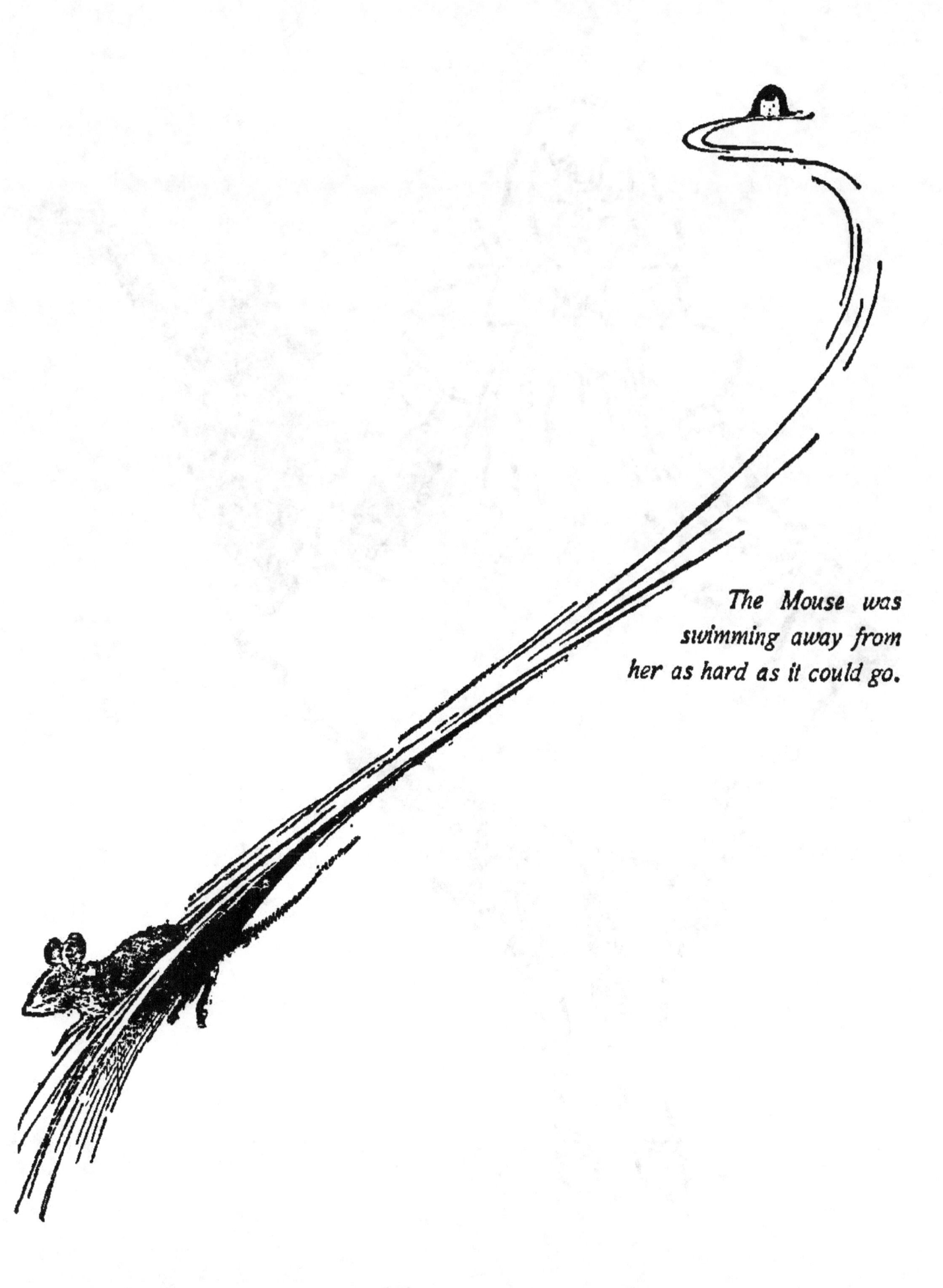

The Mouse was
swimming away from
her as hard as it could go.

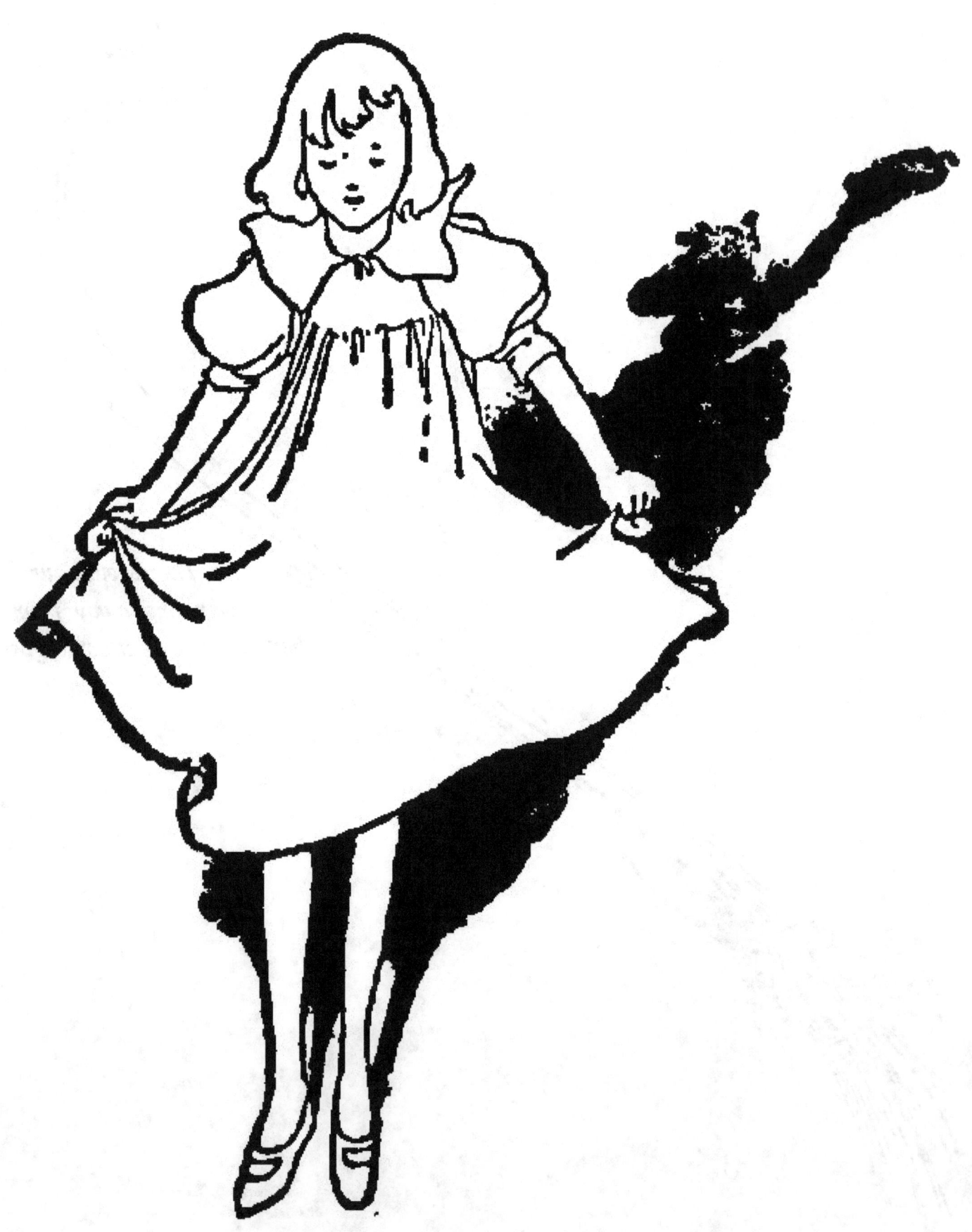

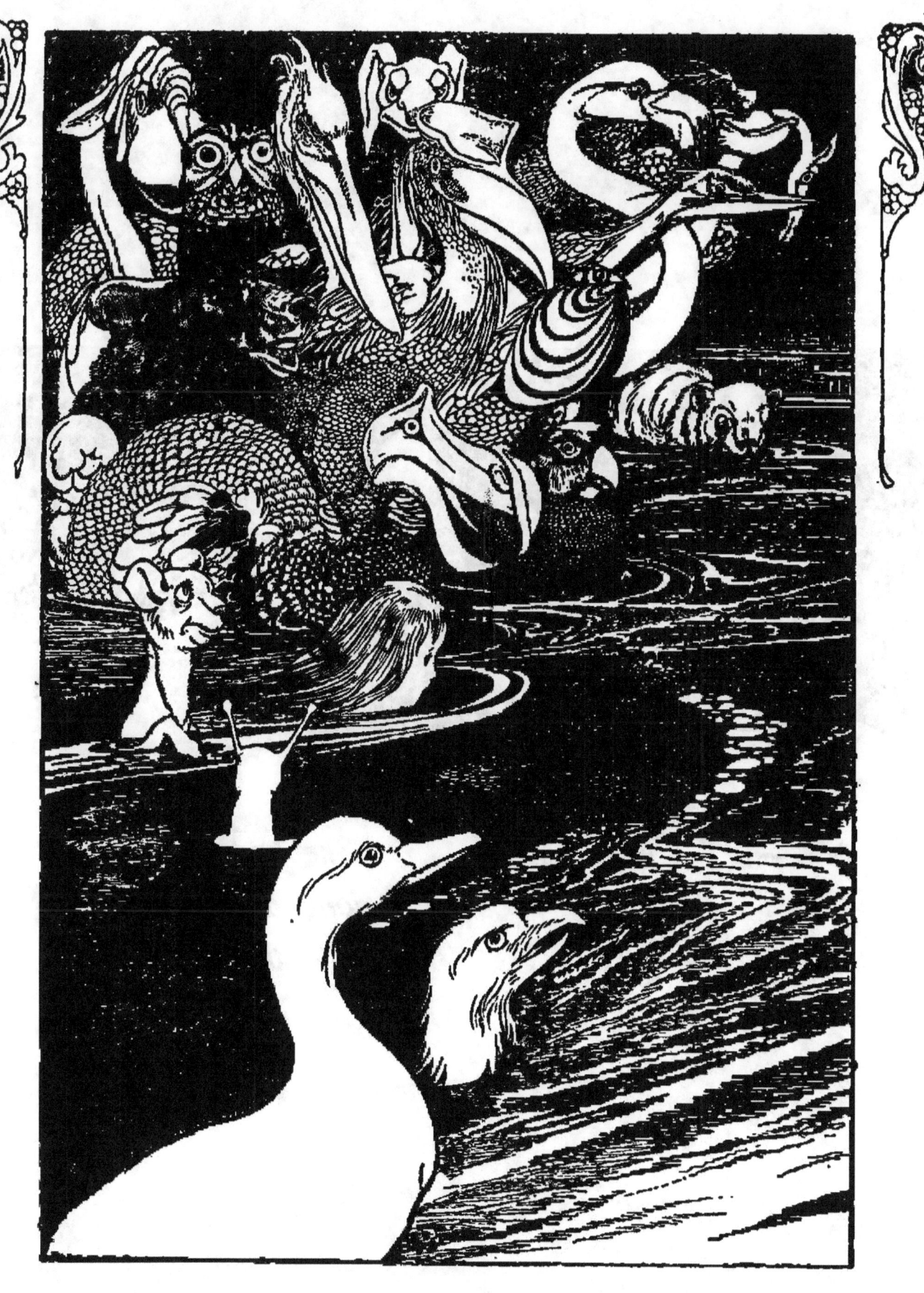

Alice led the way and the whole party swam to the shore

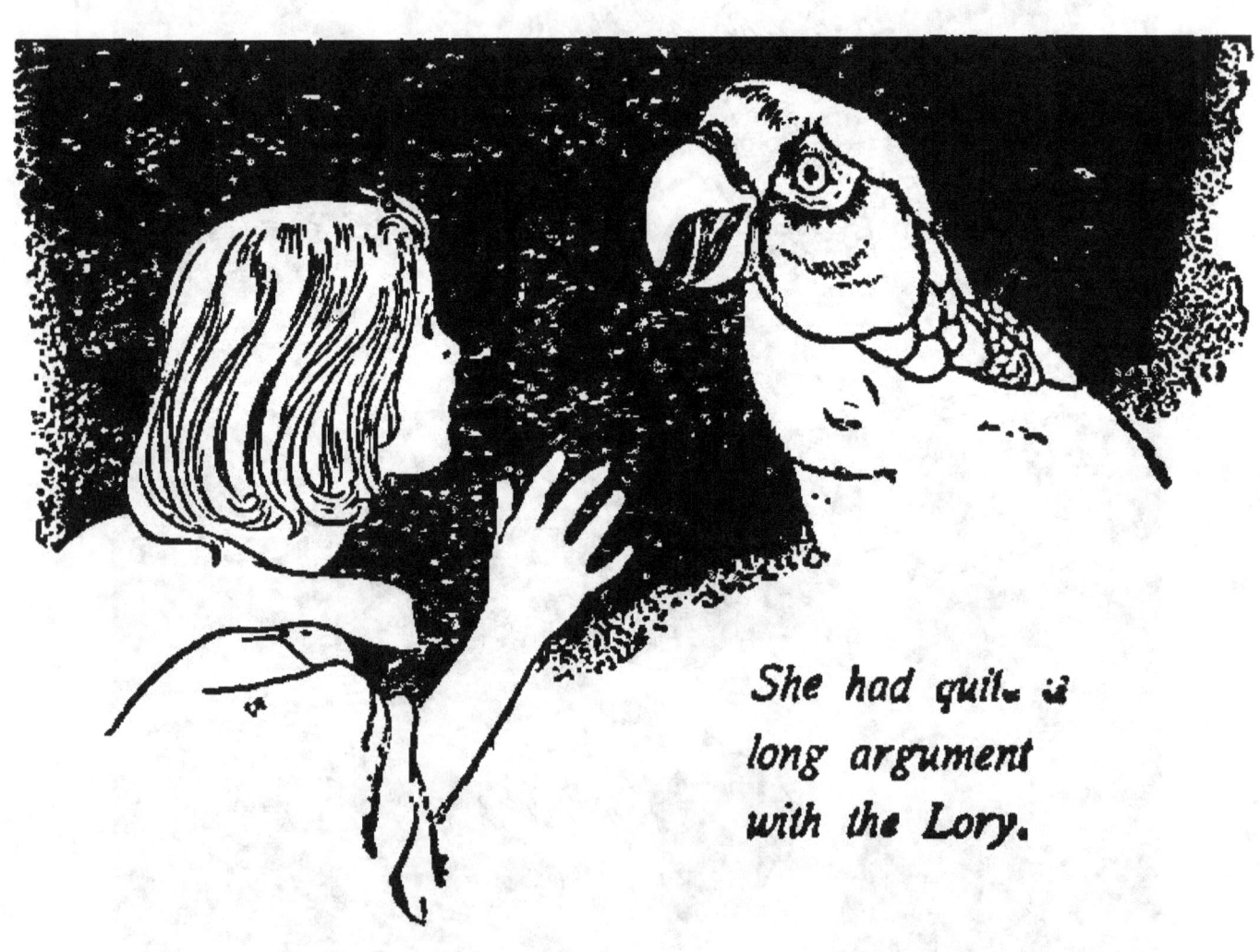

She had quite a
long argument
with the Lory.

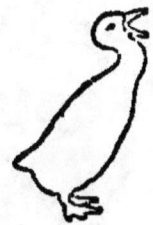

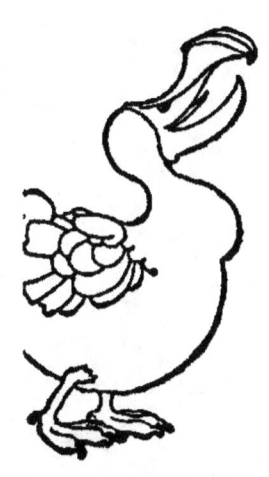

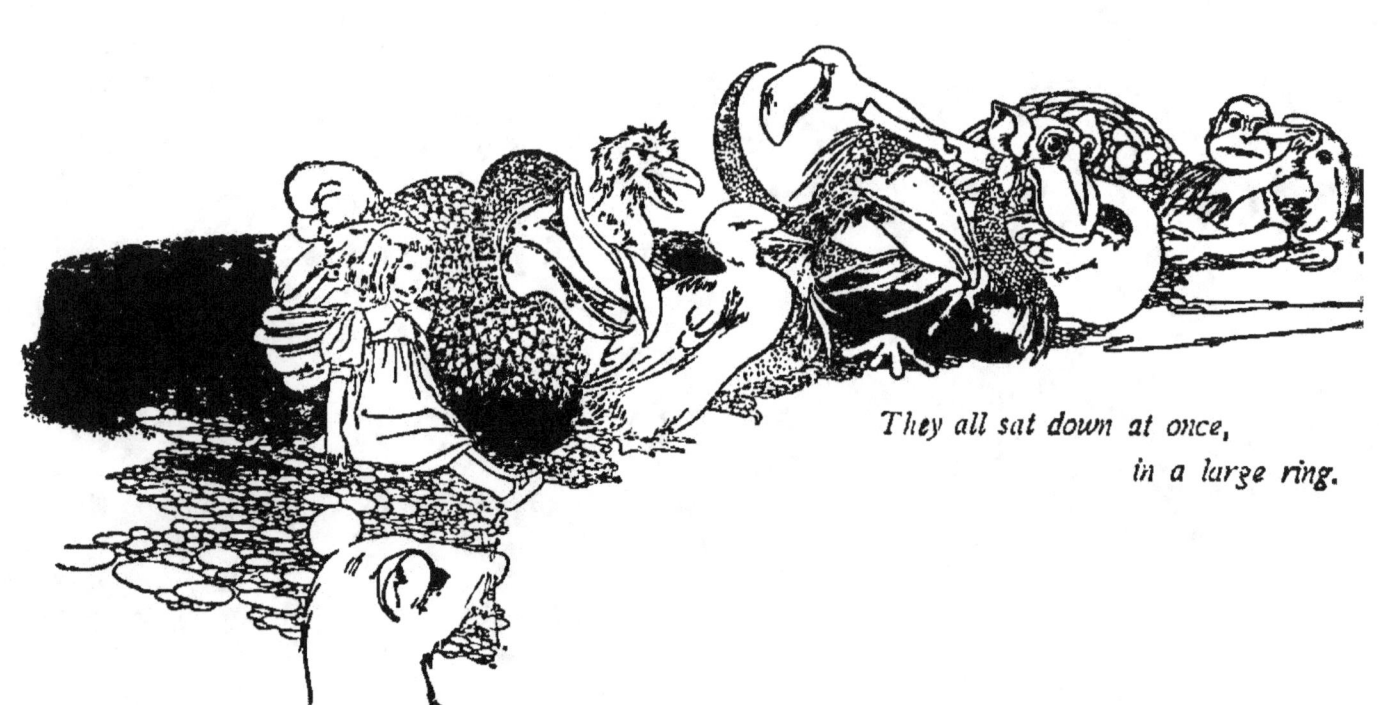

They all sat down at once,
in a large ring.

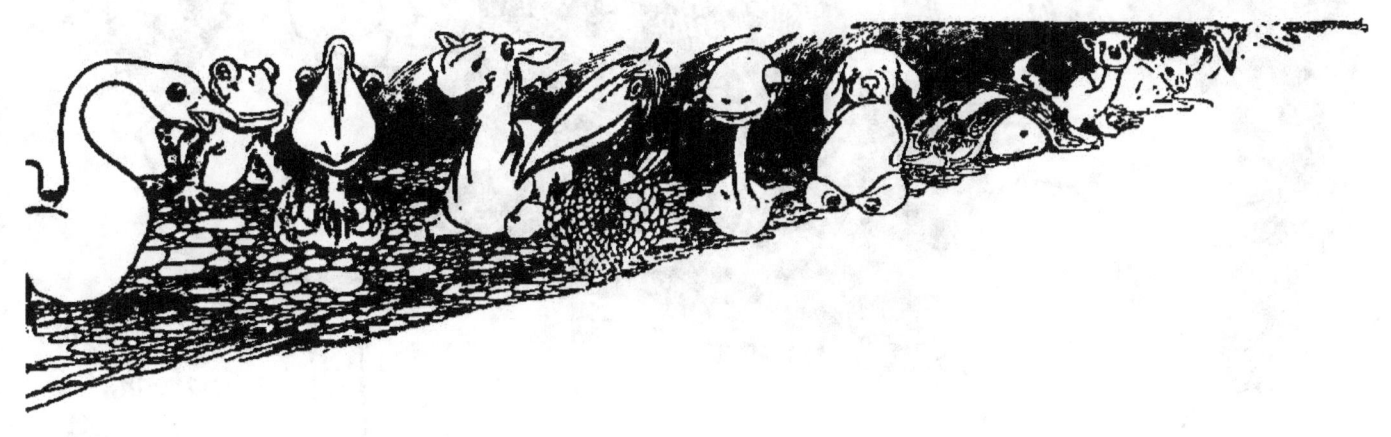

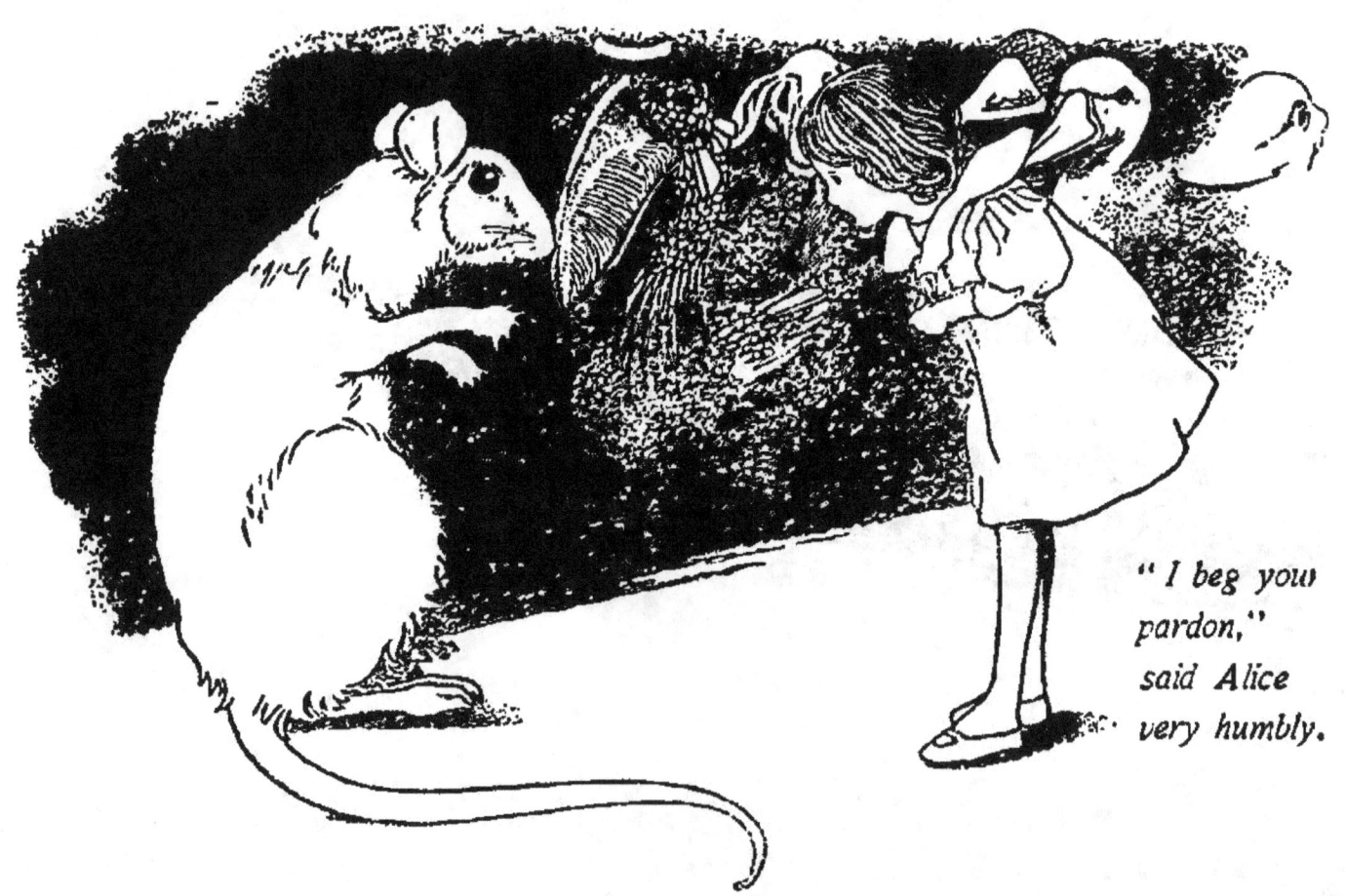

"I beg your pardon," said Alice very humbly.

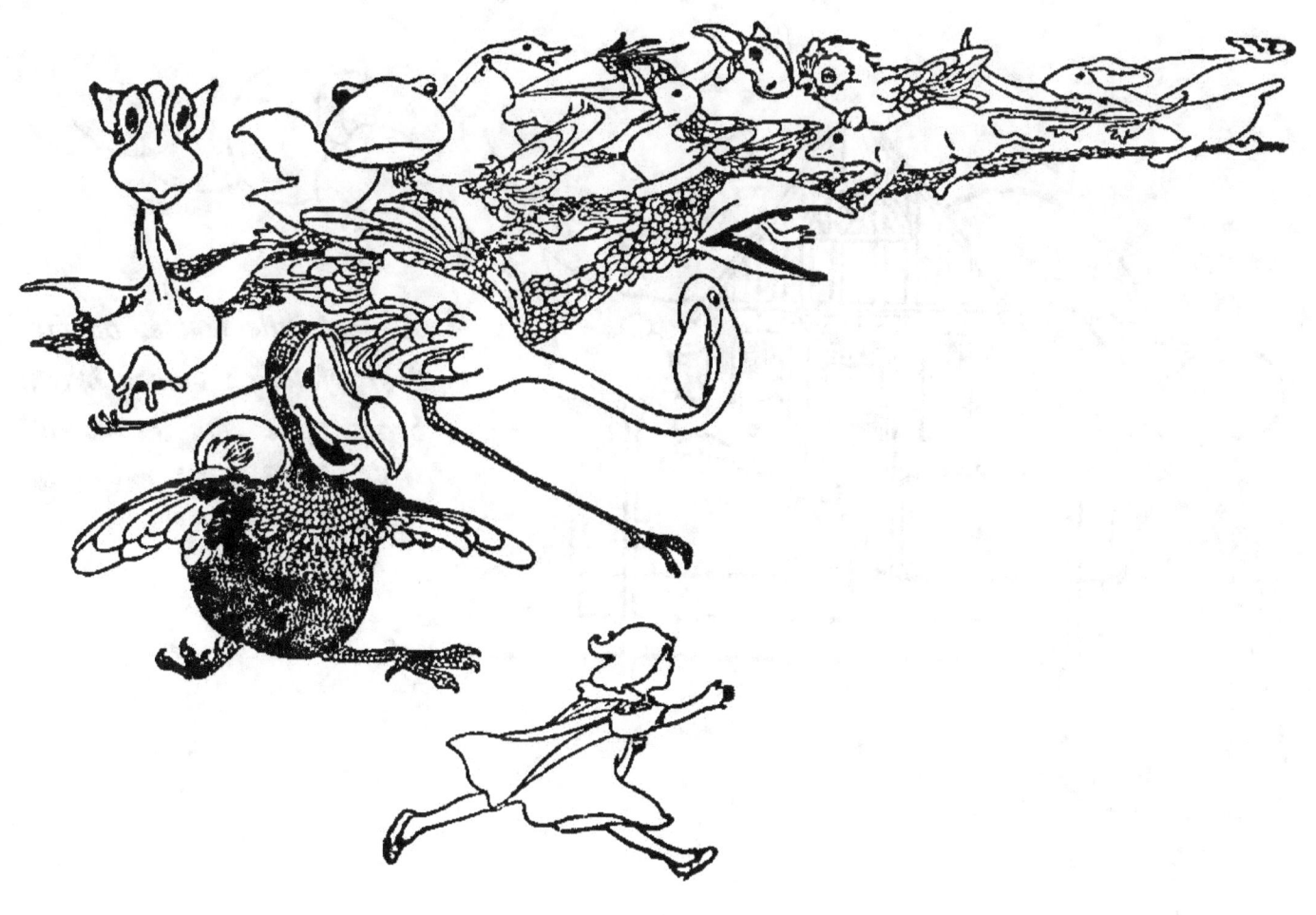

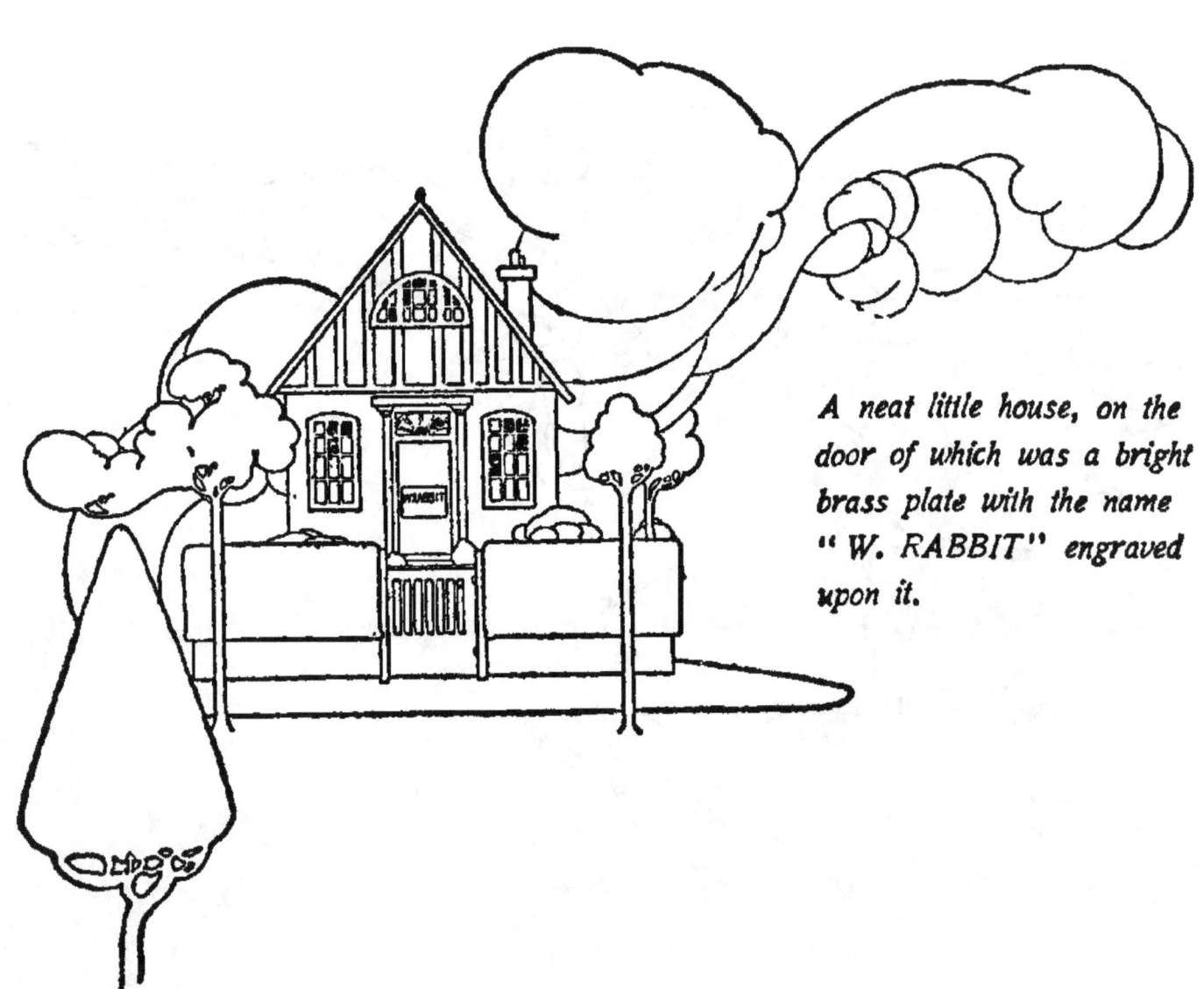

A neat little house, on the door of which was a bright brass plate with the name " W. RABBIT " engraved upon it.

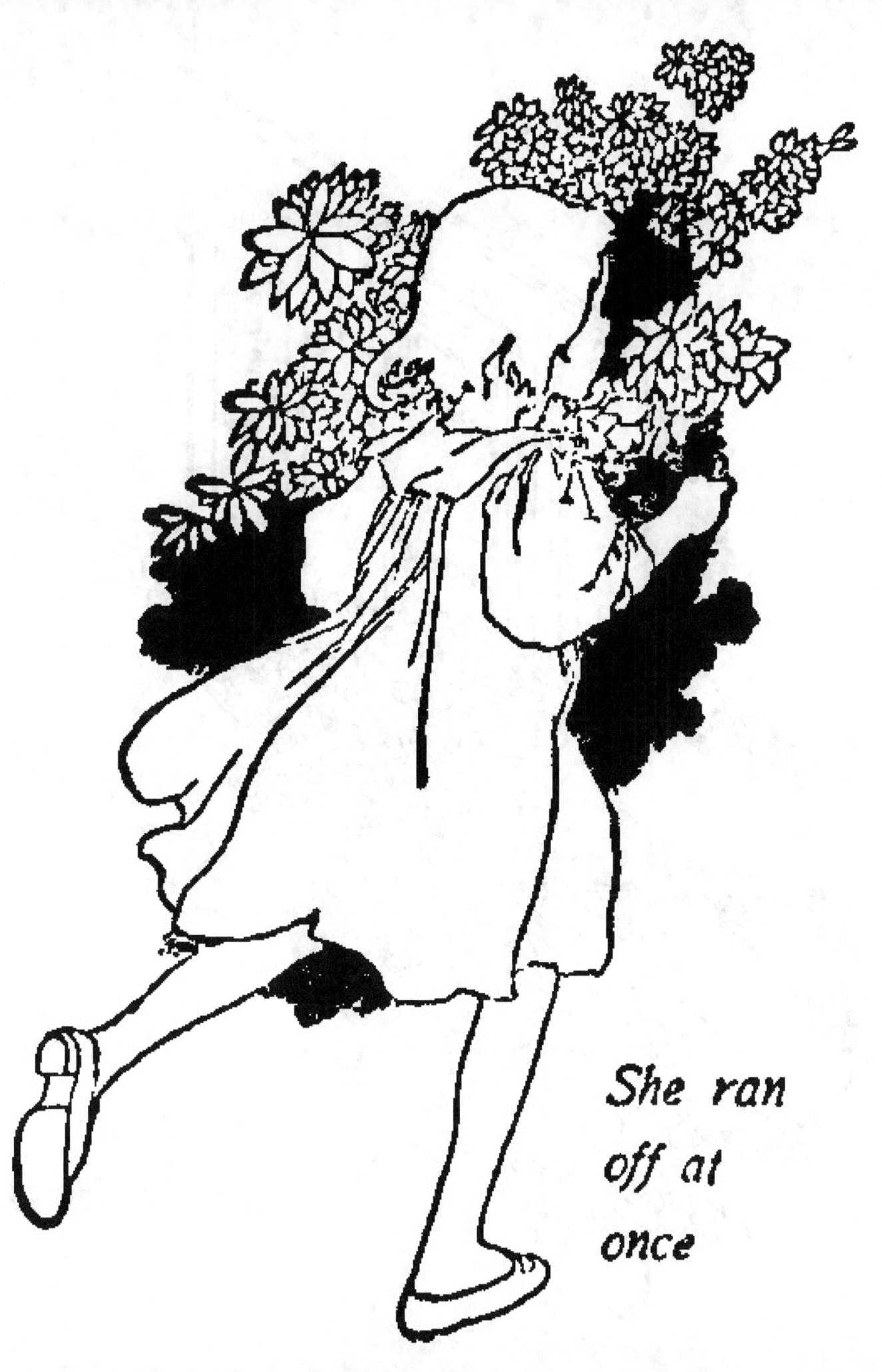

She ran
off at
once

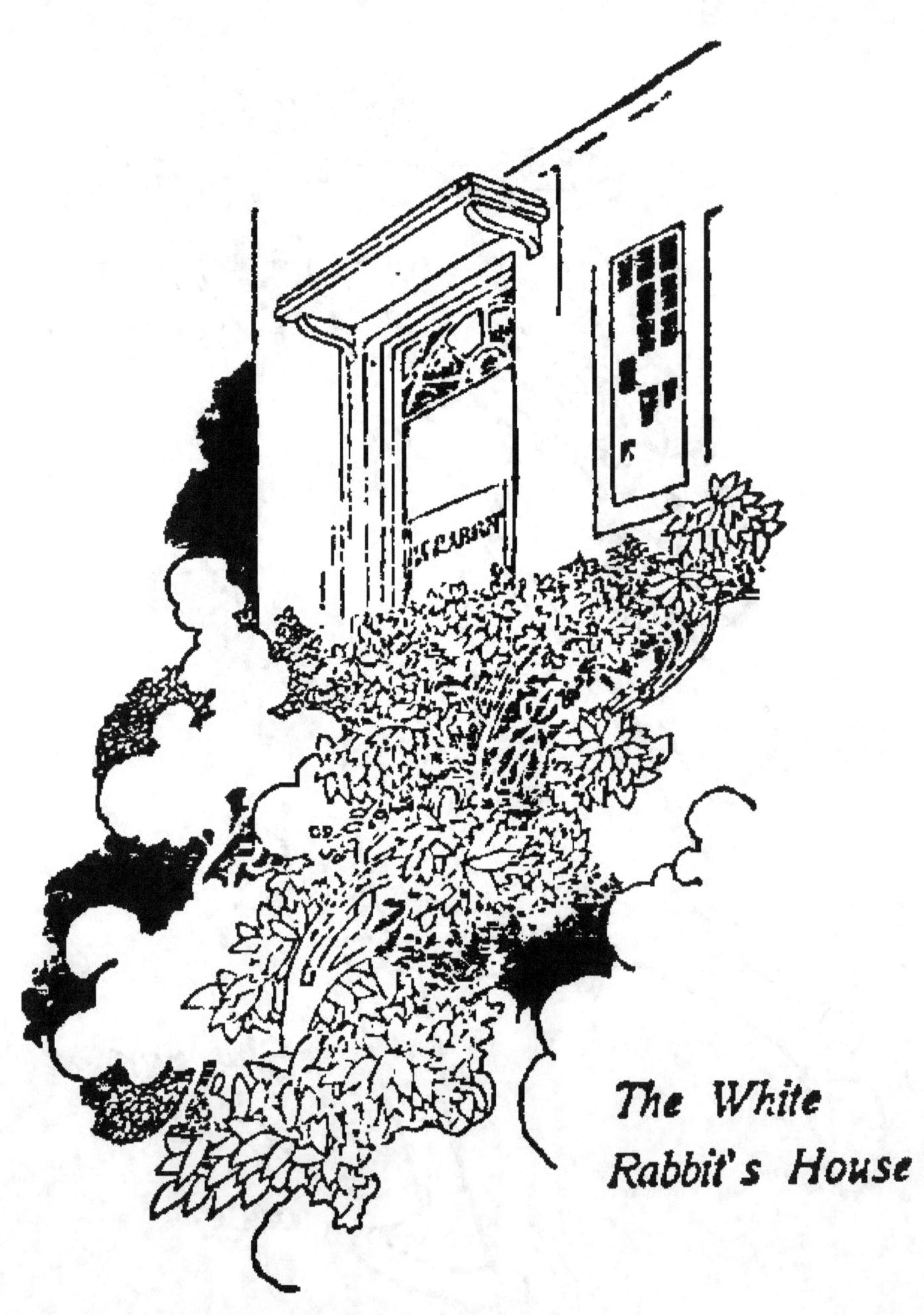

The White
Rabbit's House

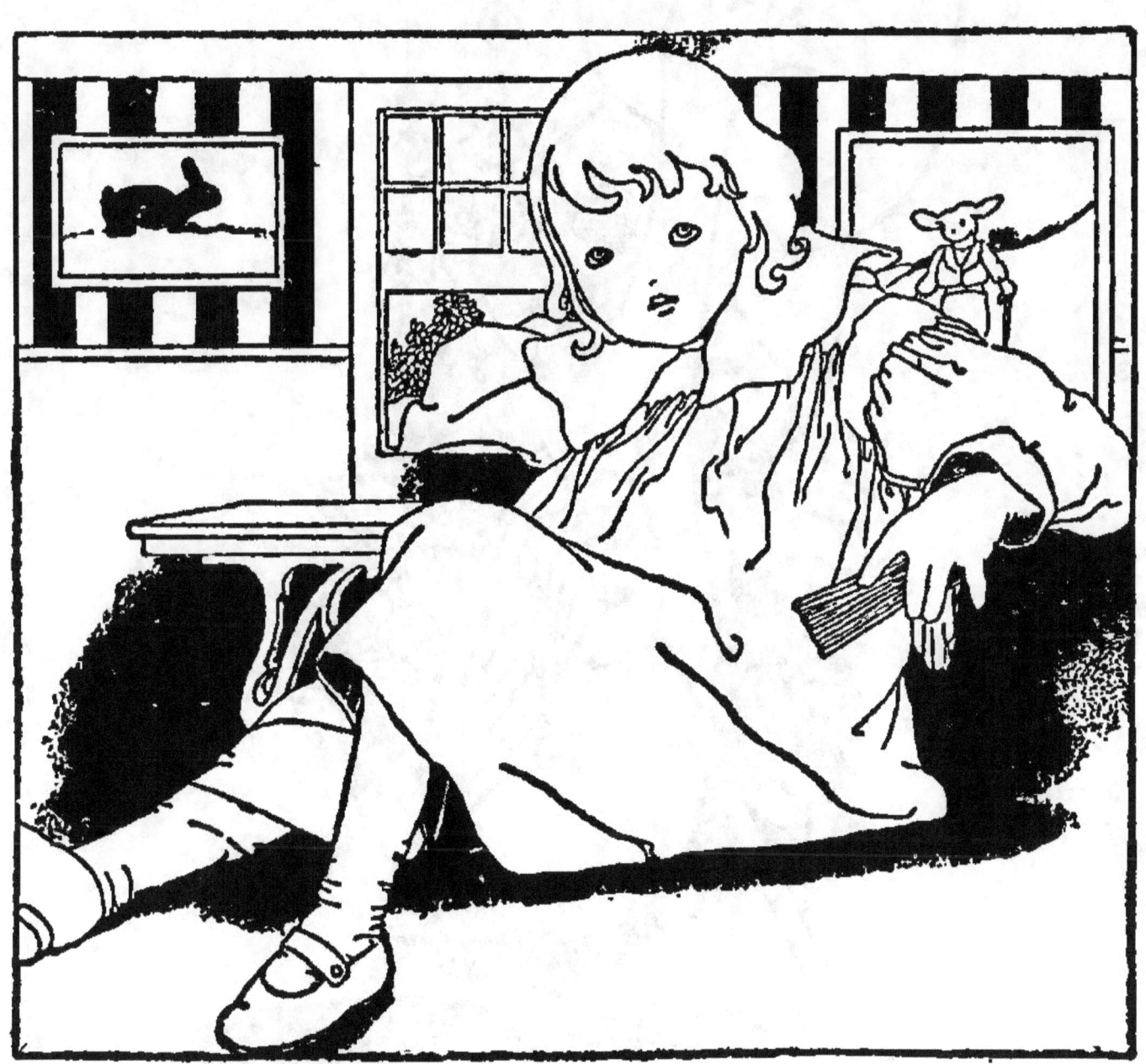

It was very
   uncomfortable.

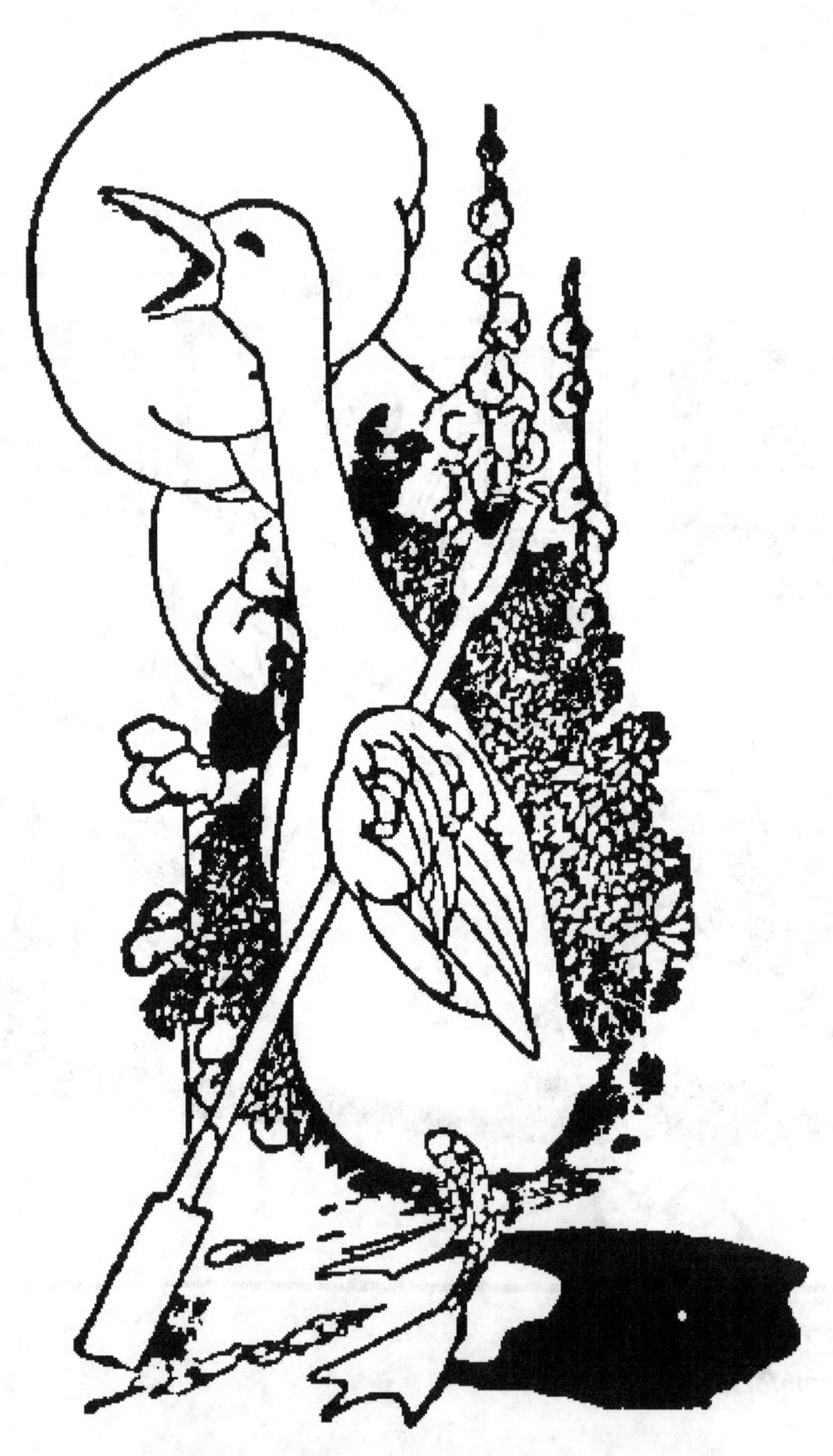

" Digging for apples,
yer honour !"

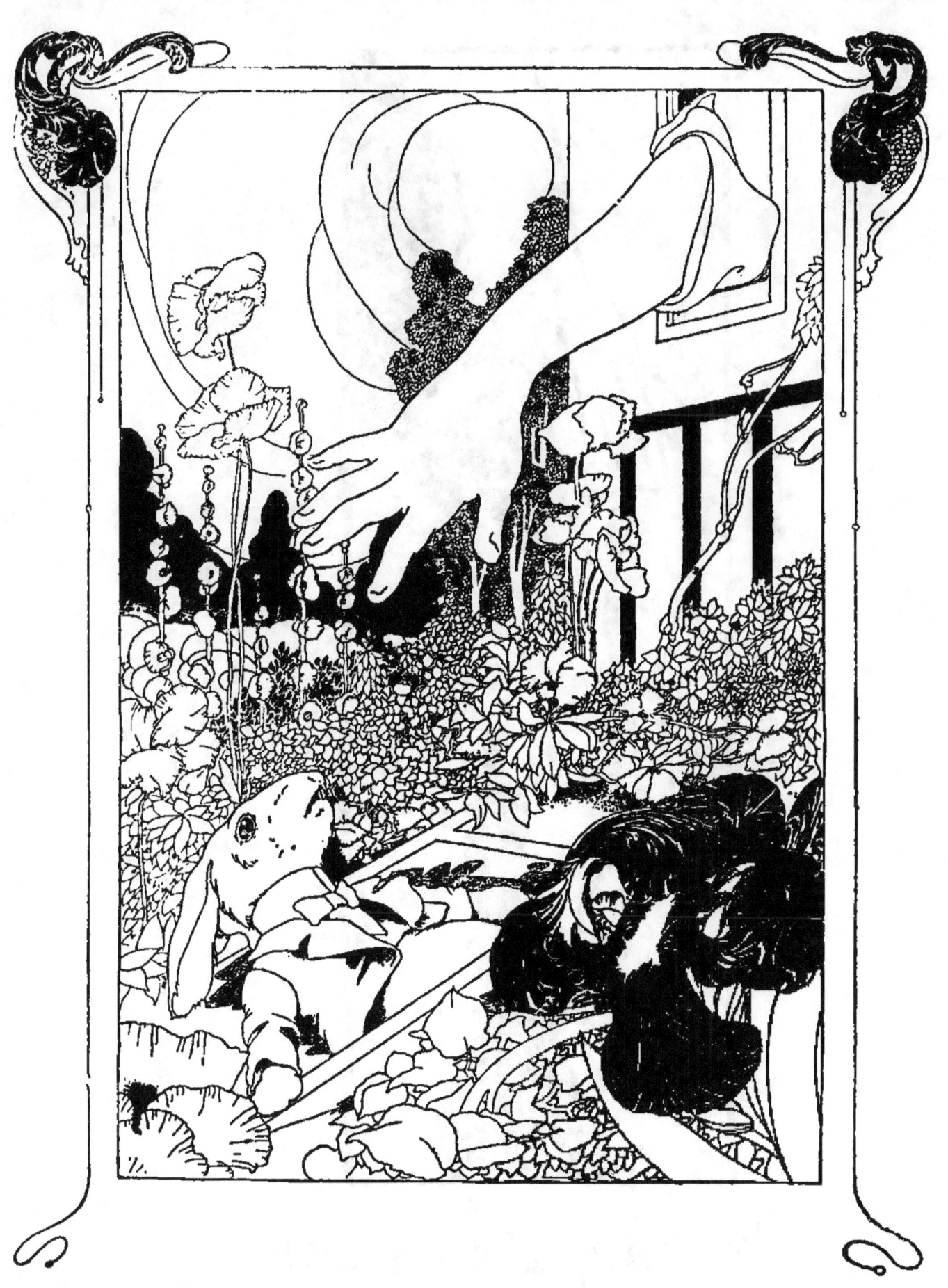

She suddenly spread out her hand, and made a snatch in the air

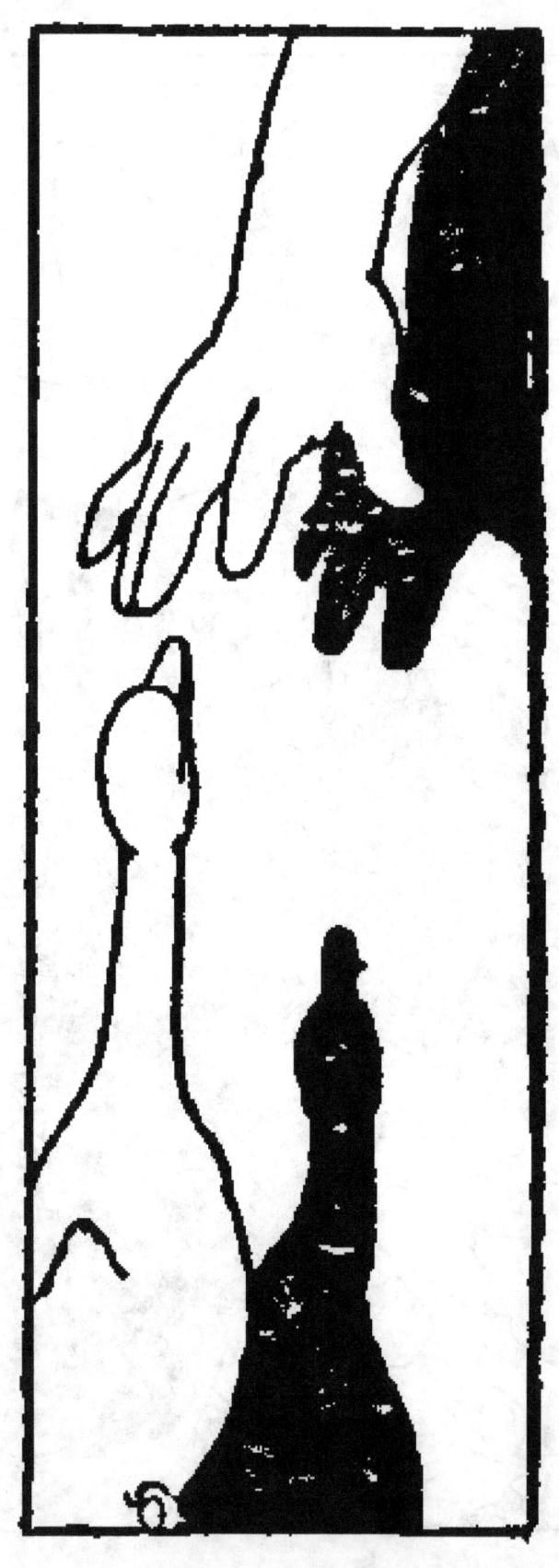

"Sure, It's an arm,
        yer honour!"

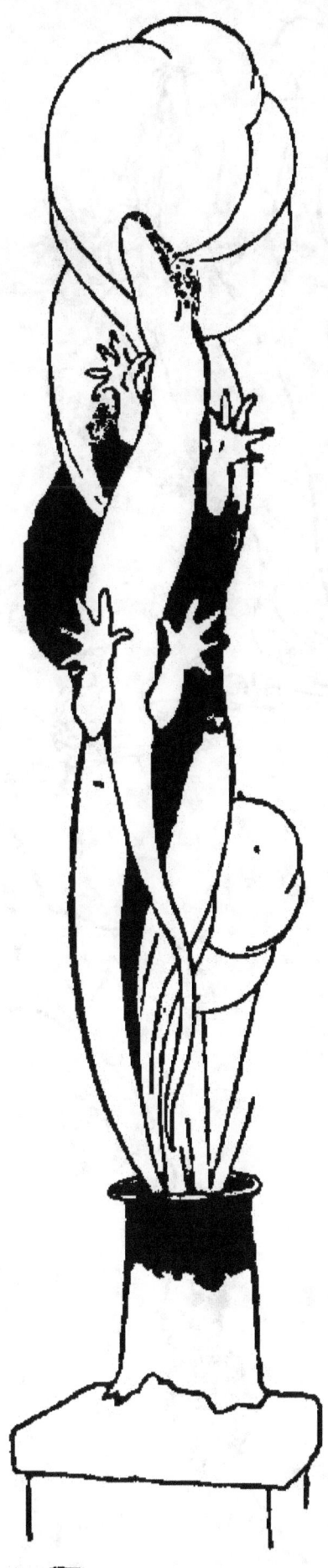

"There goes
    Bill!"

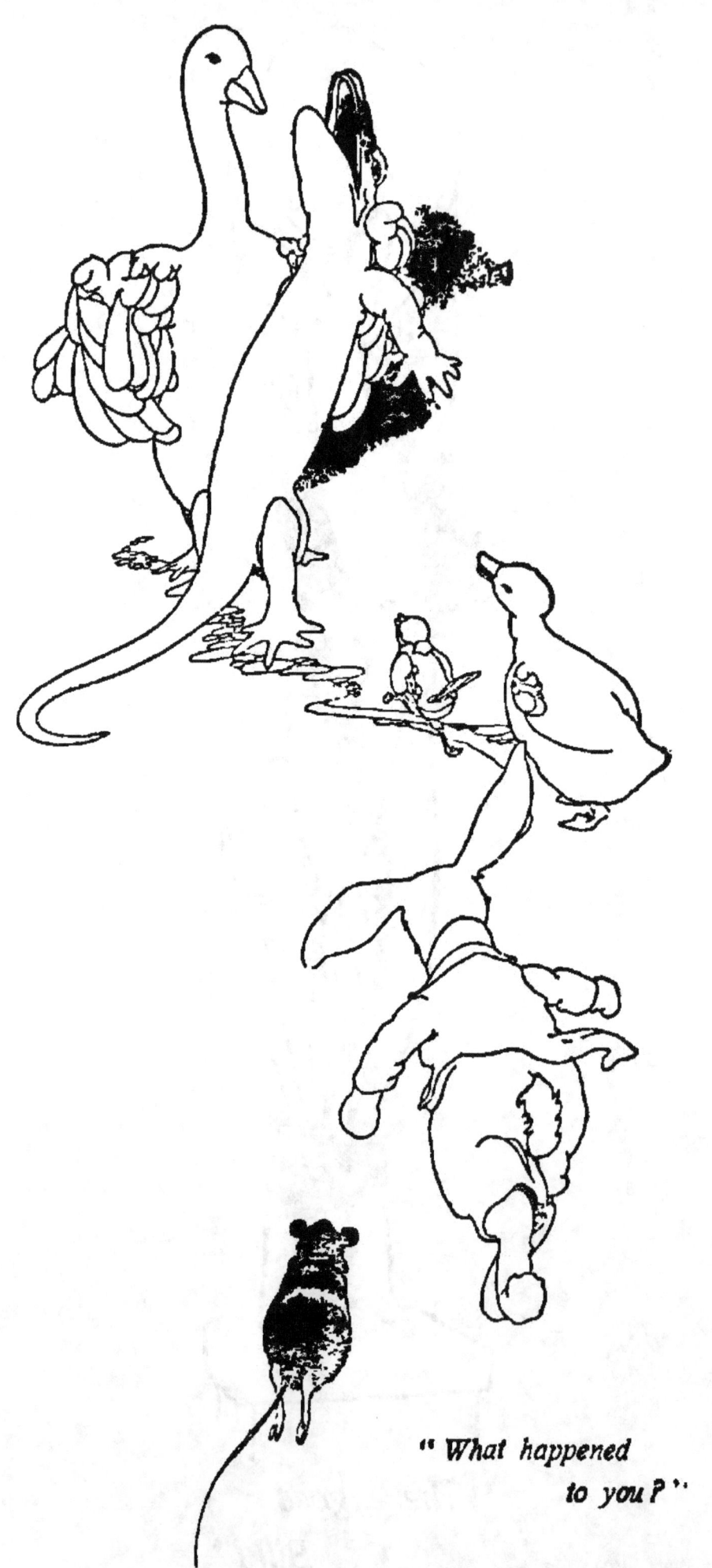

" What happened
to you ? "

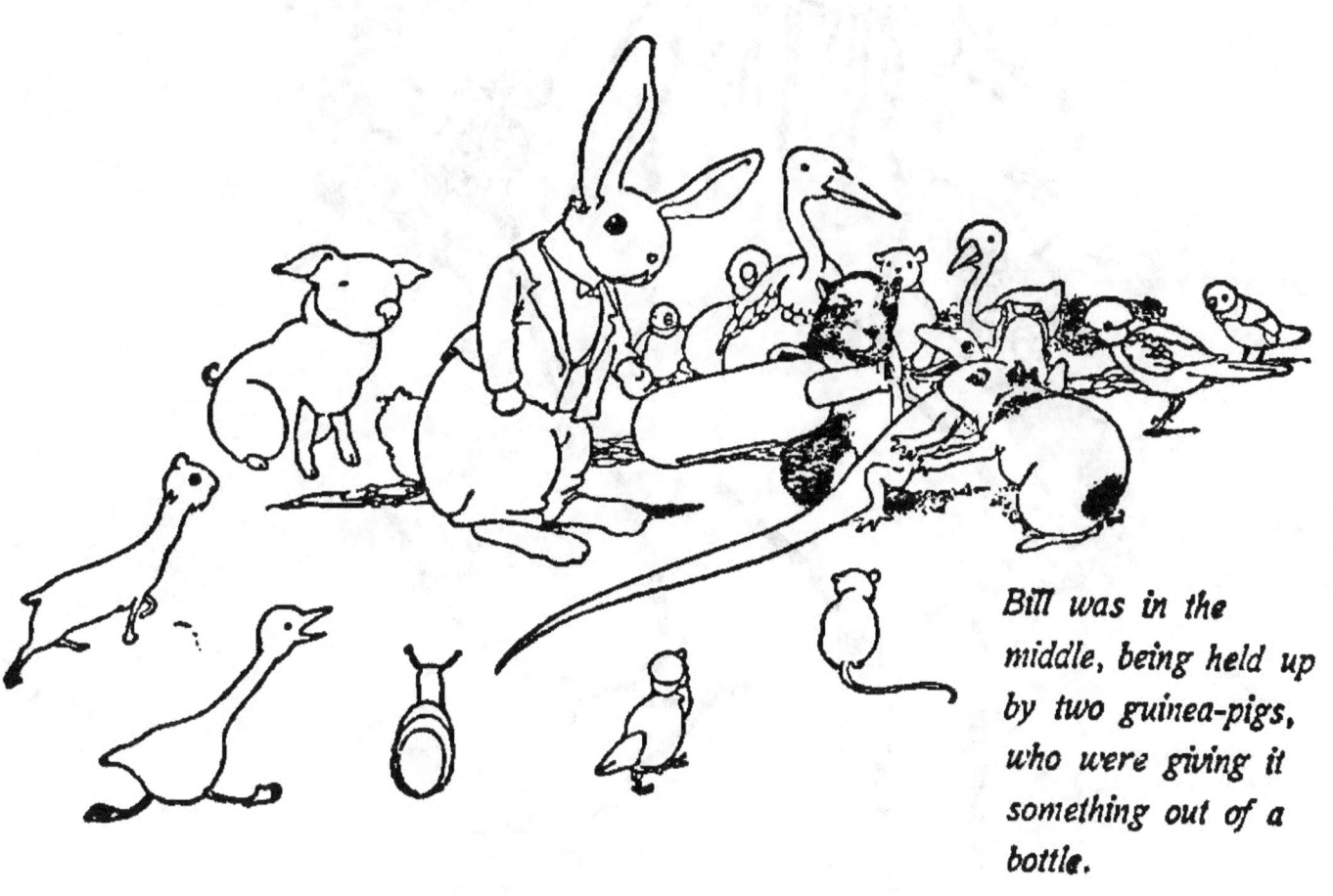

Bill was in the middle, being held up by two guinea-pigs, who were giving it something out of a bottle.

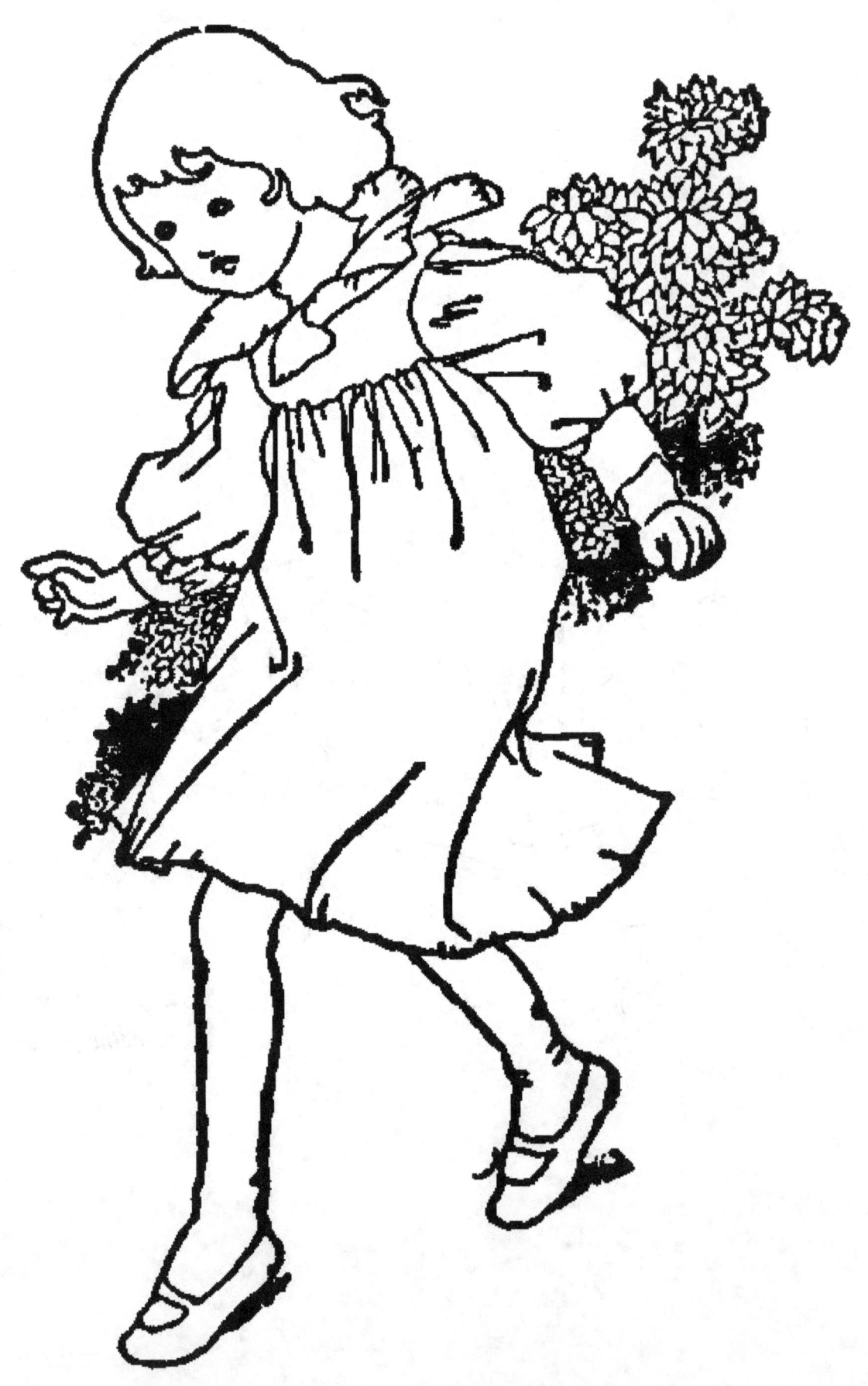

She ran off as hard

as she could.

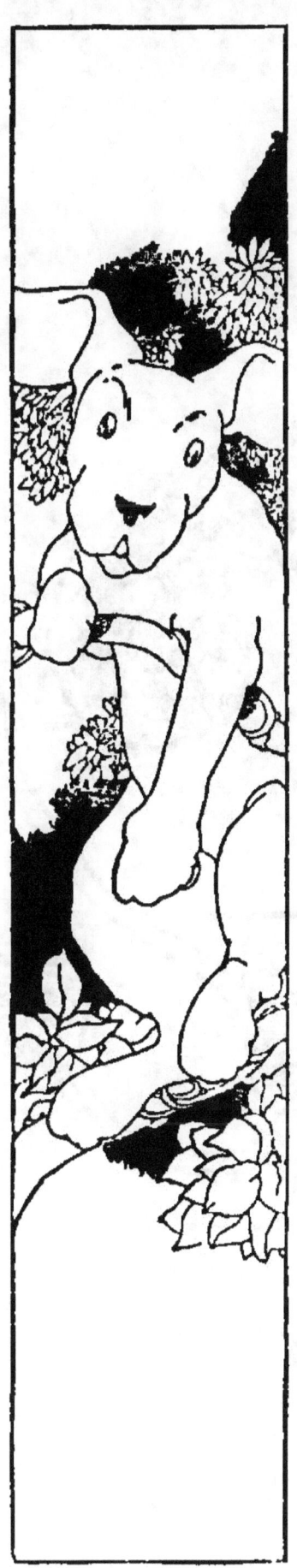

An enormous puppy
was looking down
at her.

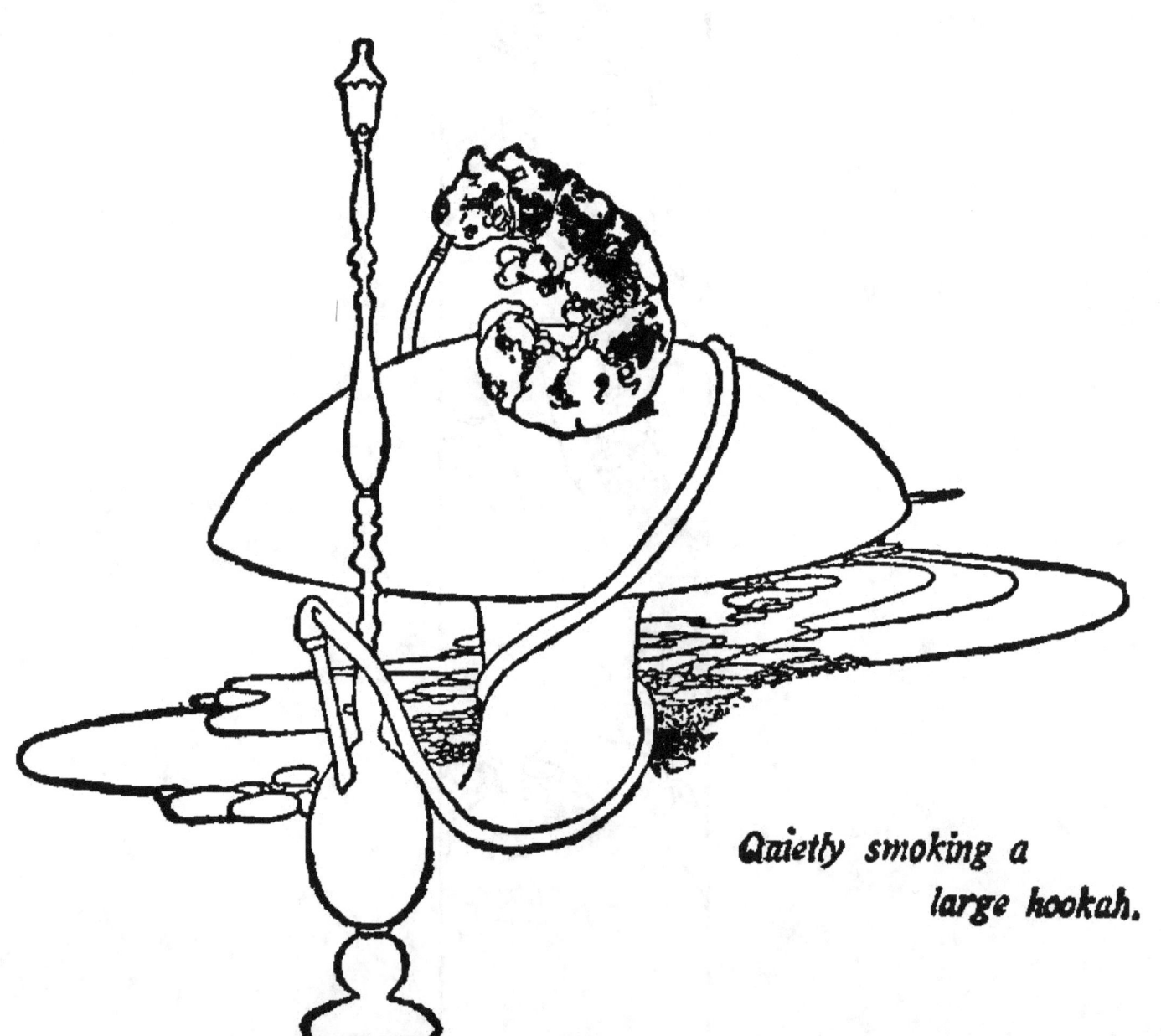

Quietly smoking a large kookah.

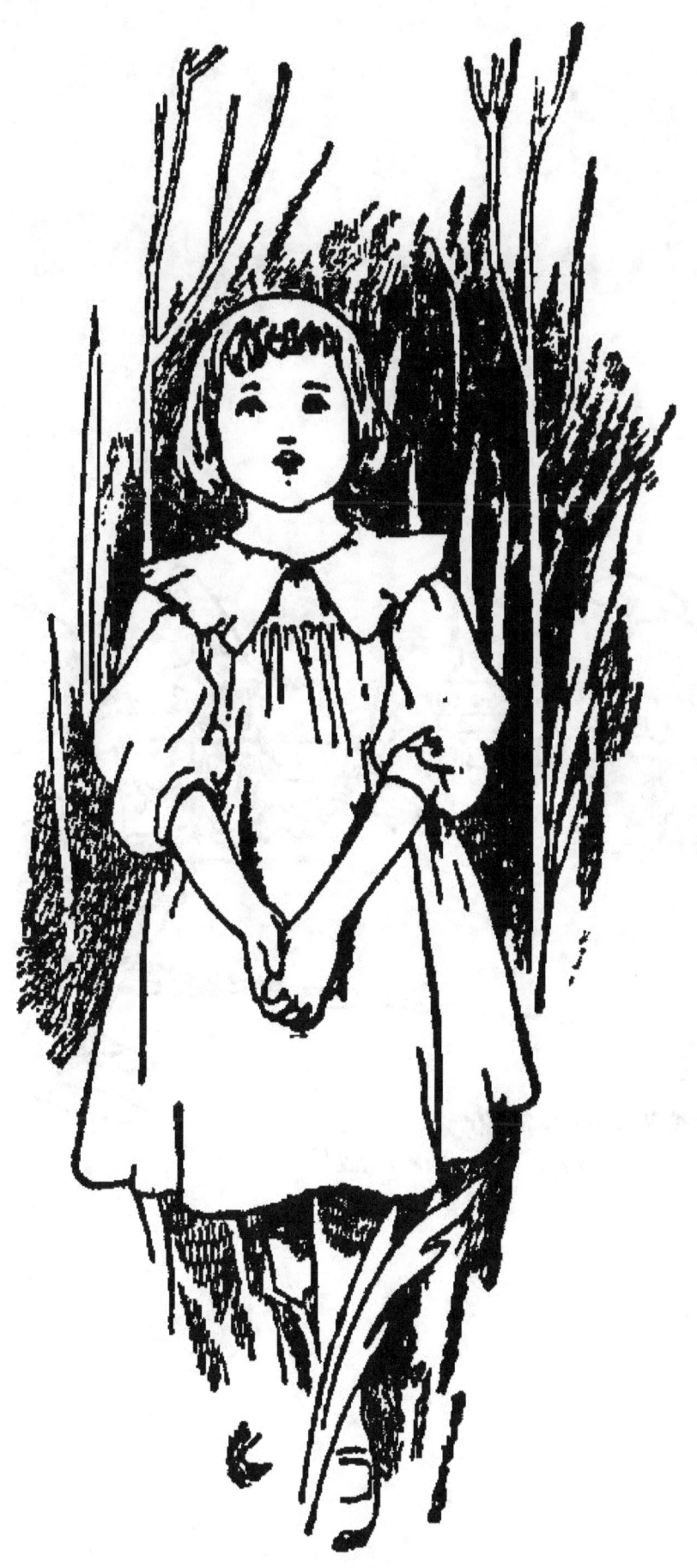

Alice folded her hands,

and began.

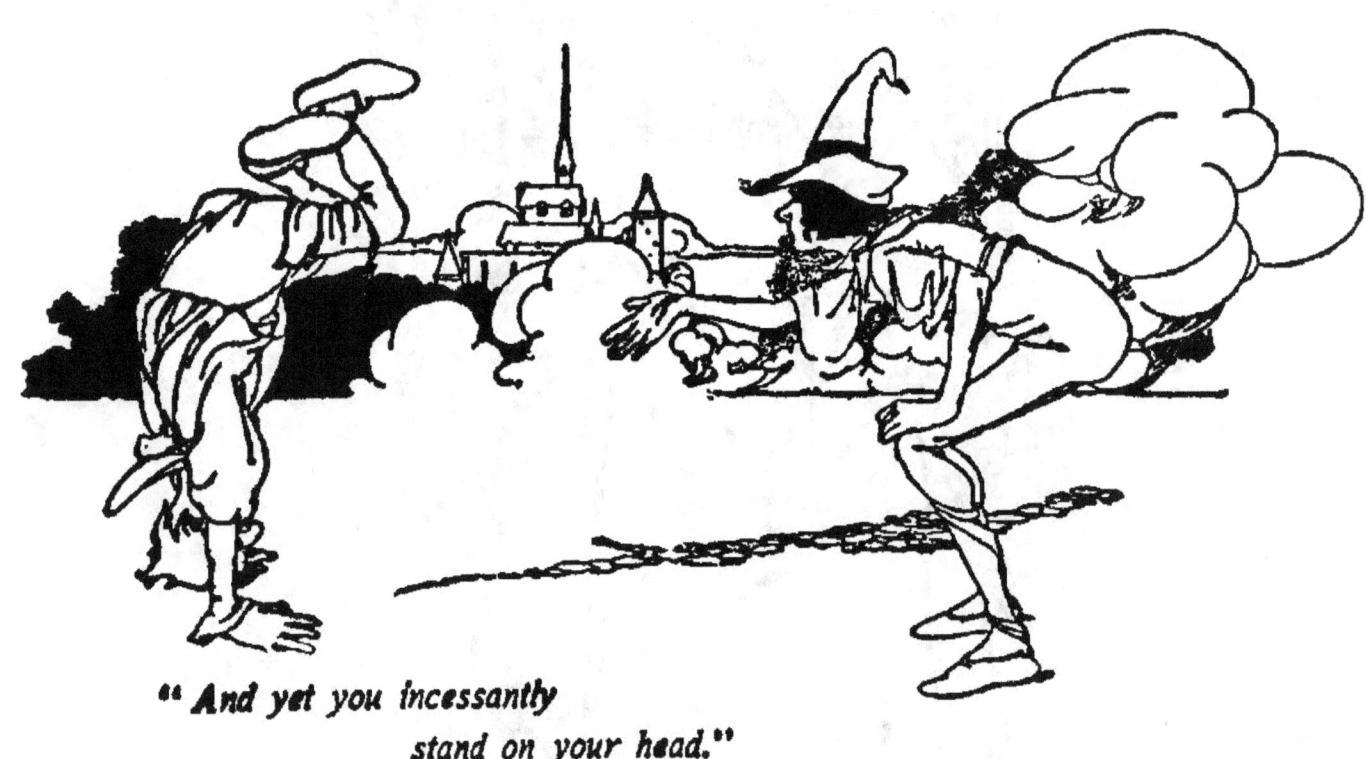

"*And yet you incessantly
stand on your head.*"

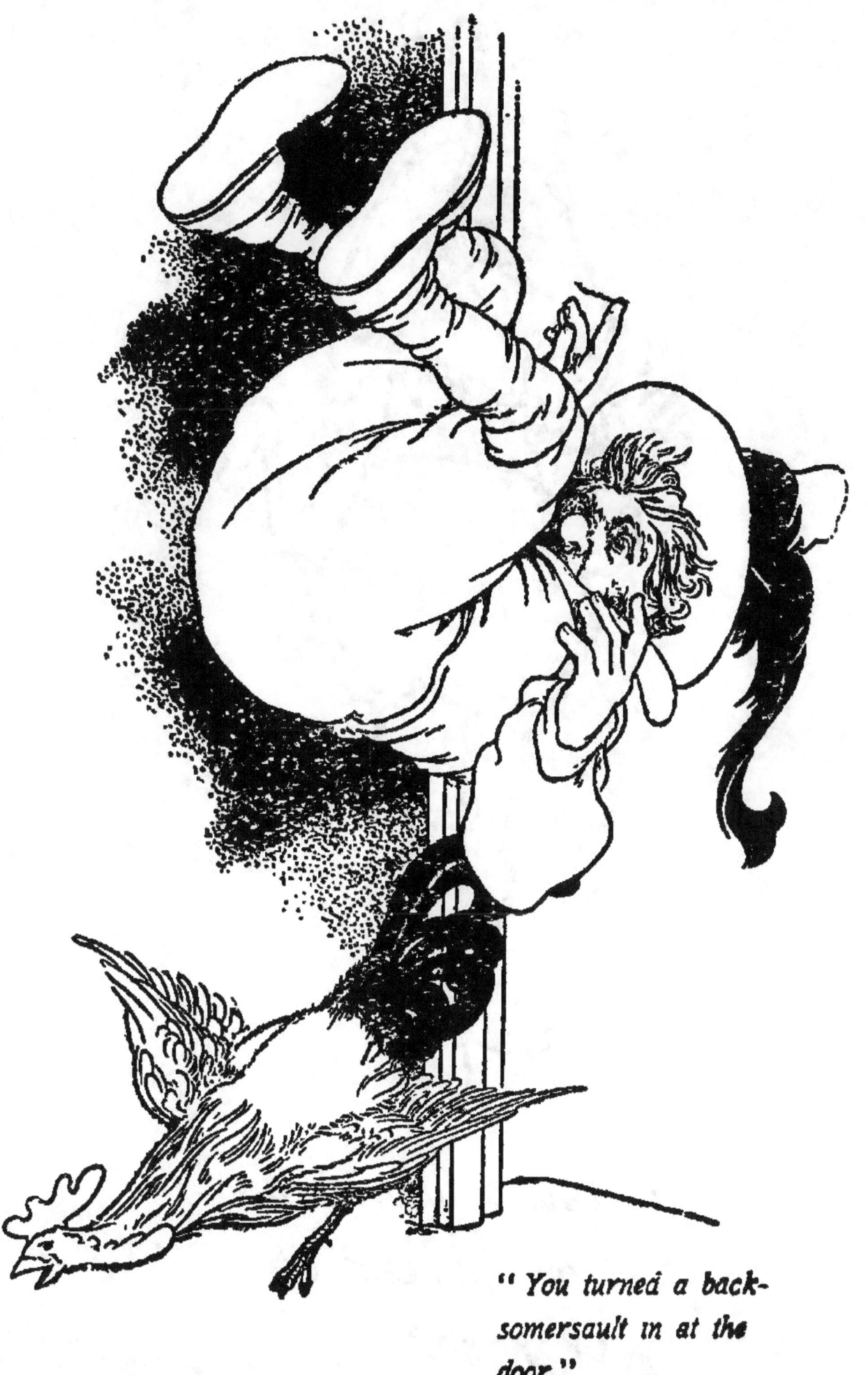

" You turned a back-somersault in at the door."

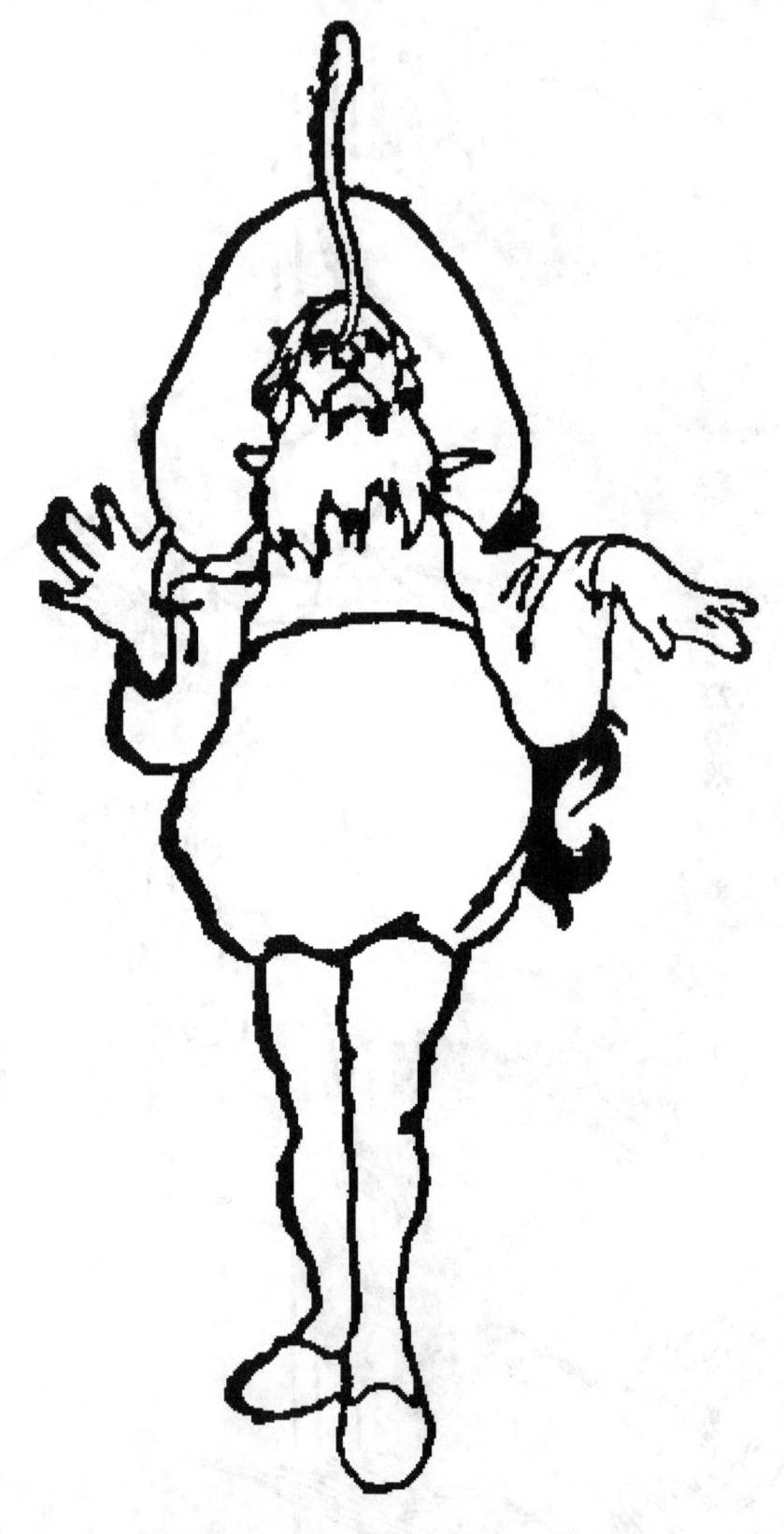

" You balanced an
eel on the end of
your nose."

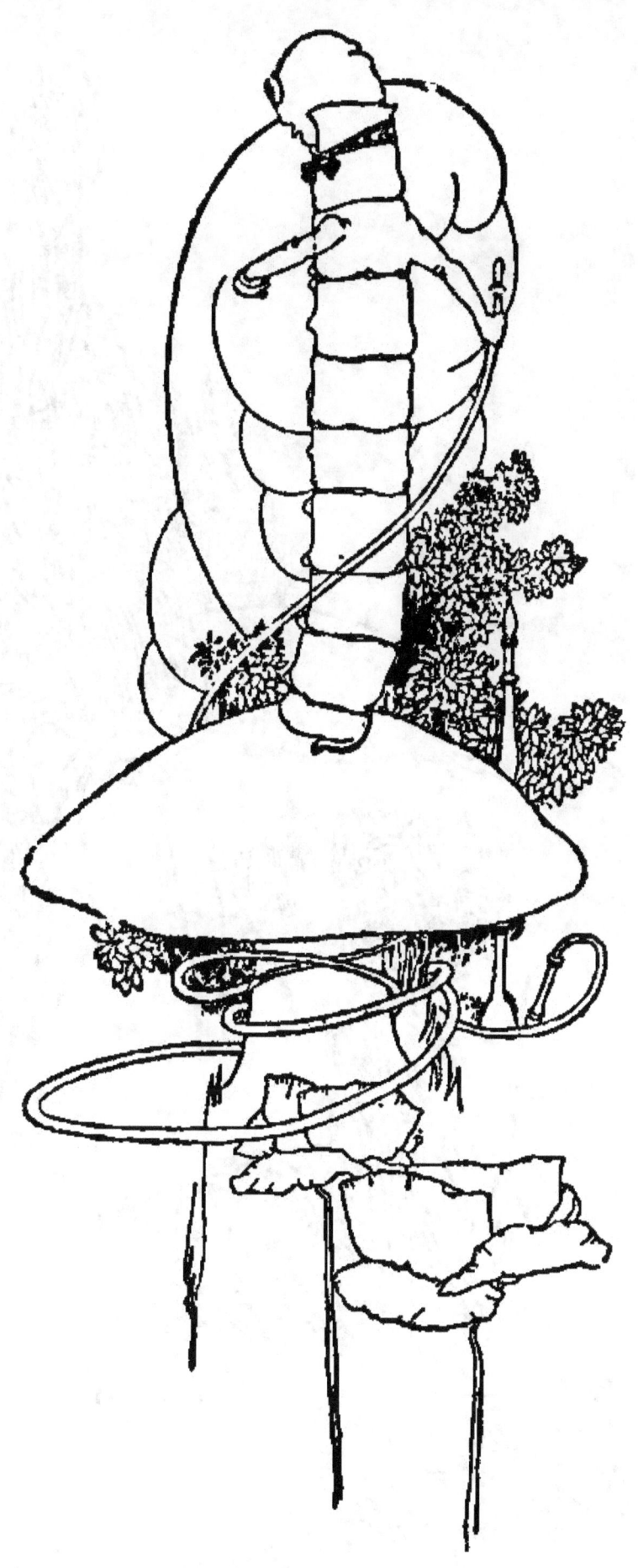

*" It is a very good
height indeed "*

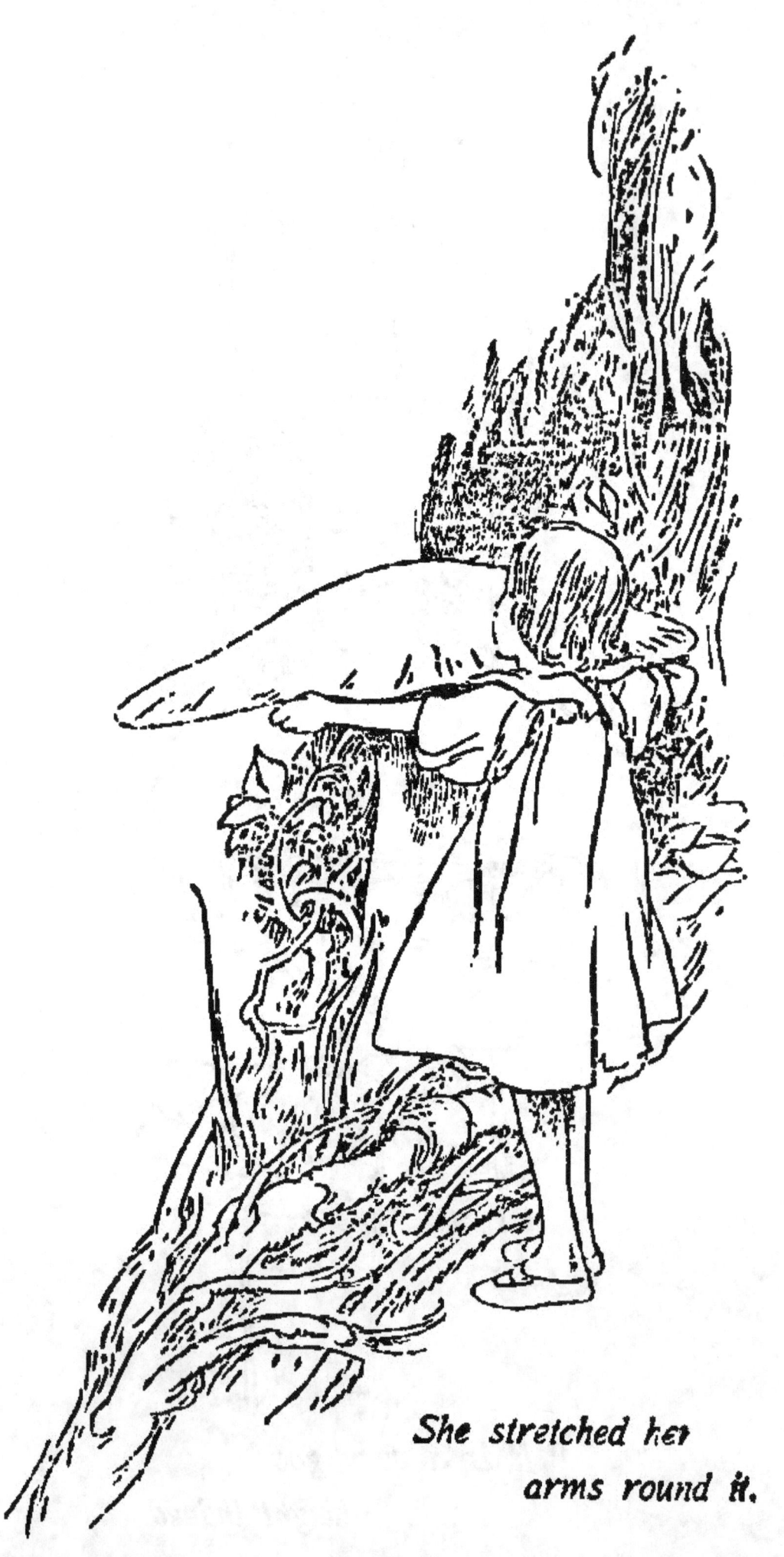

She stretched her
arms round it.

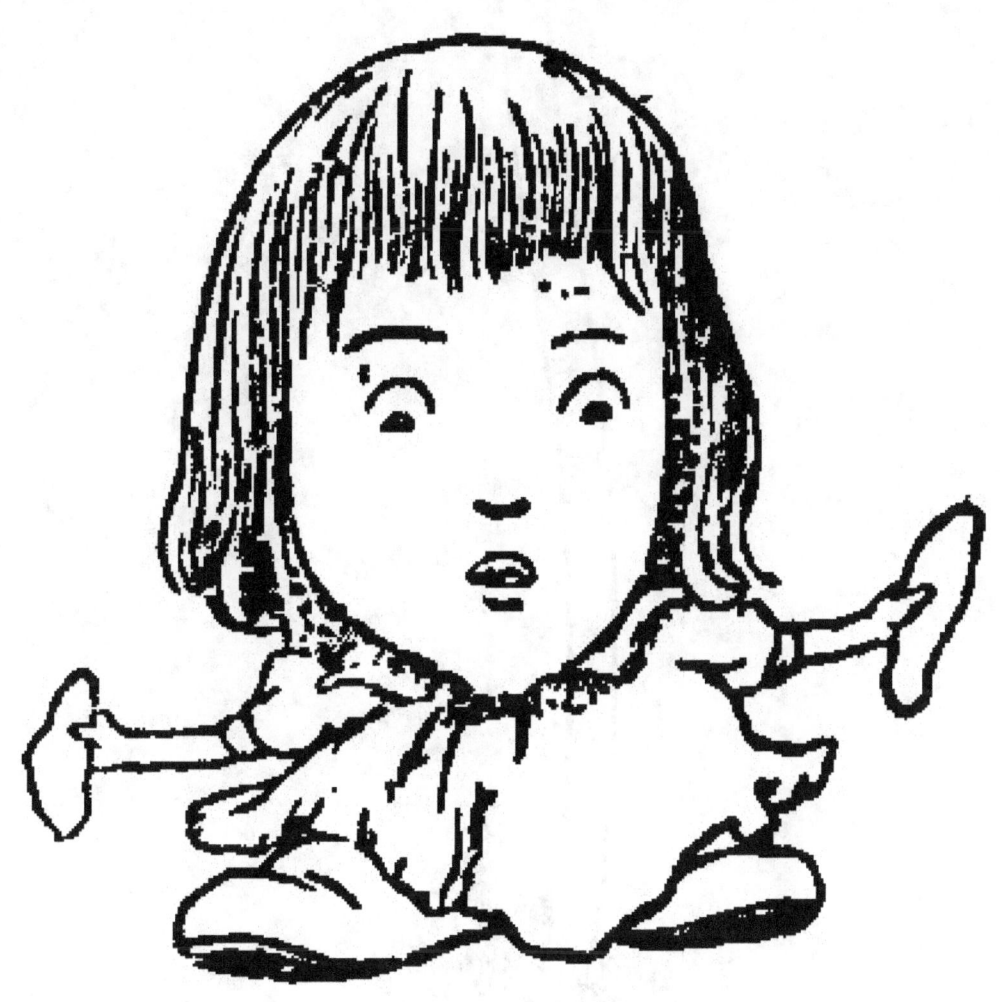

She was

shrinking rapidly.

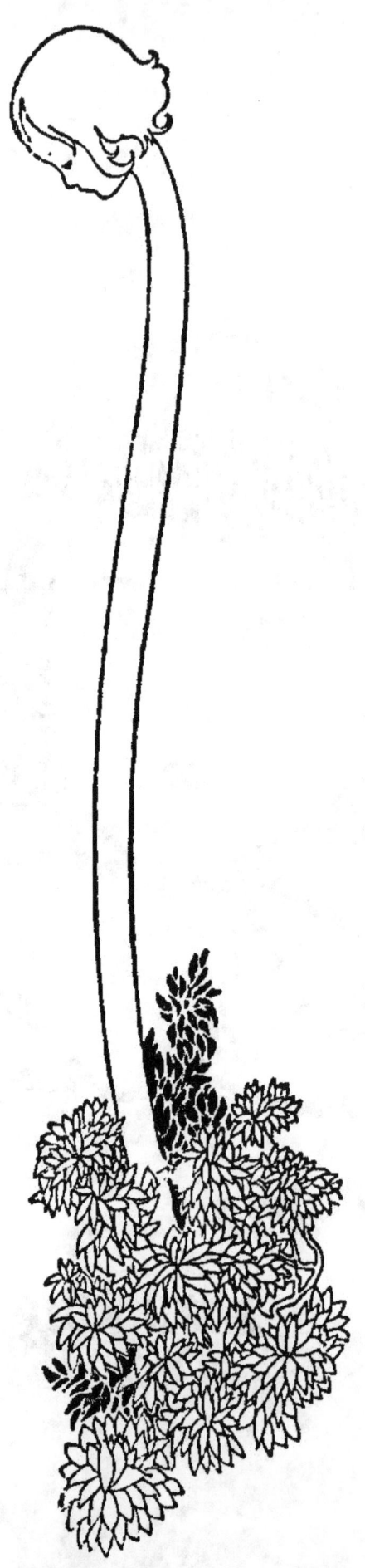

*All she could see . . . . was
an immense length of neck*

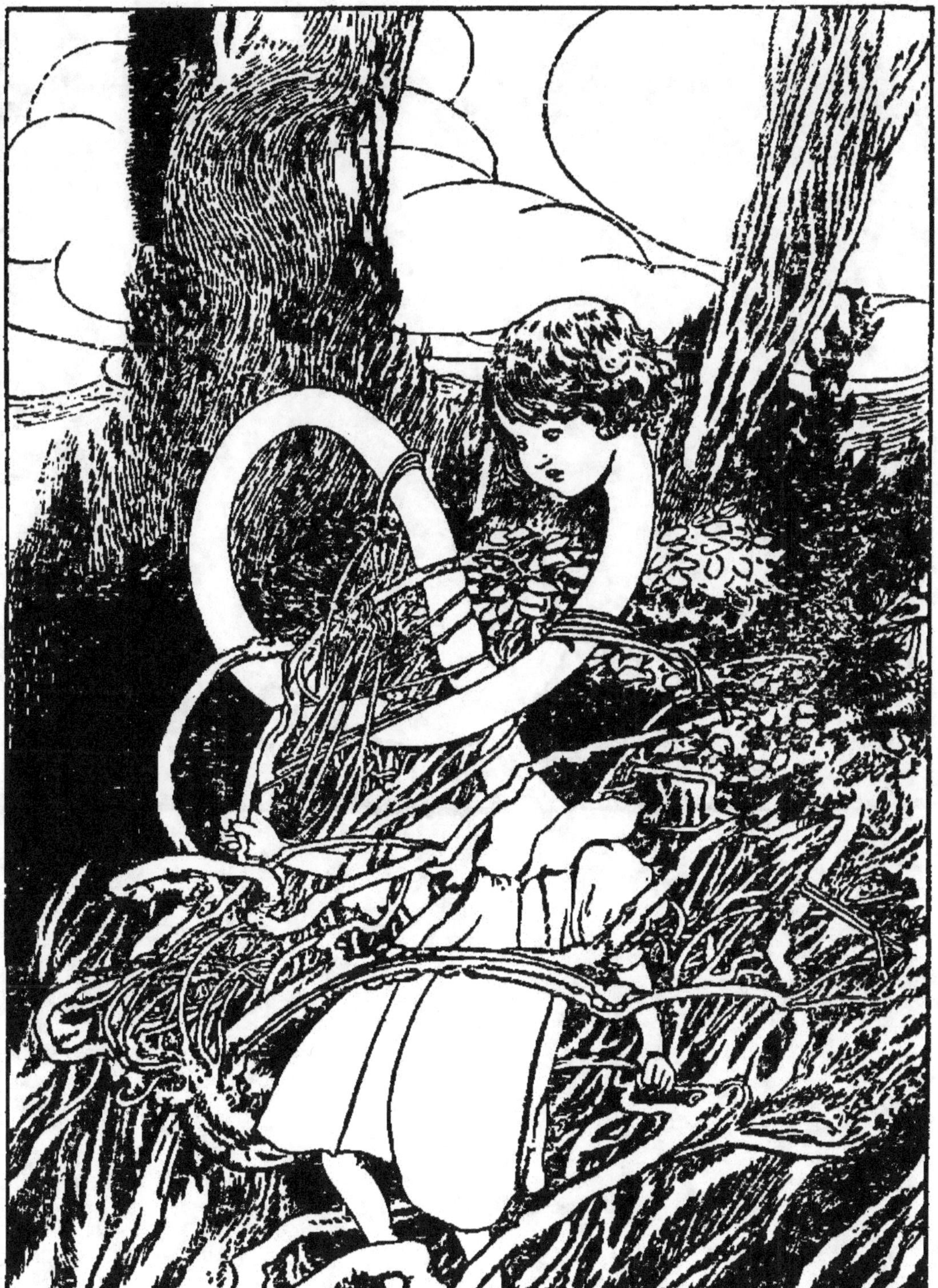

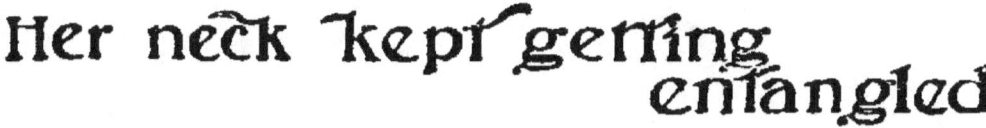

Her neck kept getting
                entangled

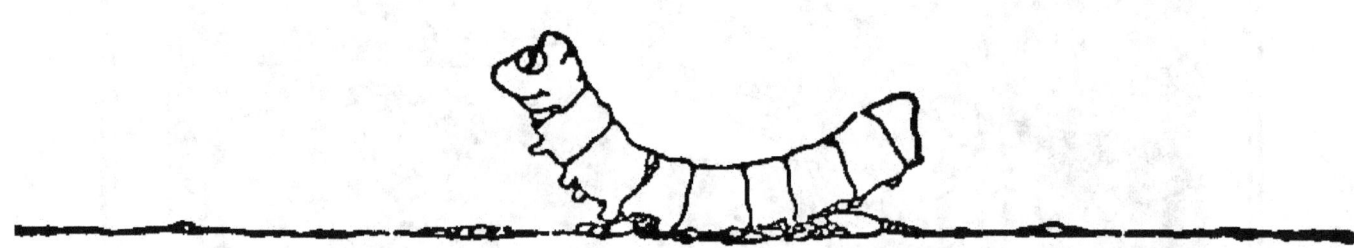

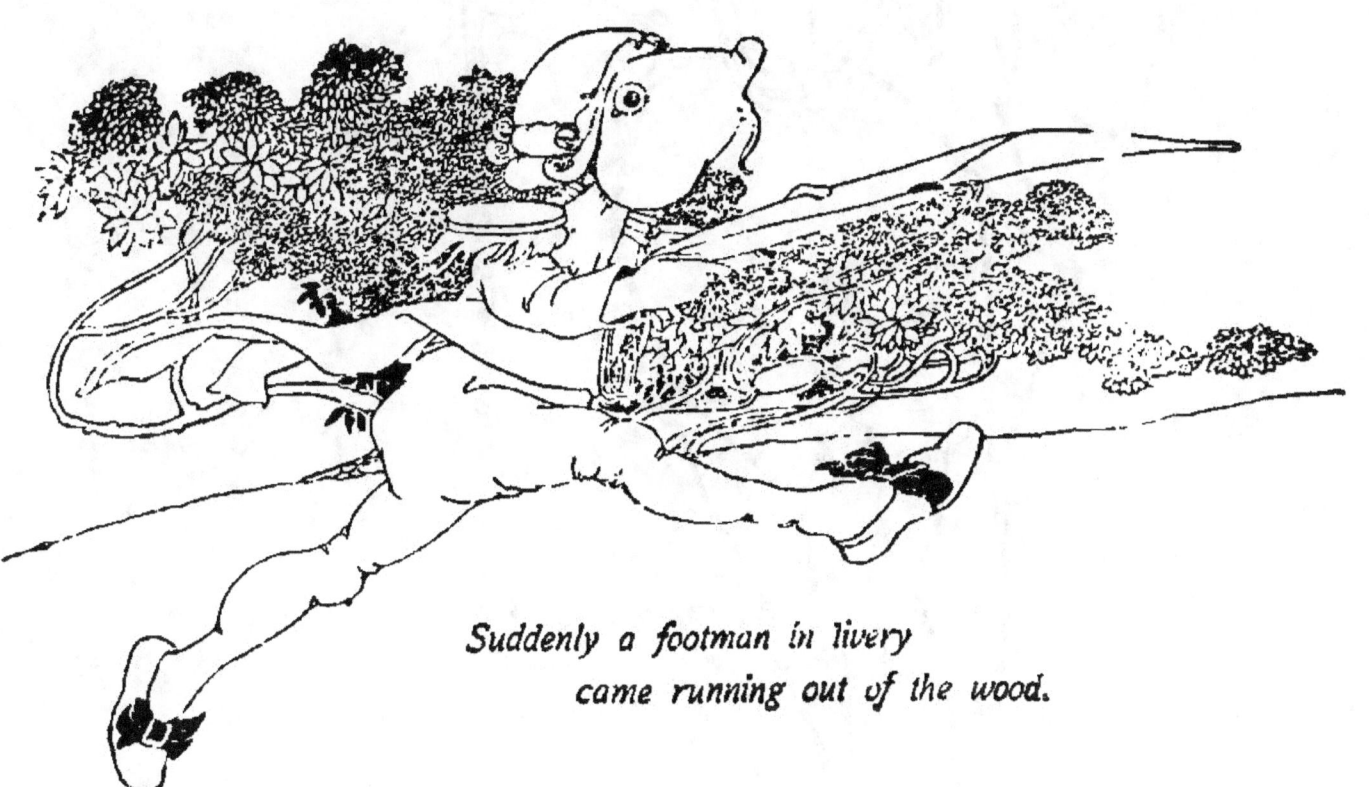

Suddenly a footman in livery
came running out of the wood.

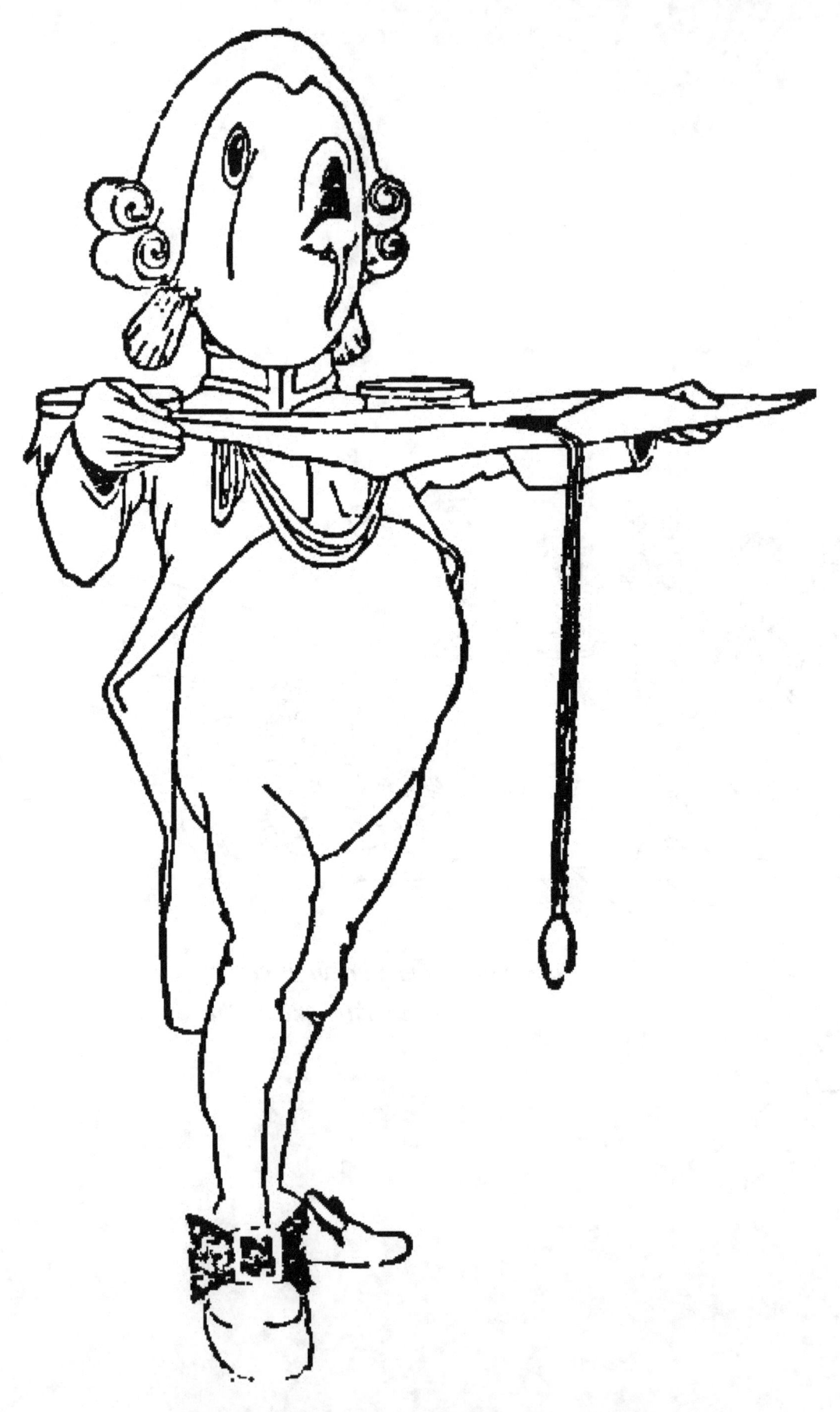

" *For the Duchess. An invitation from the Queen* "

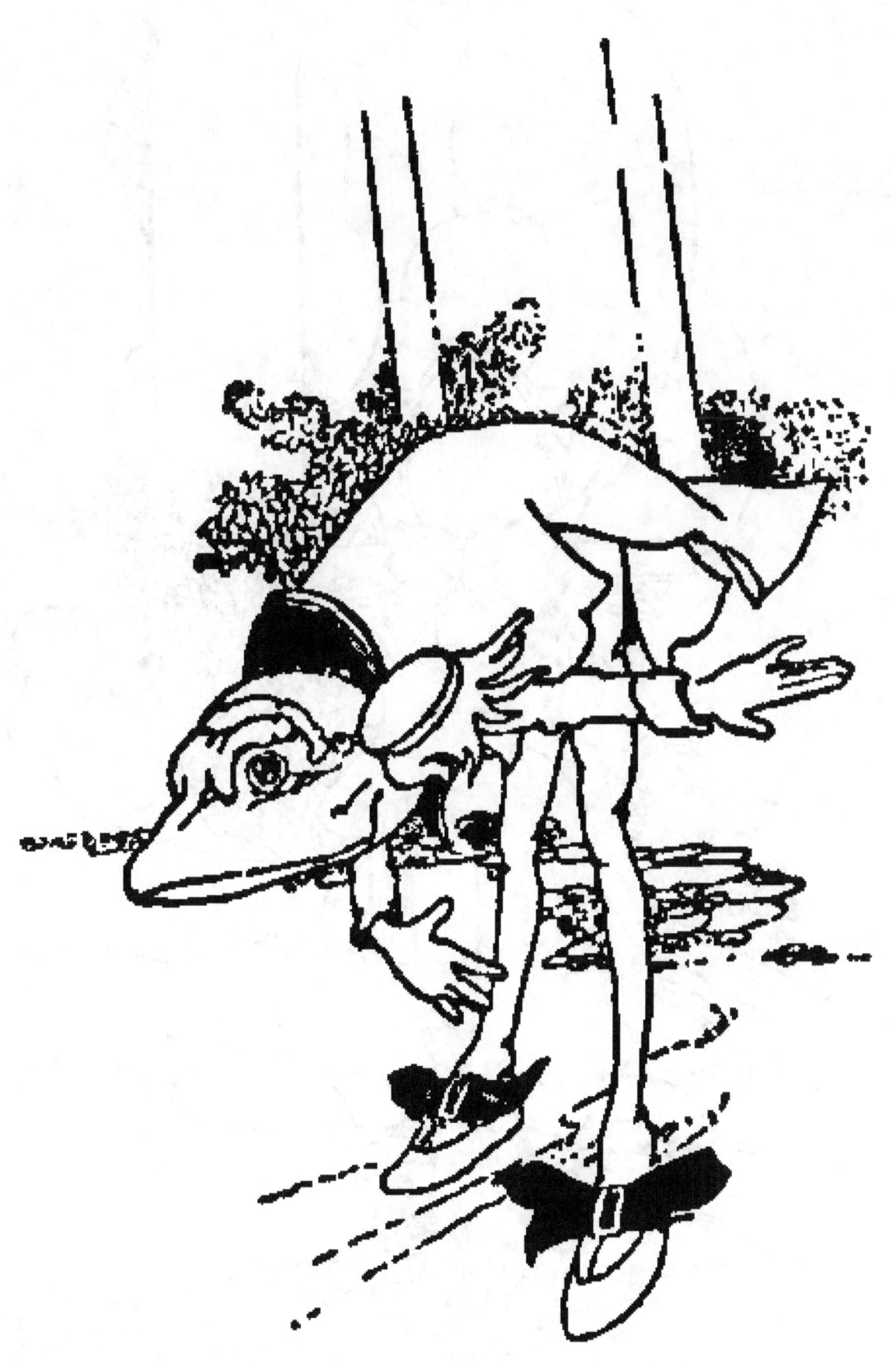

"From the Queen."

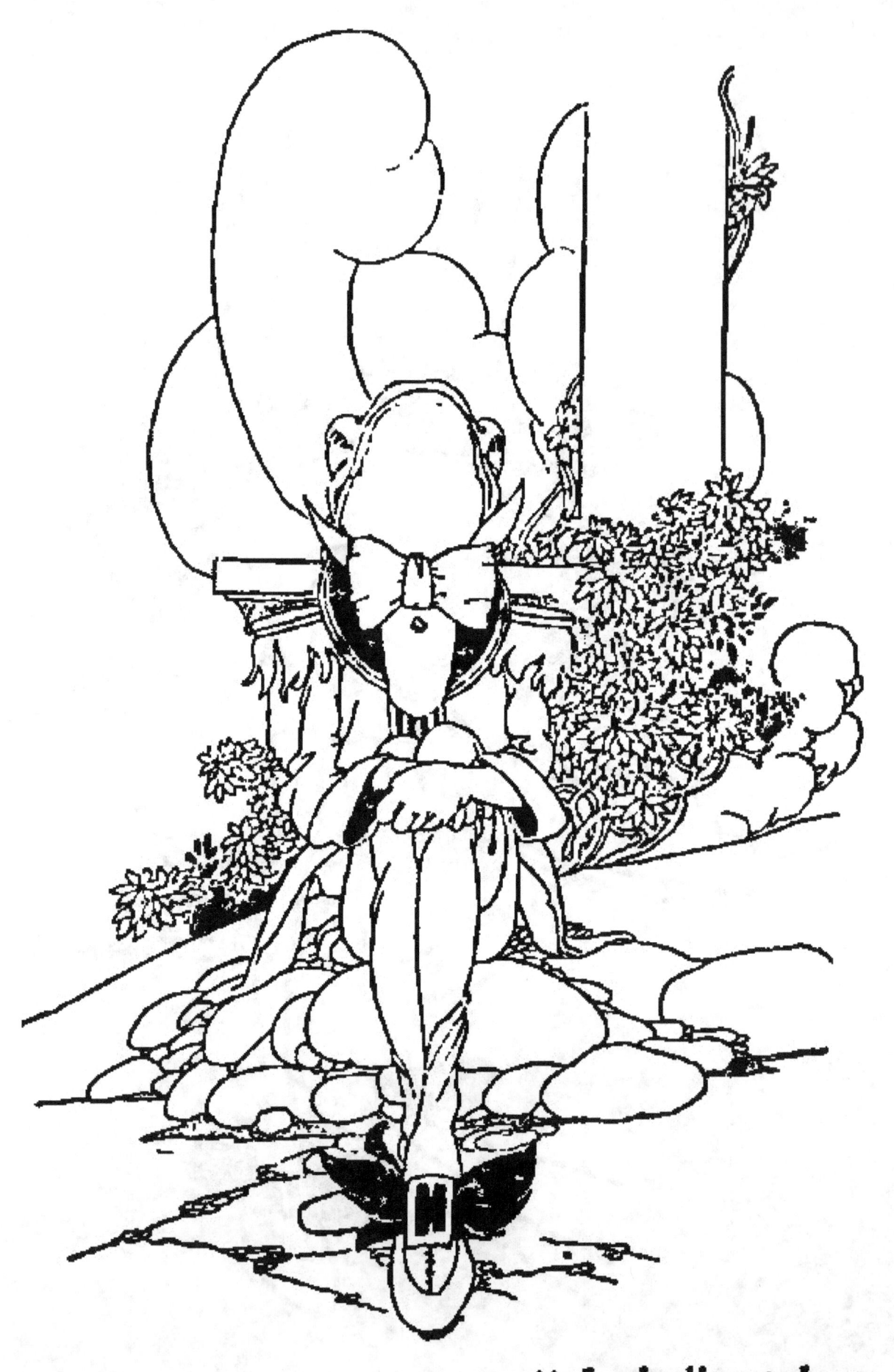

" I shall sit here
till to-morrow."

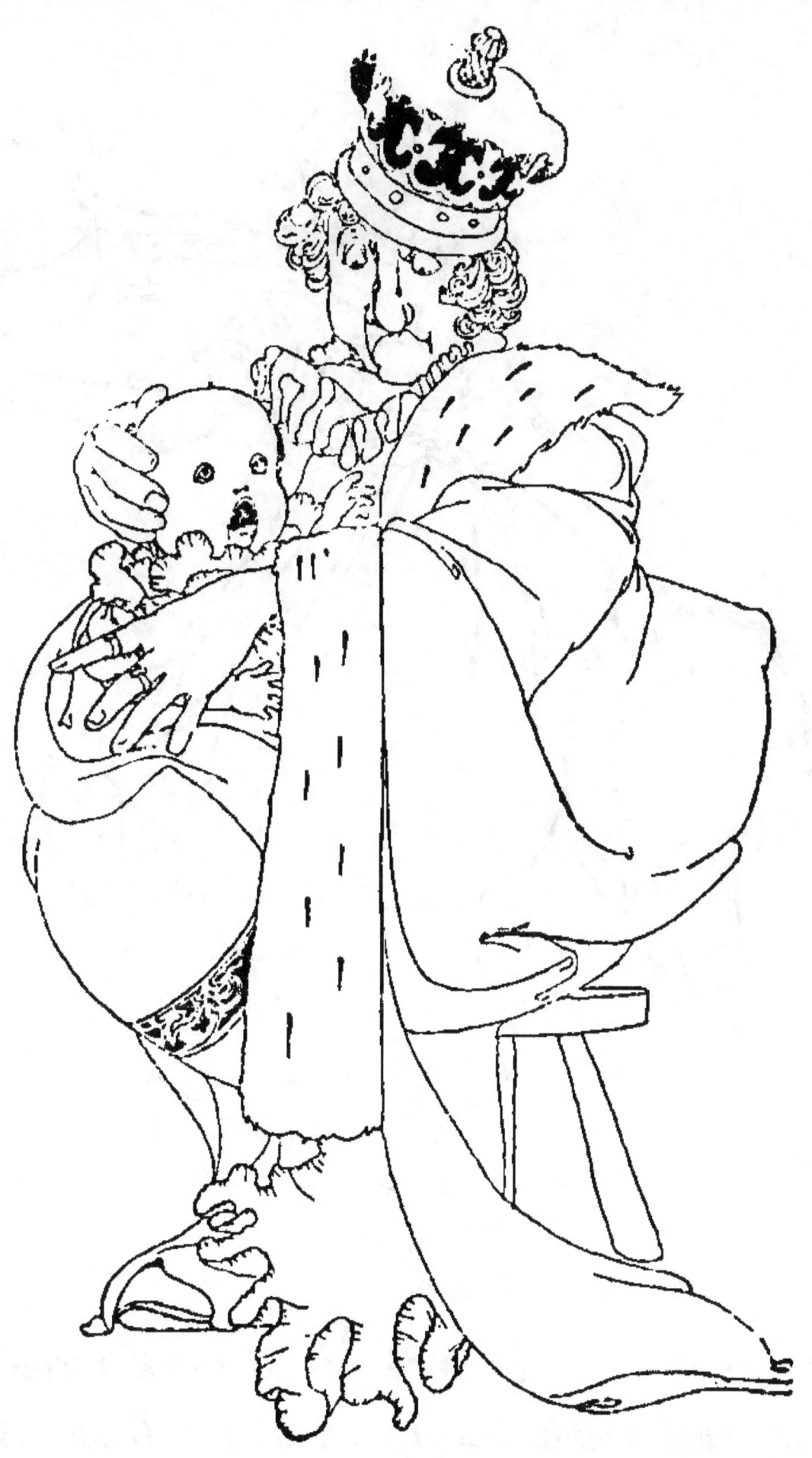

The Duchess

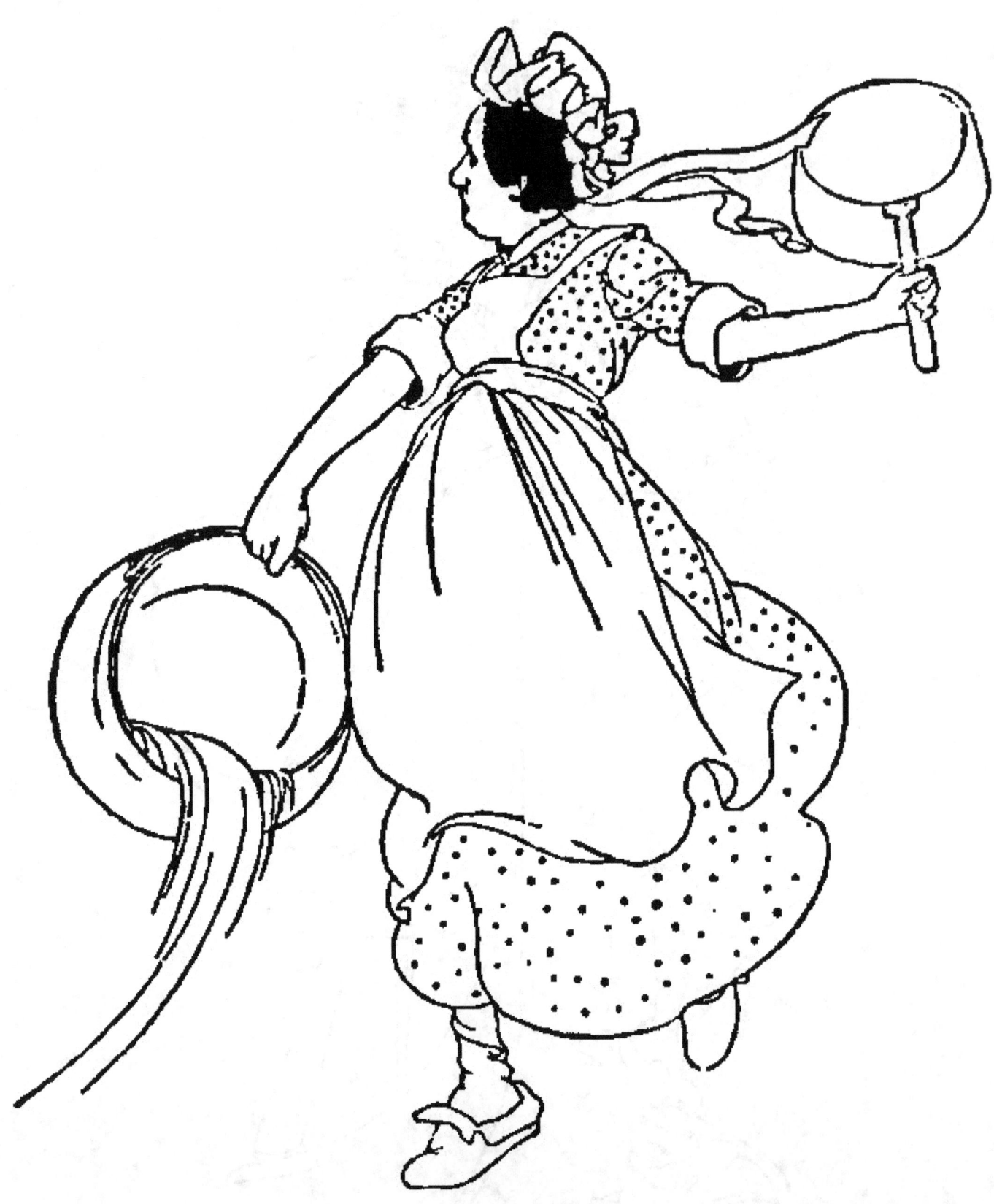

The cook . . at once set to work throwing
everything within her reach at the Duchess.

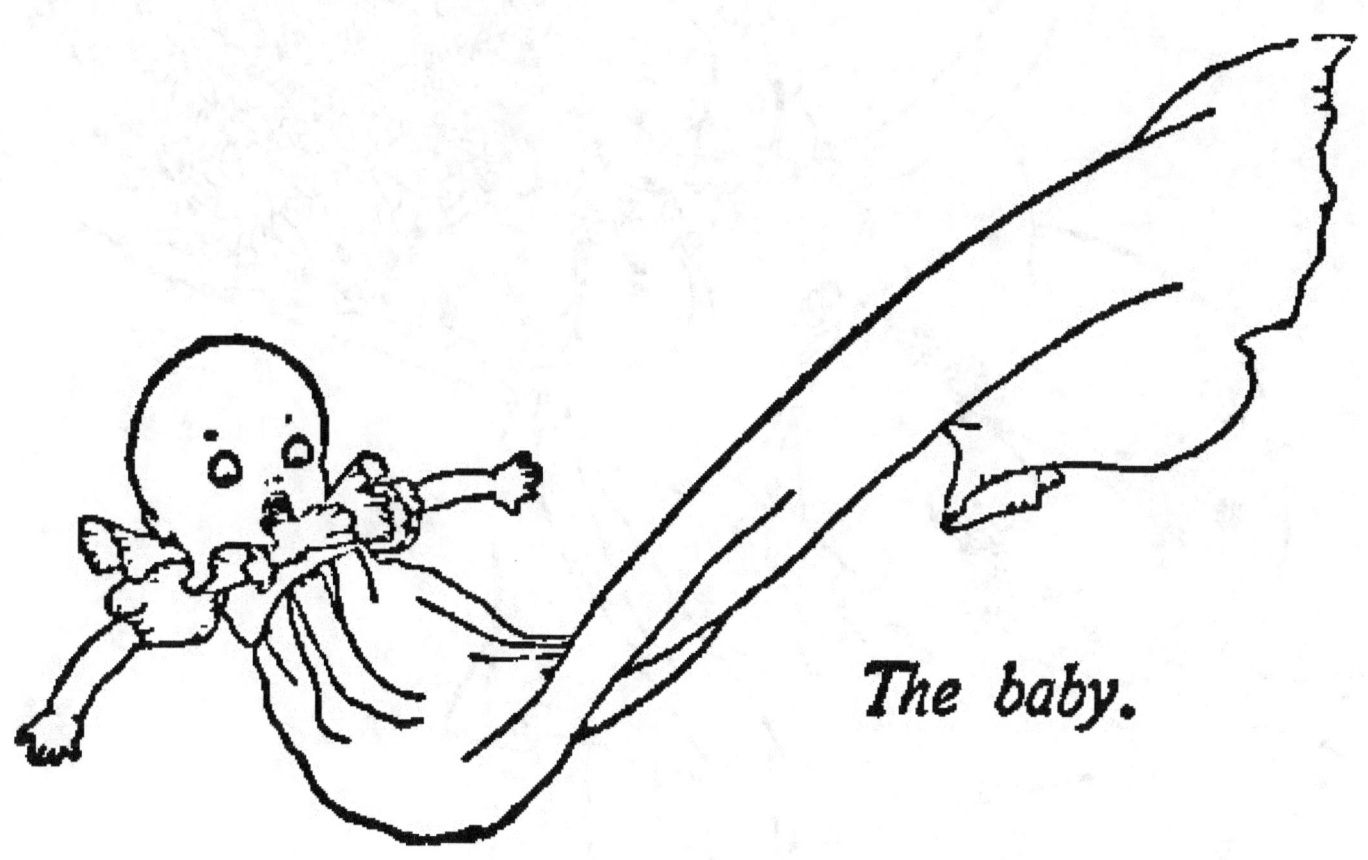

The baby.

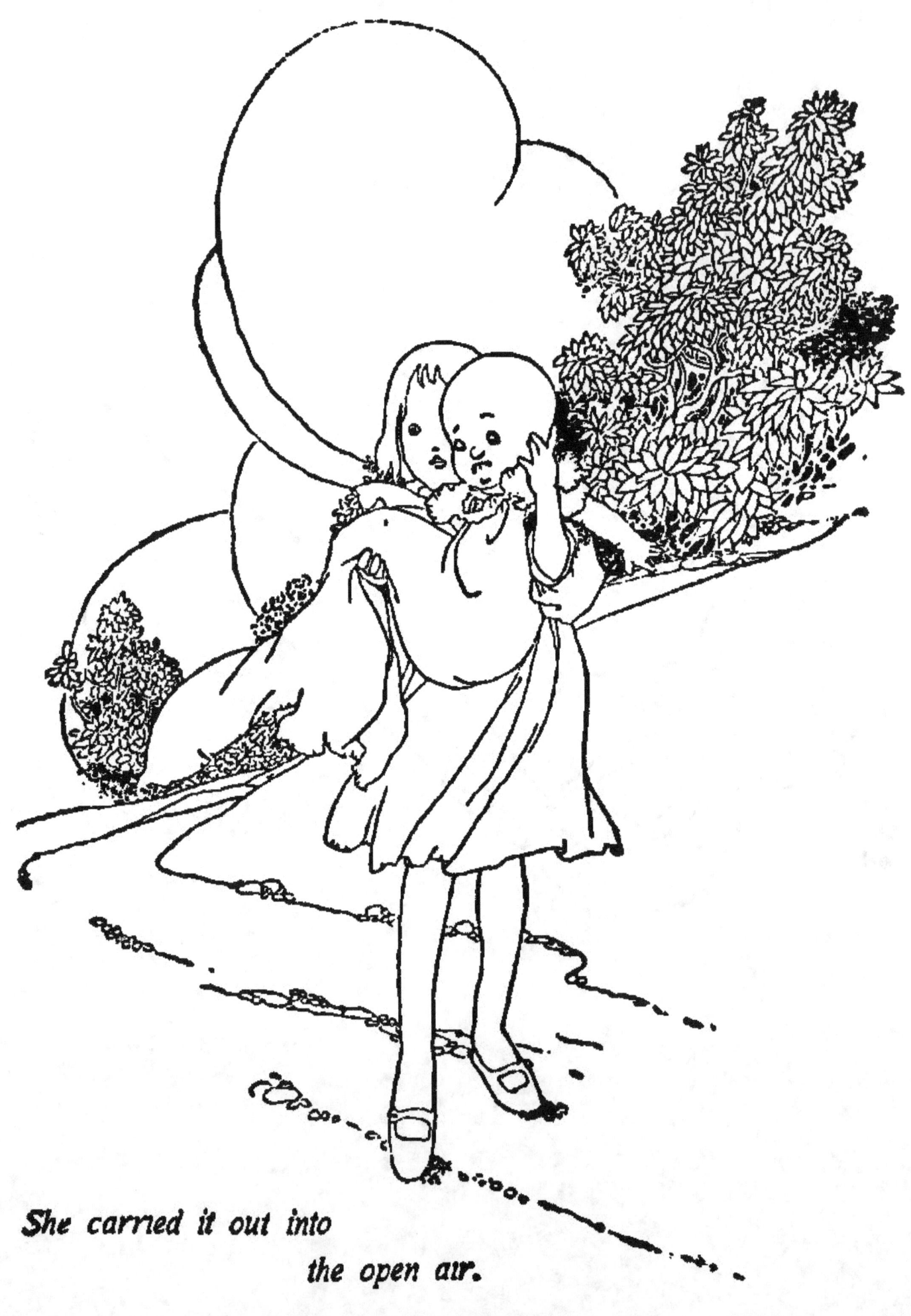

She carried it out into

  the open air.

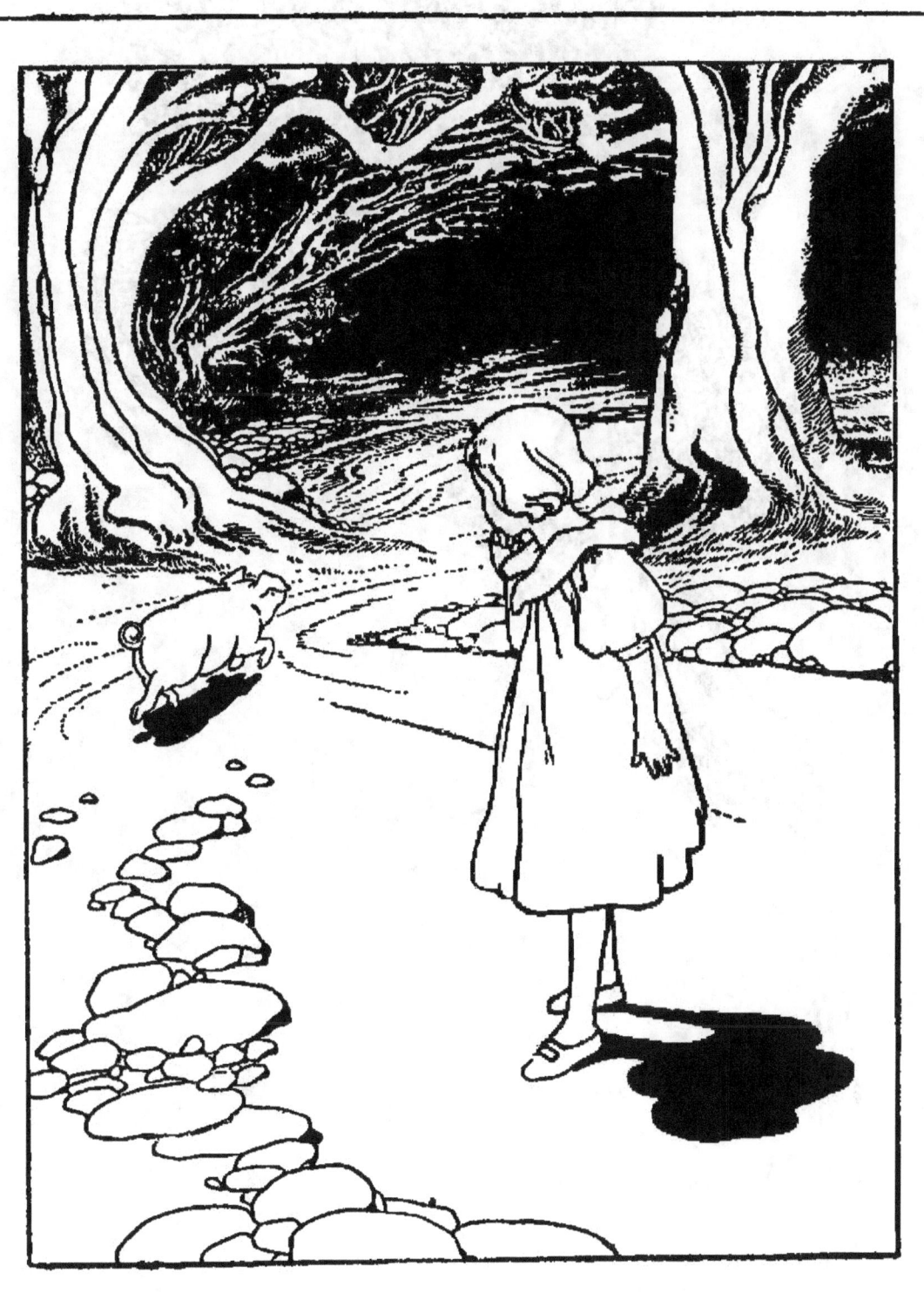

She ✱✱✱ felt quite relieved
to see it trot quietly away

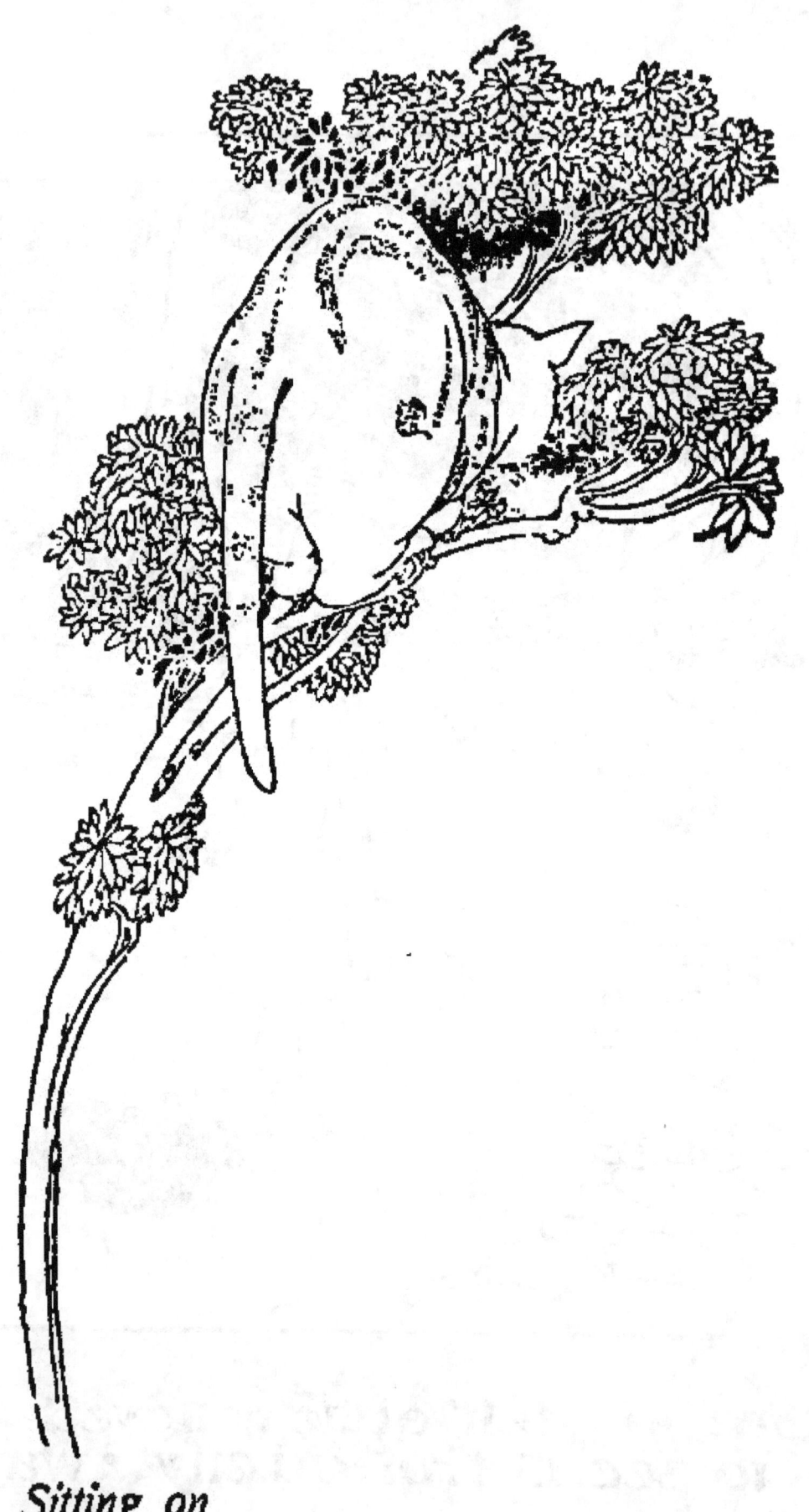

Sitting on
a bough
of a tree.

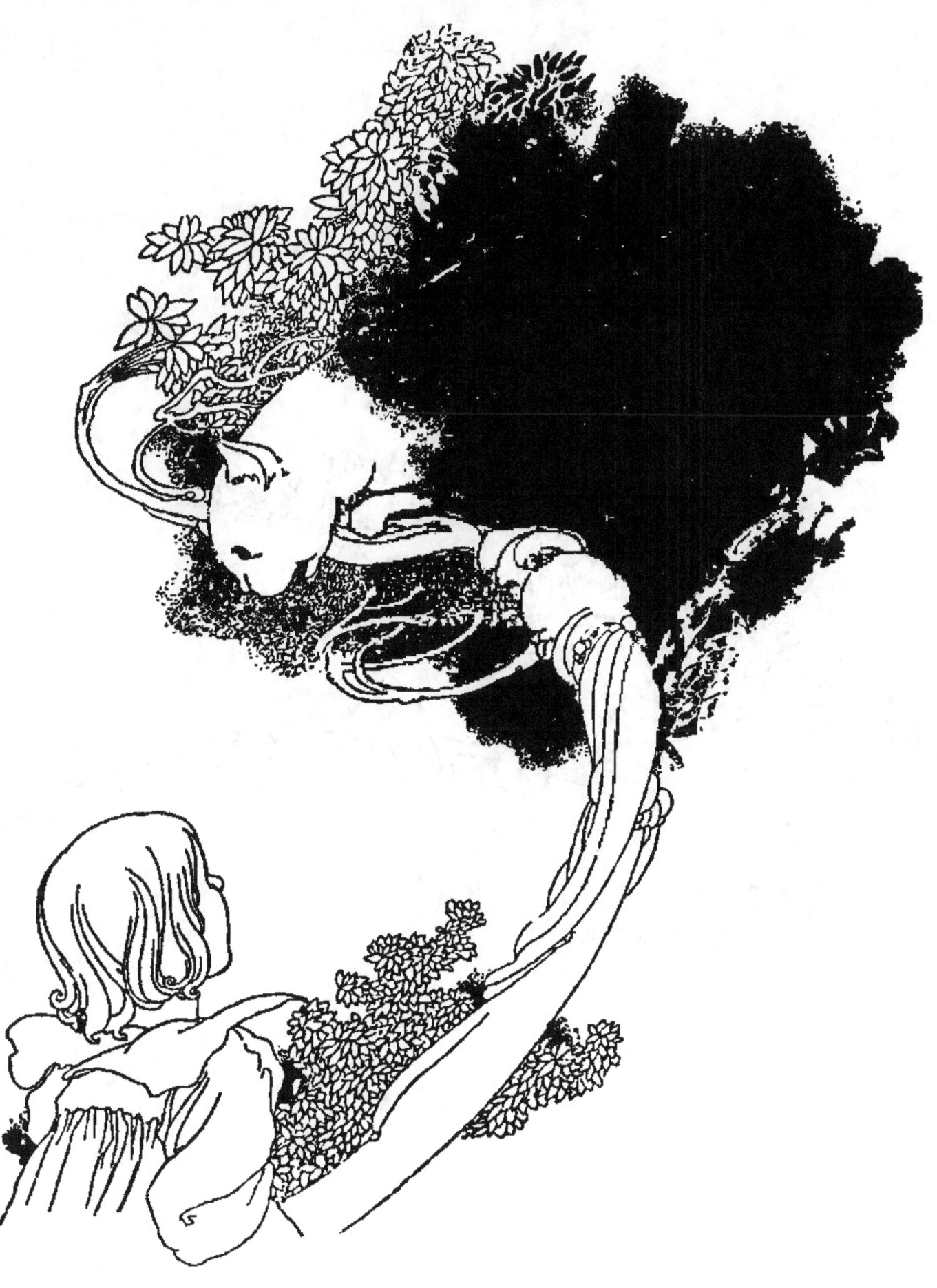

" *Did you say pig,*
          or fig ? "

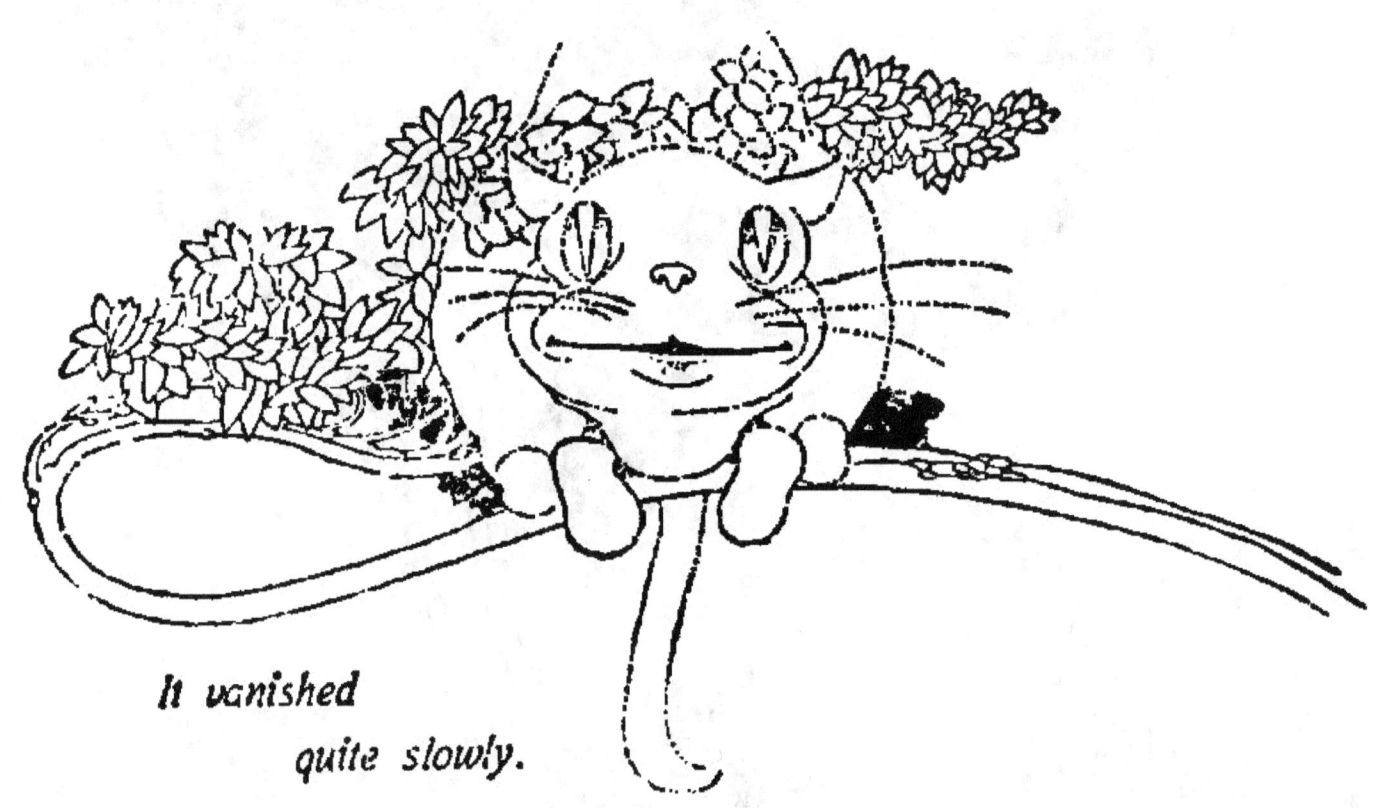

It vanished
    quite slowly.

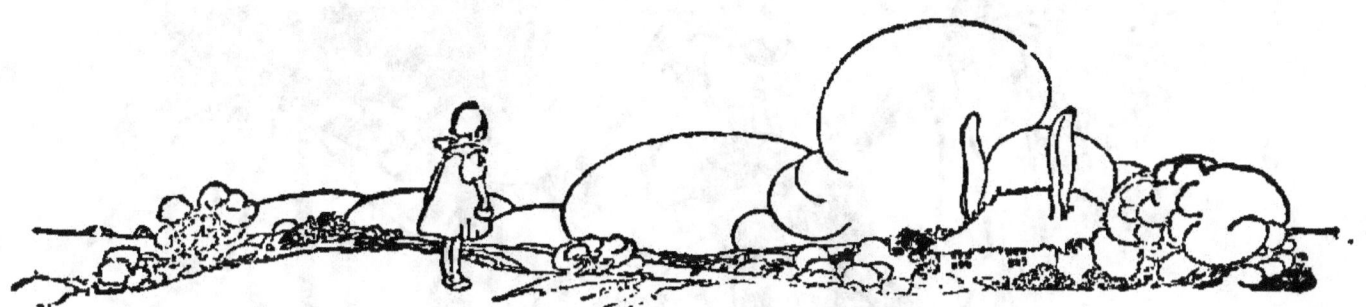

The March
Hare's house

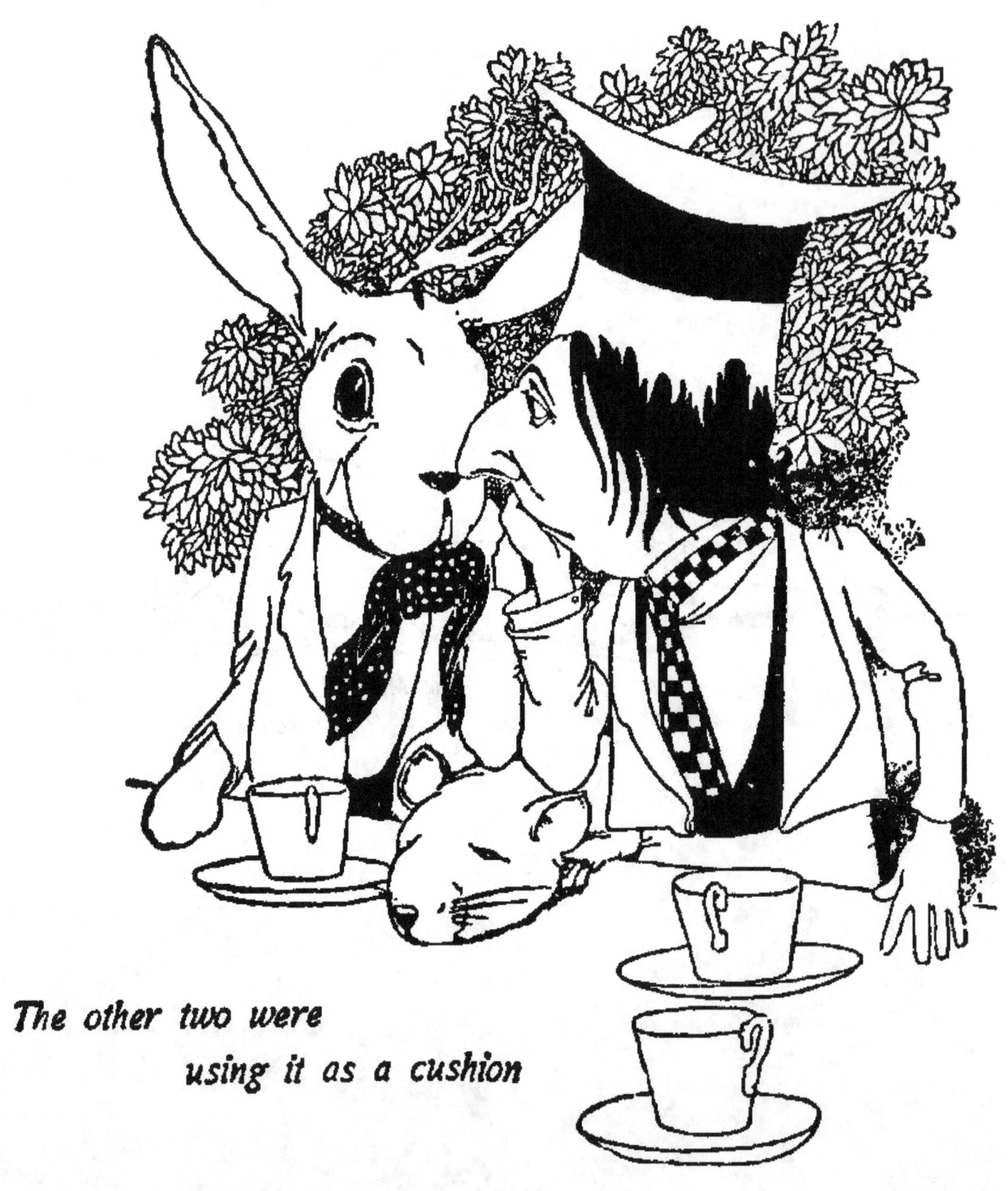

The other two were

using it as a cushion

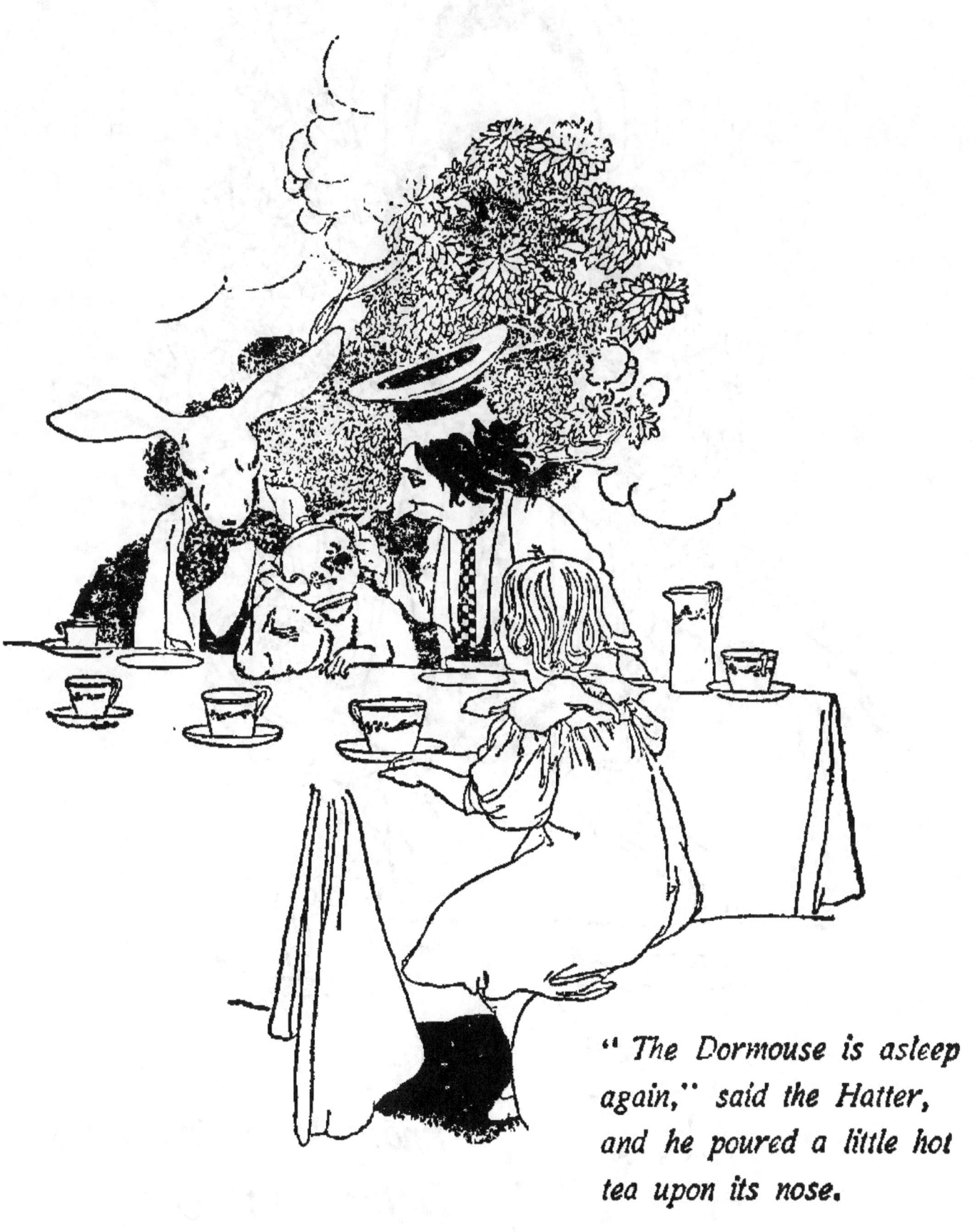

" The Dormouse is asleep
again," said the Hatter,
and he poured a little hot
tea upon its nose.

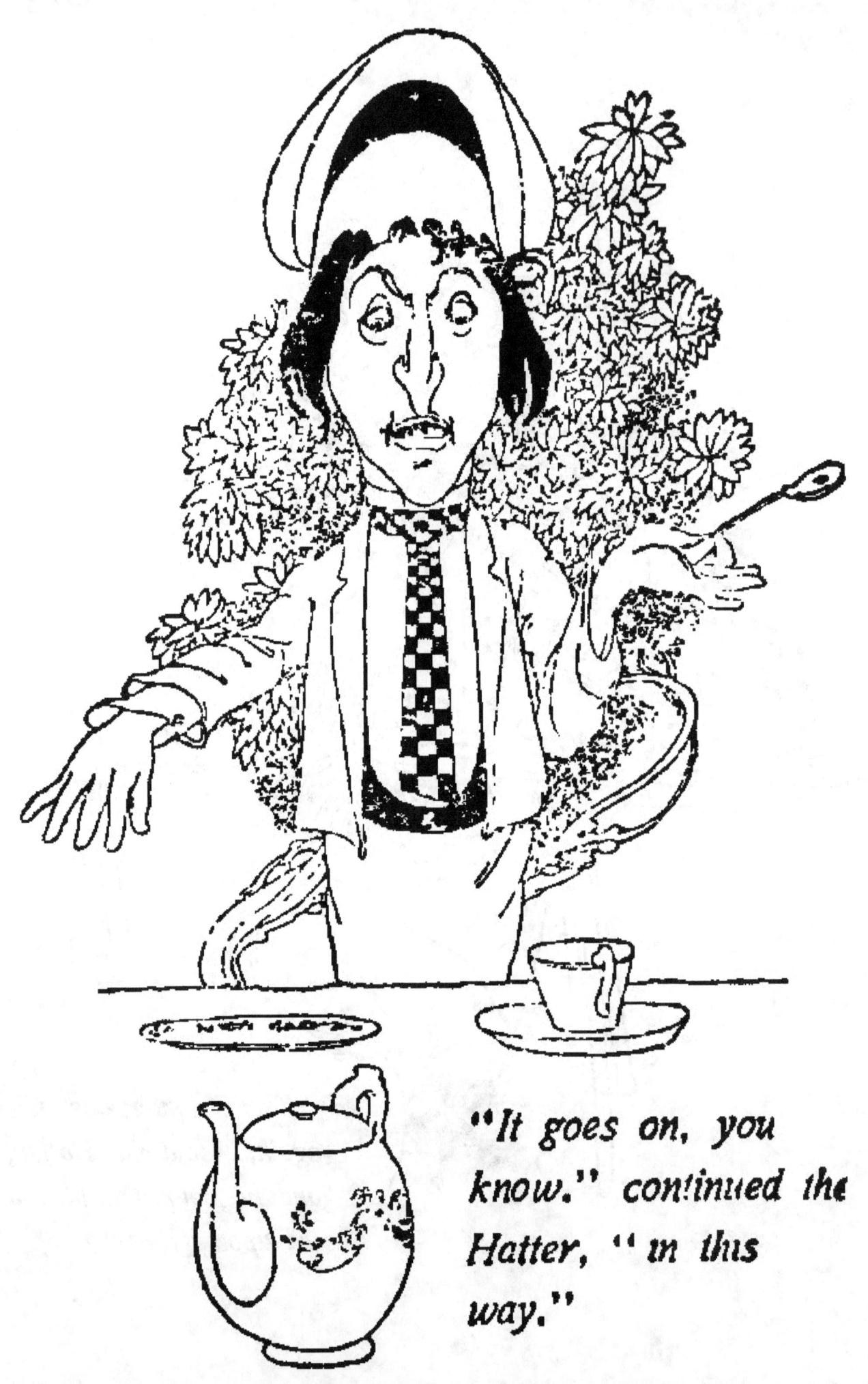

"It goes on, you know." continued the Hatter, "in this way."

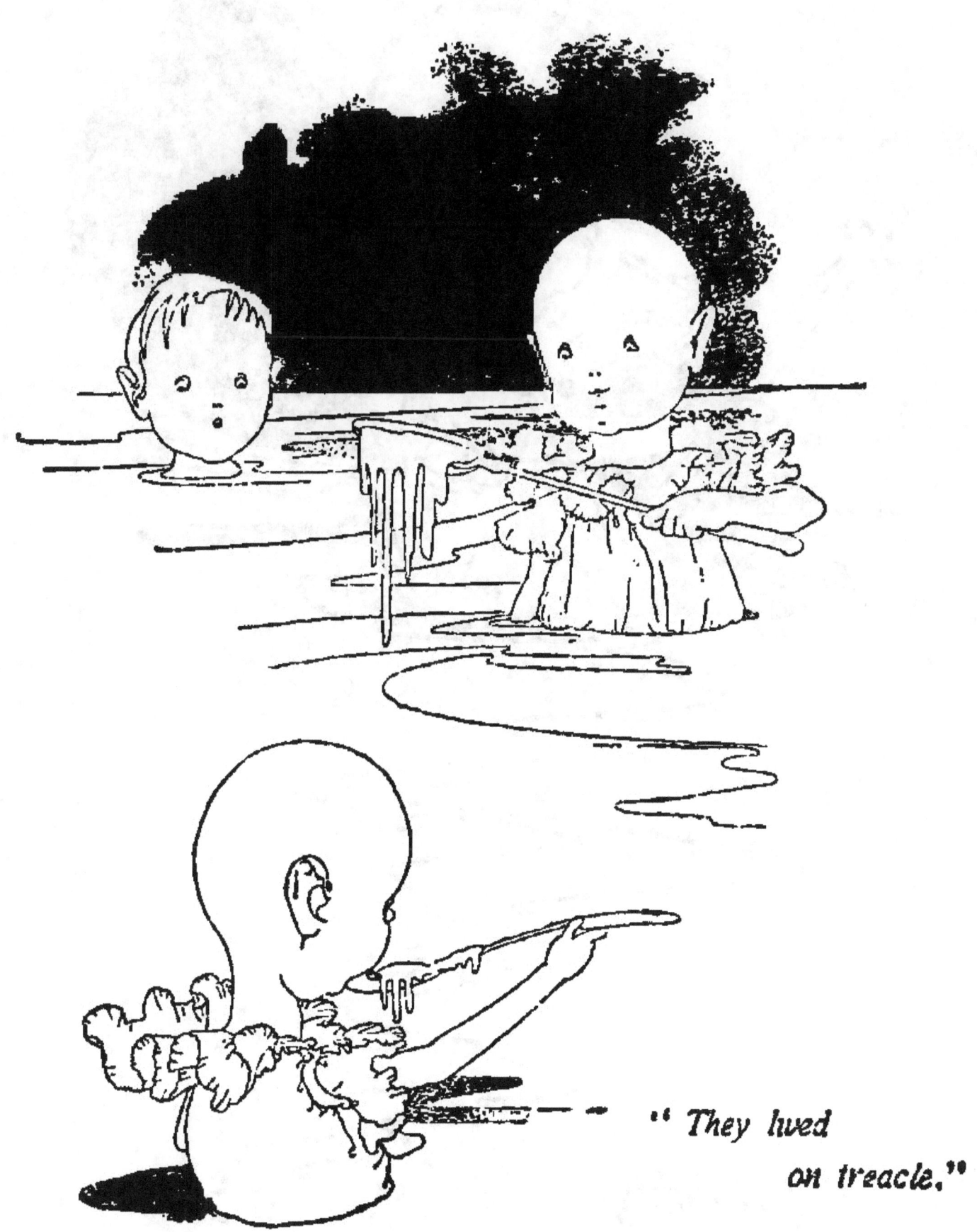

" They lived
on treacle."

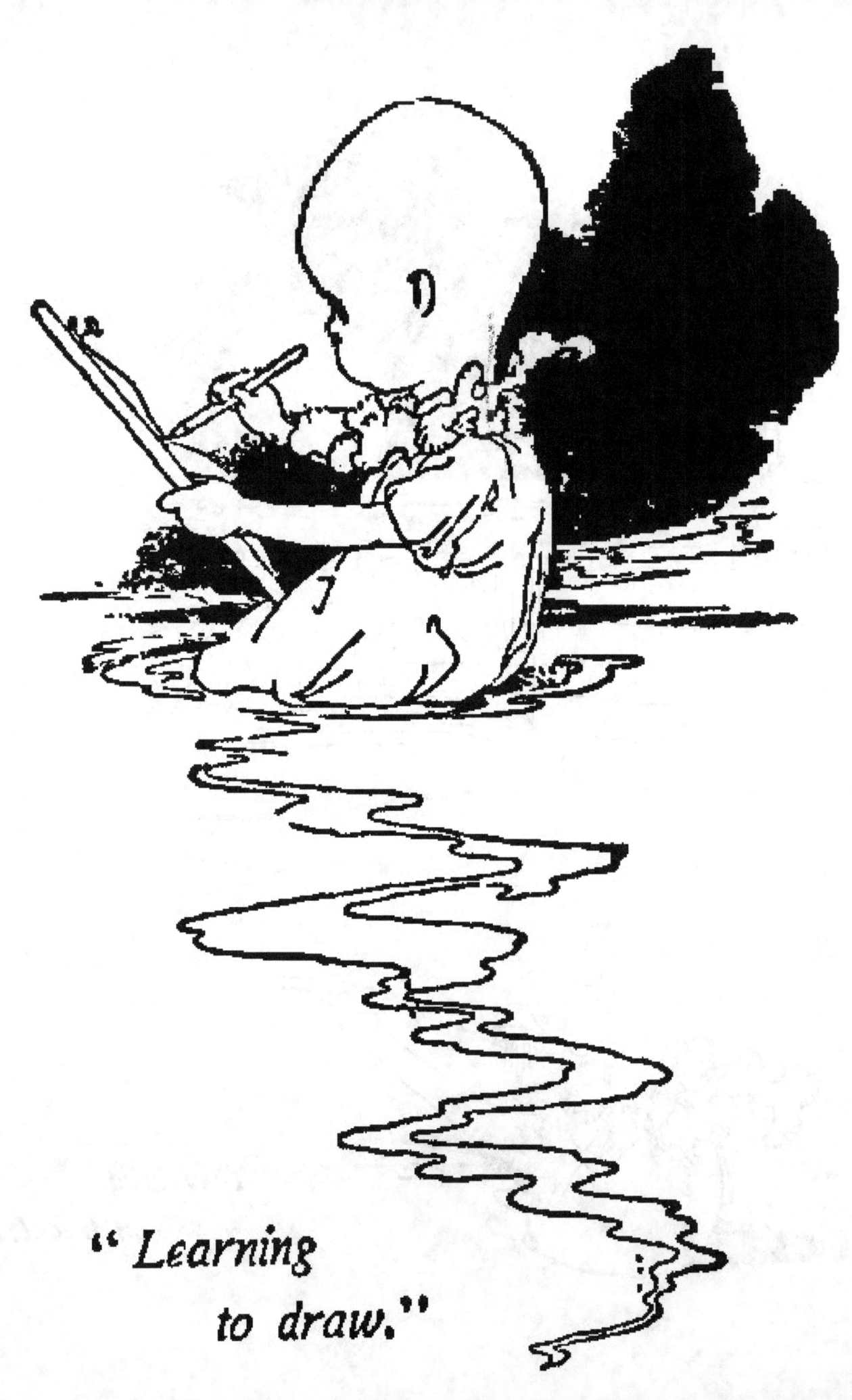

" Learning
   to draw."

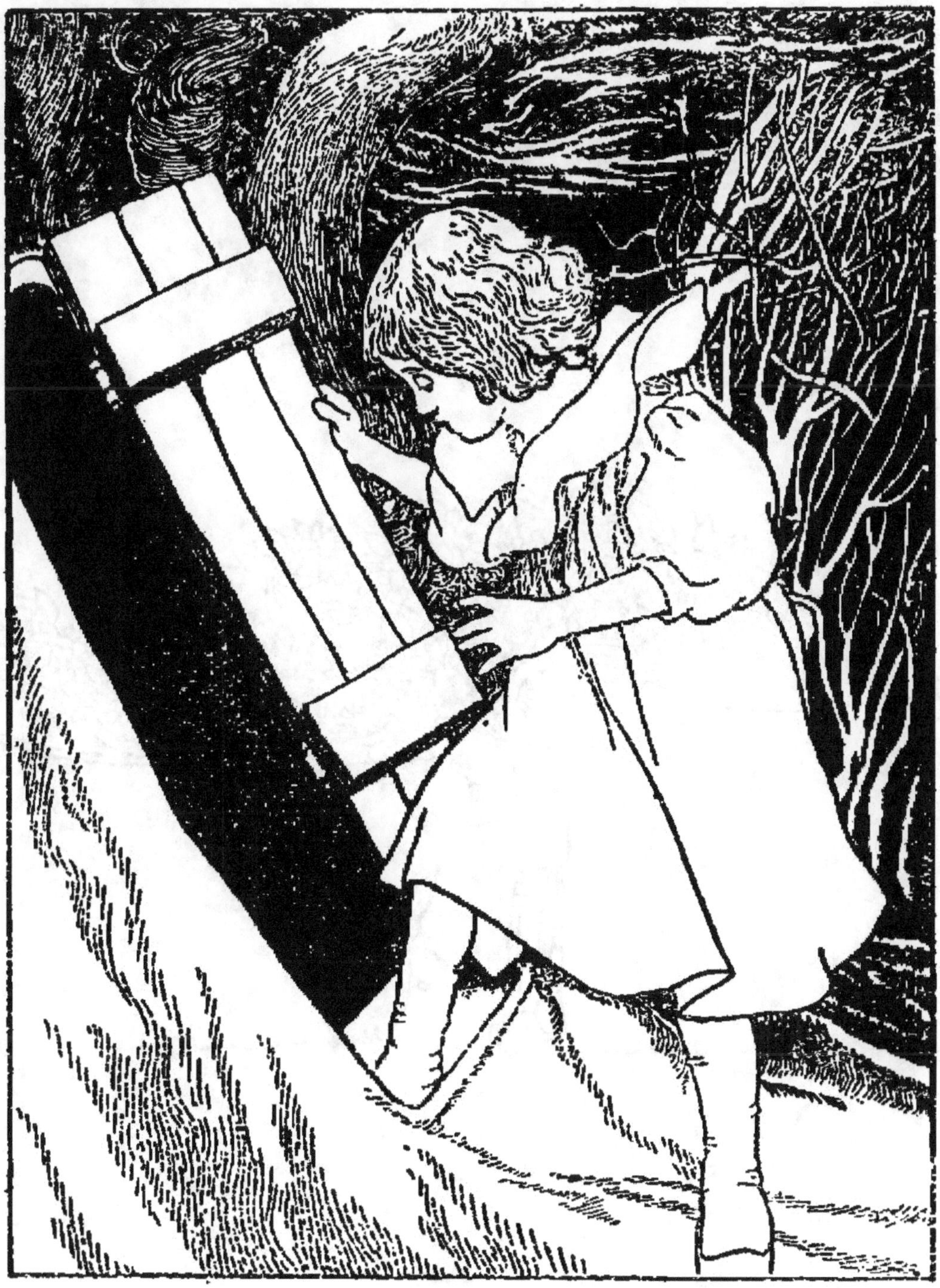

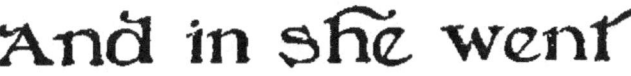

And in she went

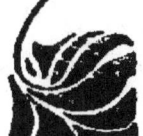
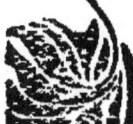

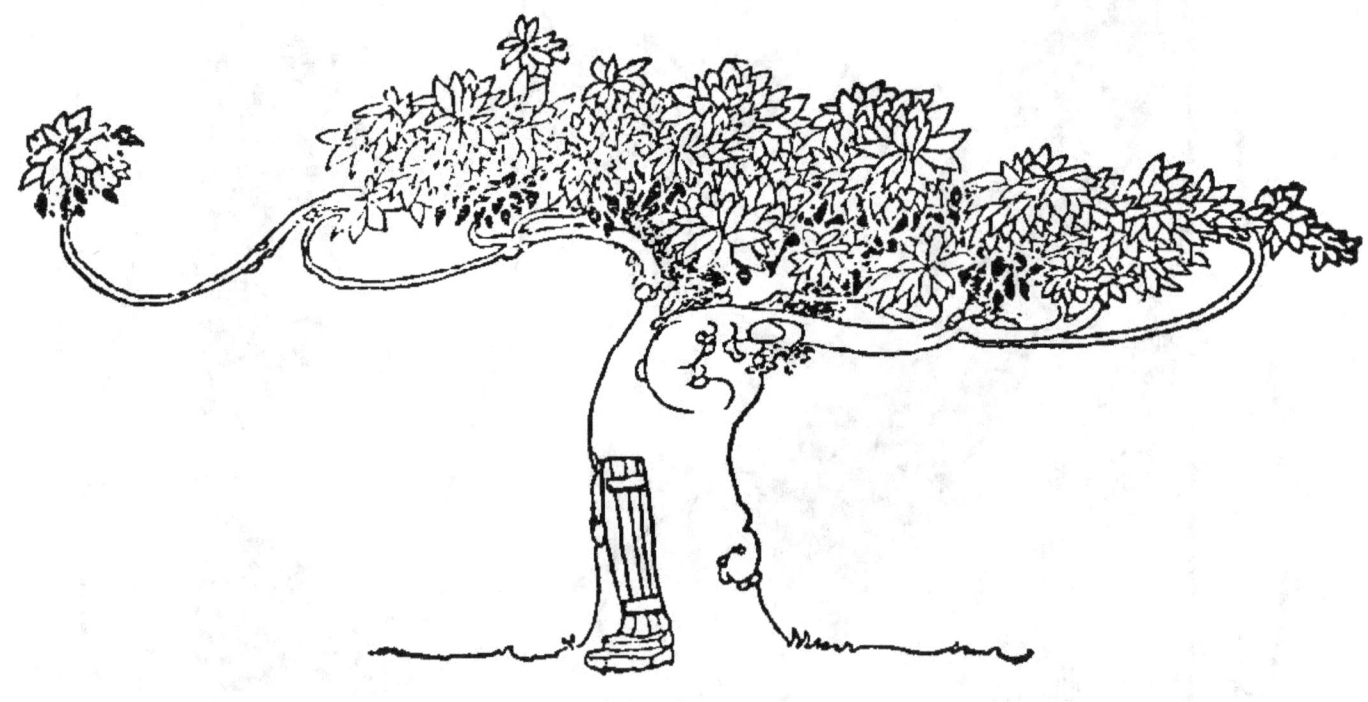

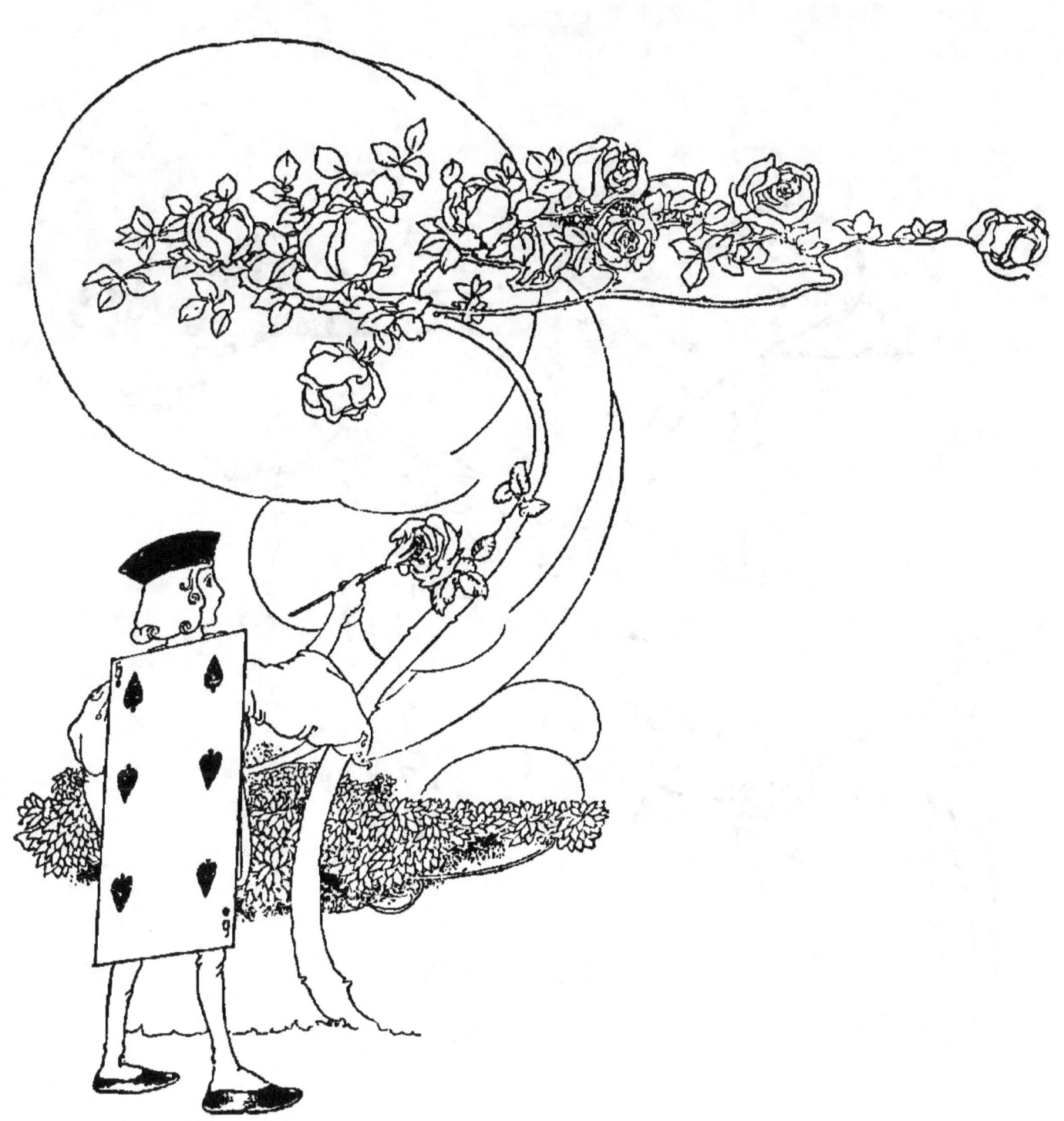

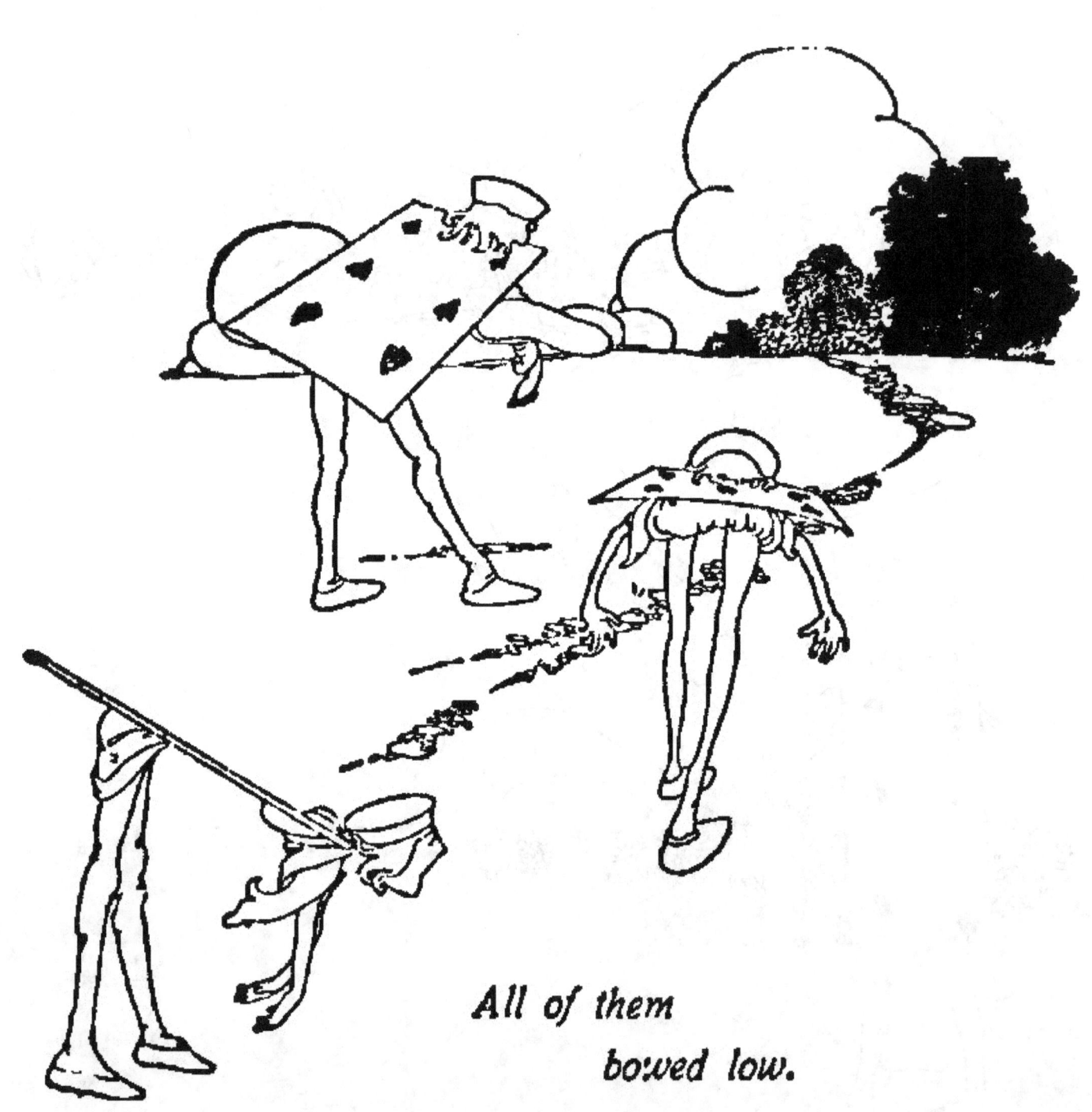

All of them
bowed low.

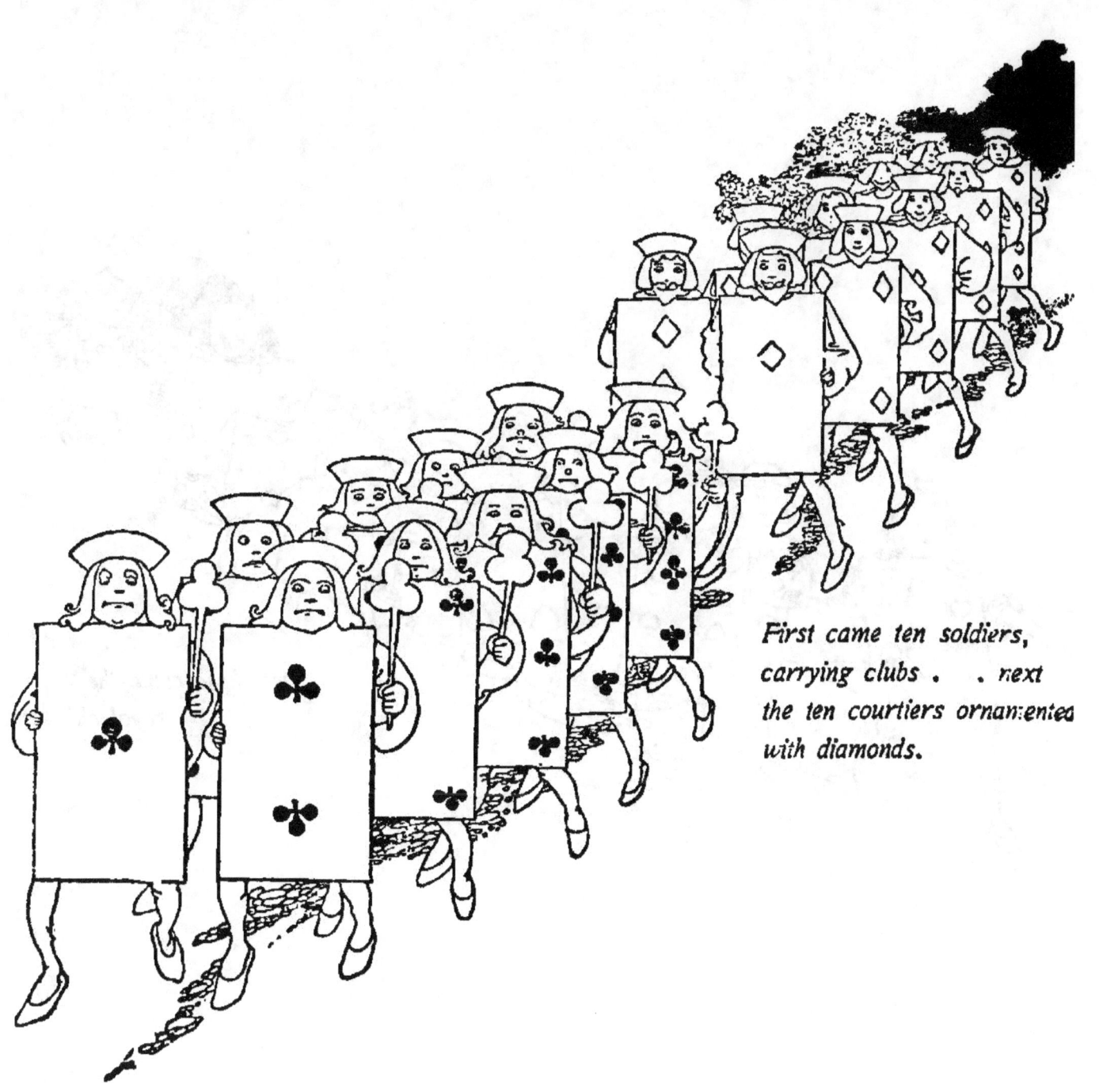

First came ten soldiers, carrying clubs . . . next the ten courtiers ornamented with diamonds.

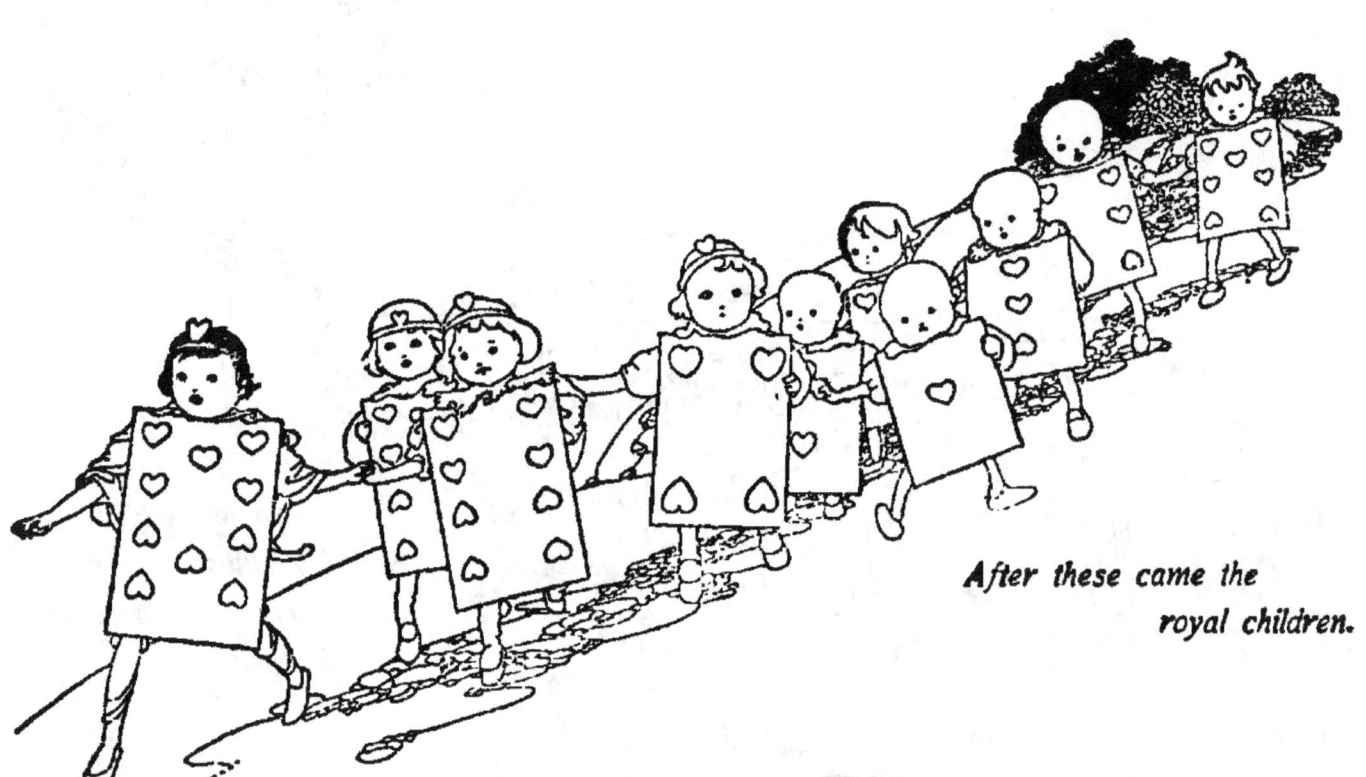

After these came the
     royal children.

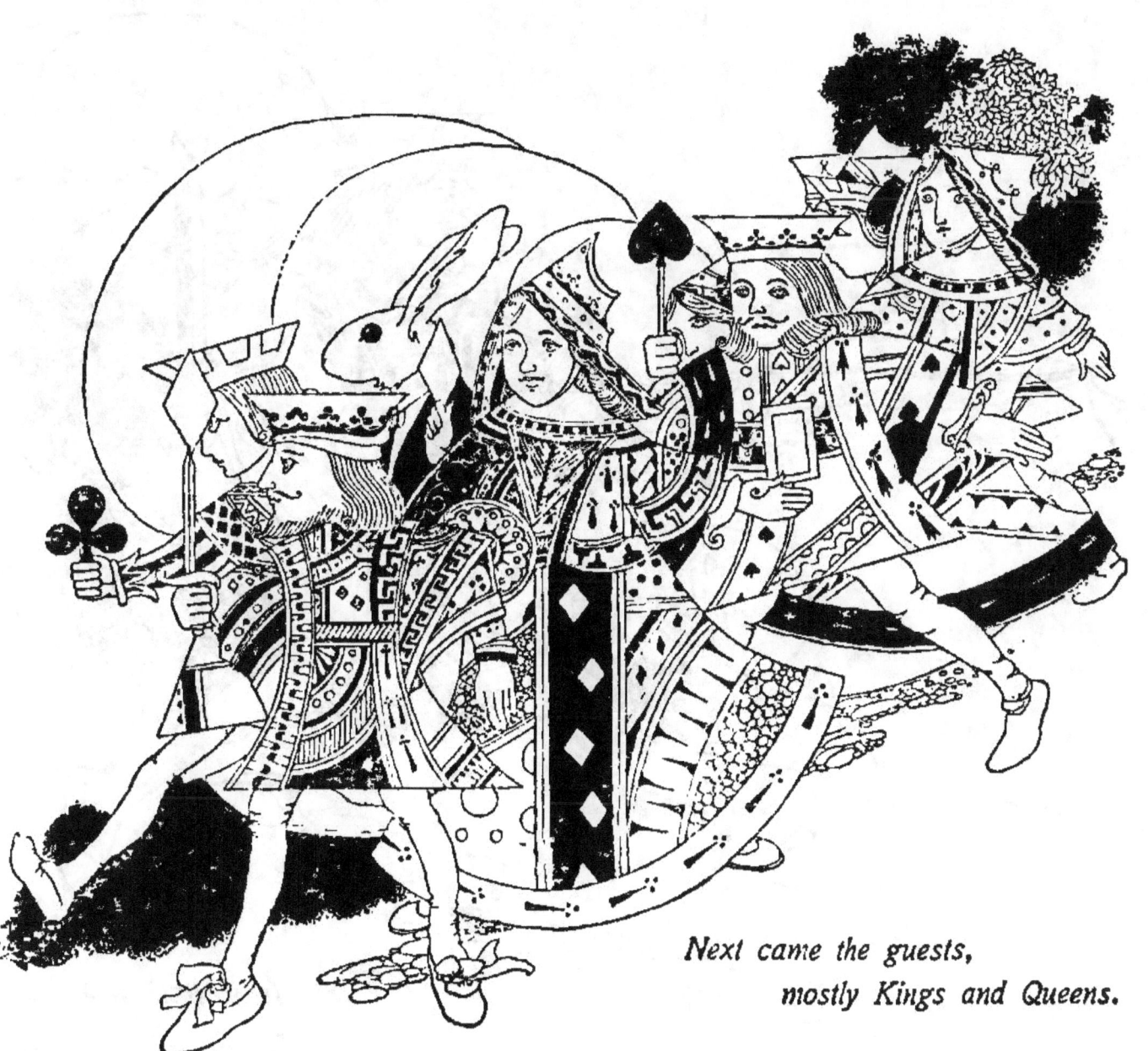

Next came the guests,
mostly Kings and Queens.

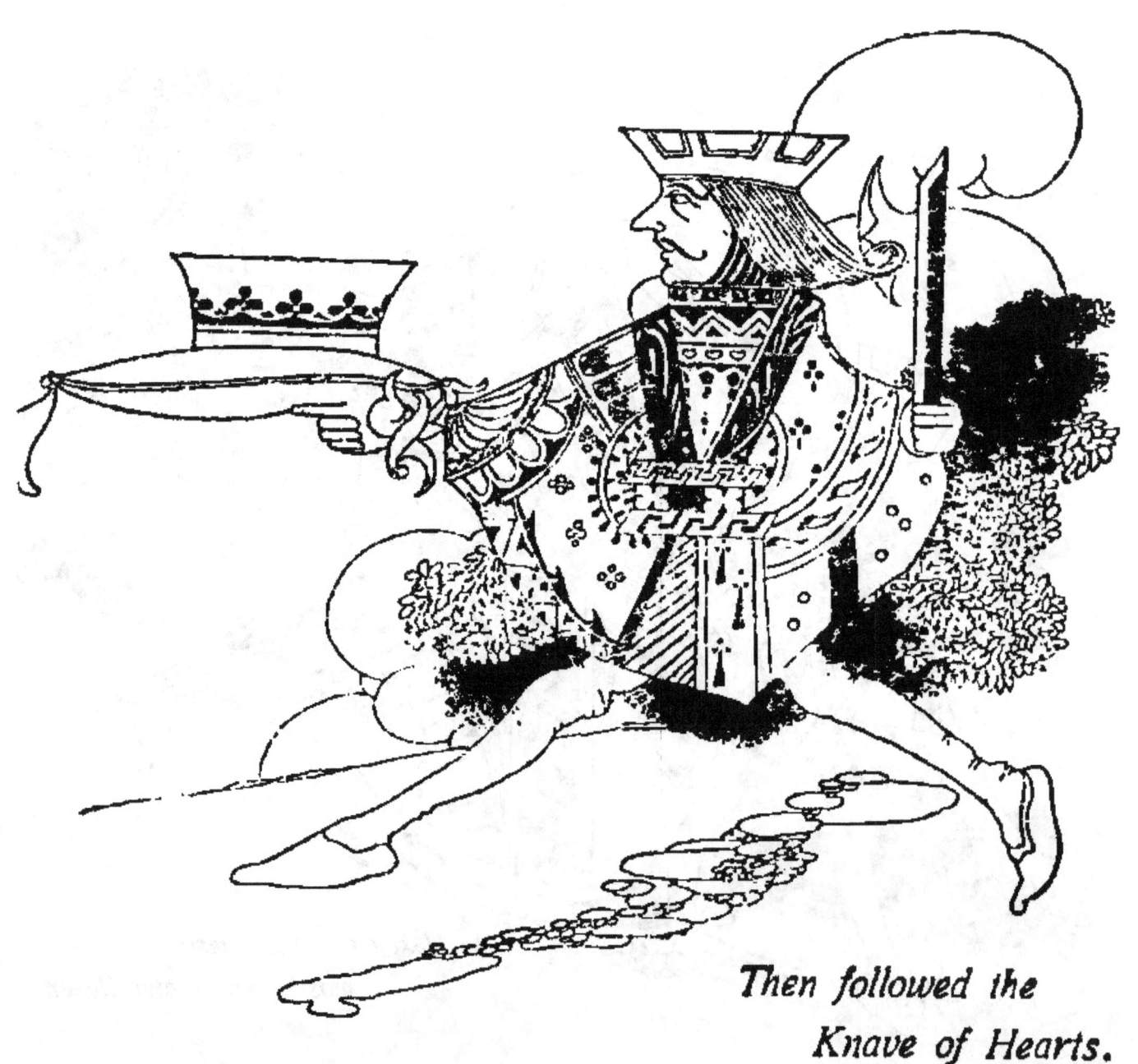

Then followed the
Knave of Hearts.

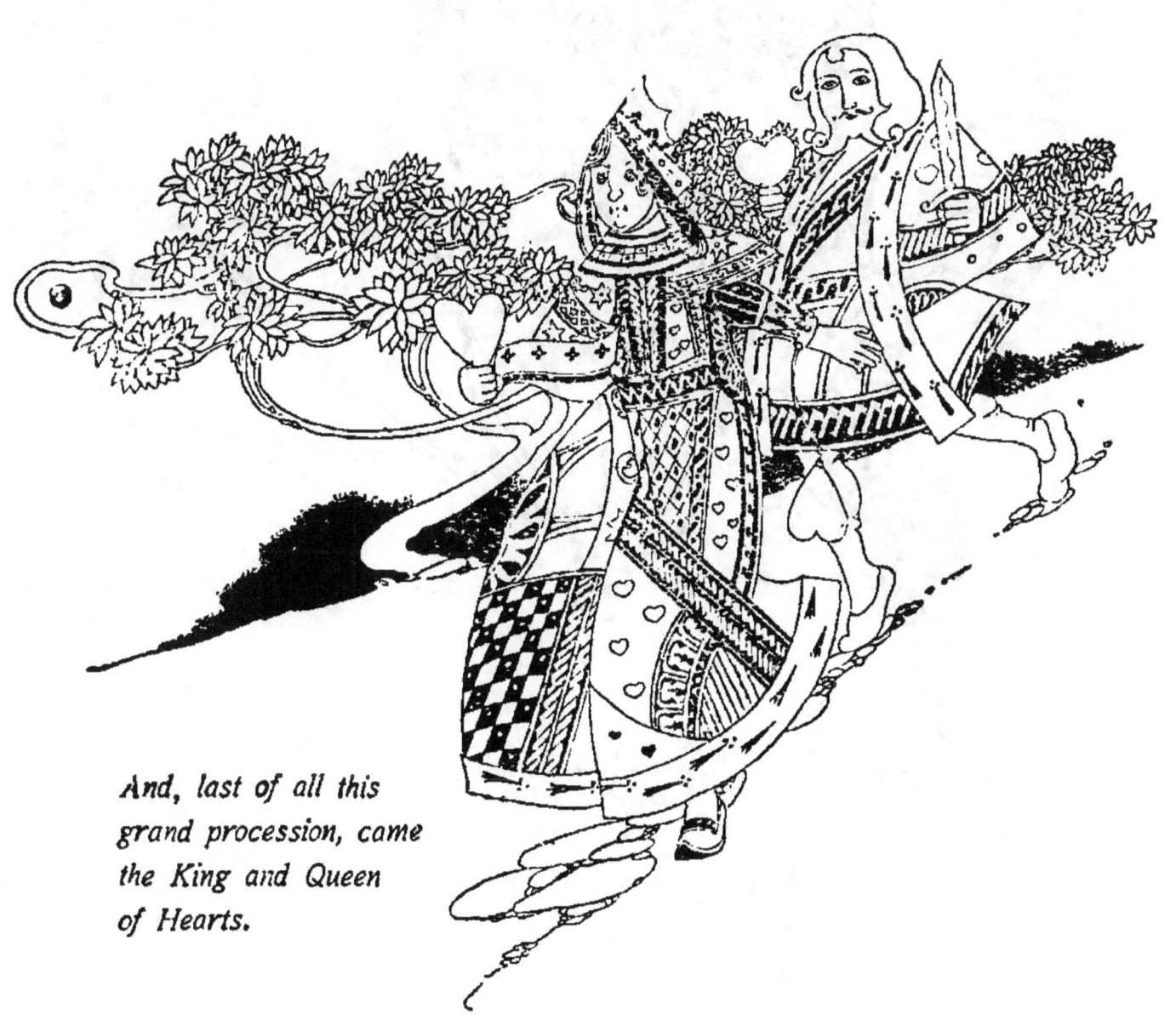

And, last of all this
grand procession, came
the King and Queen
of Hearts.

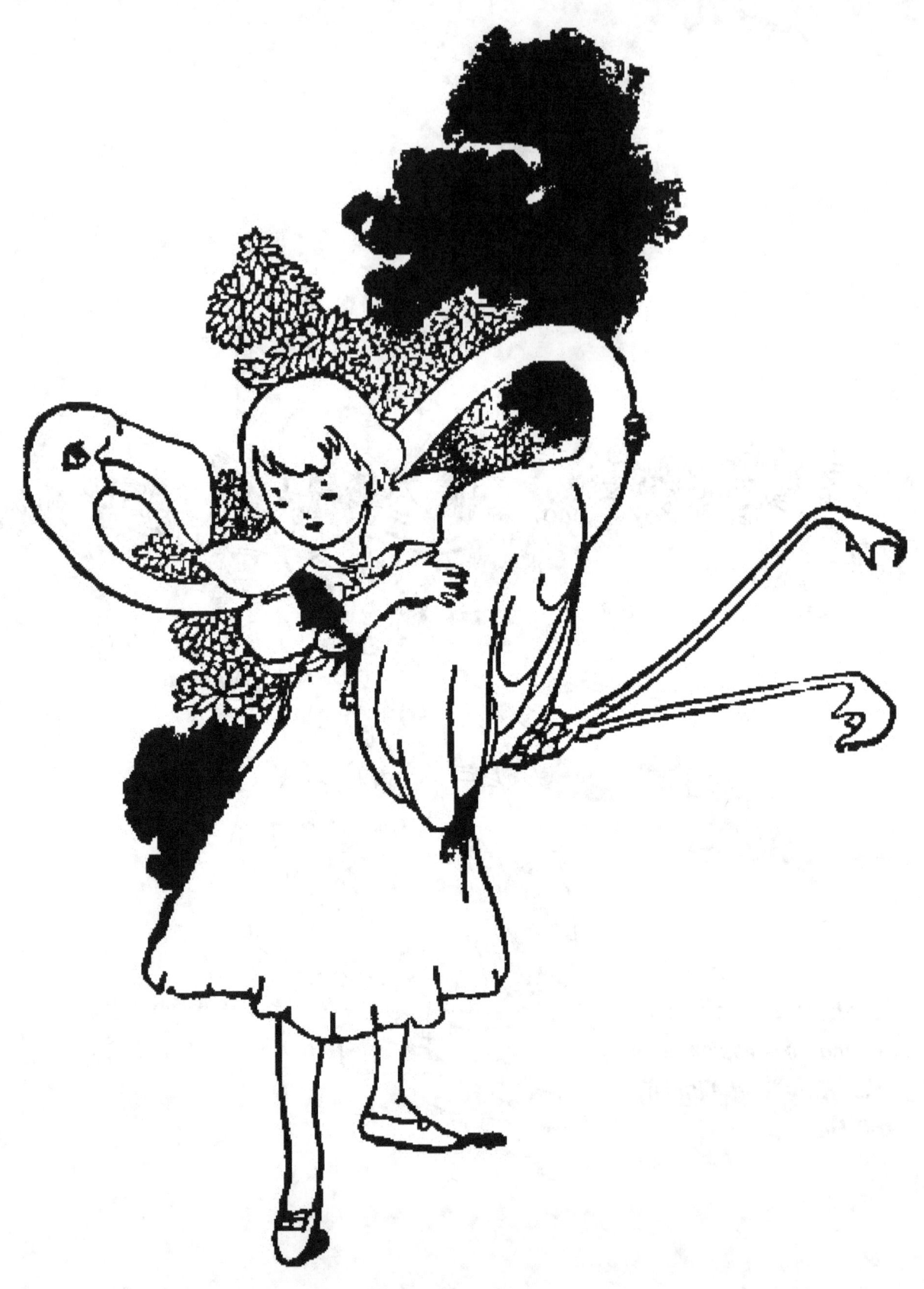

It would twist
itself round and look
up into her face.

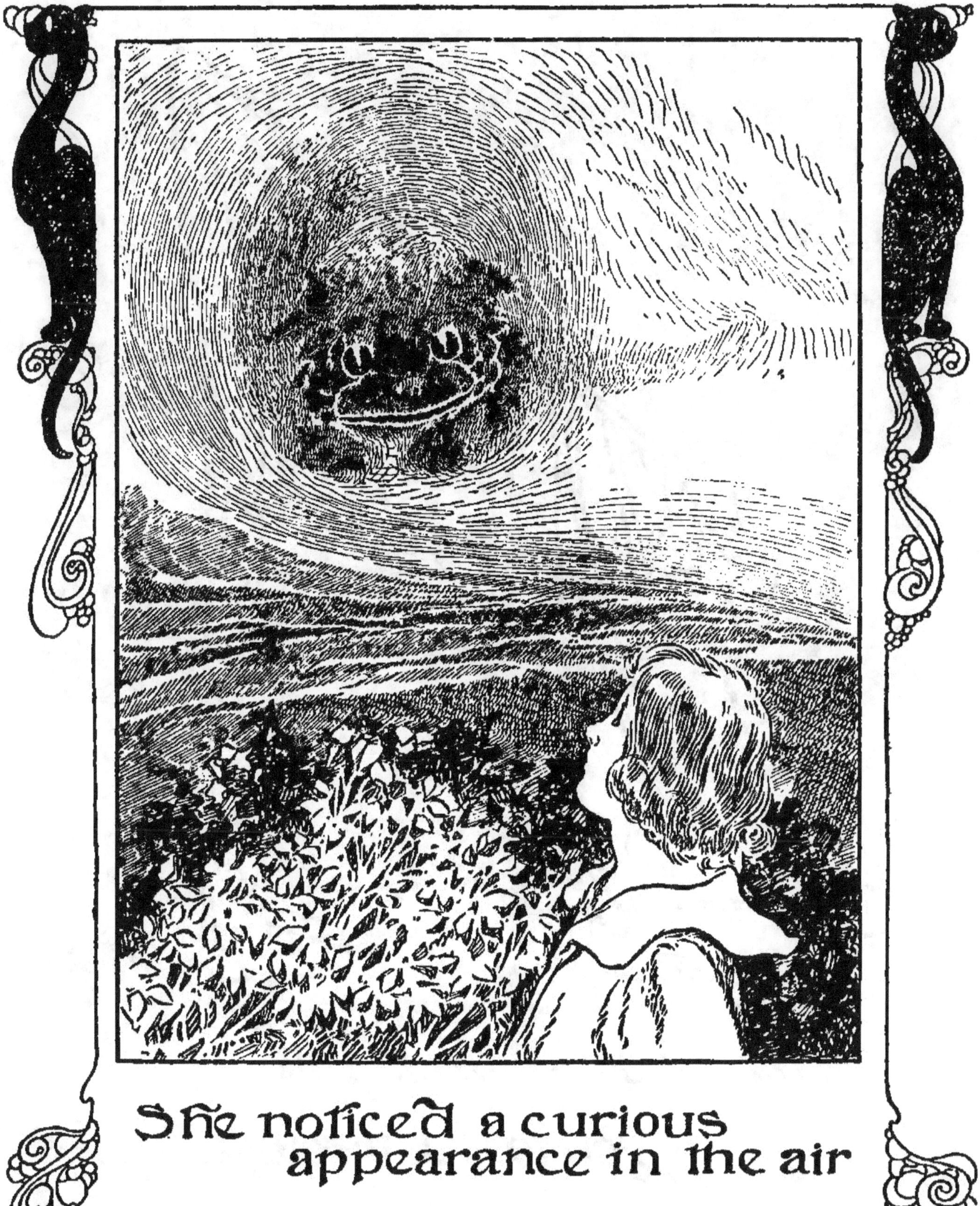

She noticed a curious
appearance in the air

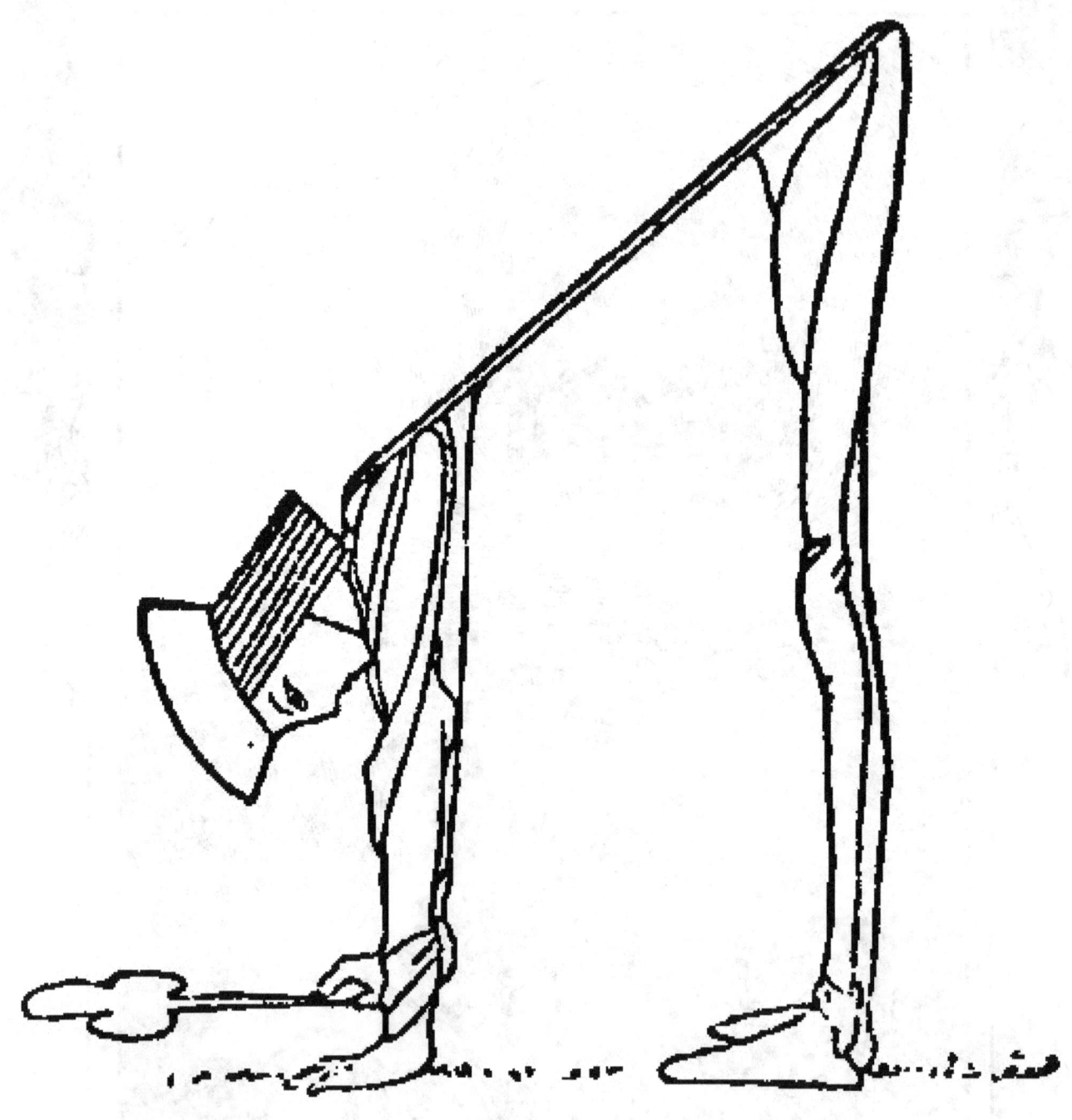

"There's the arch I've
got to go through."

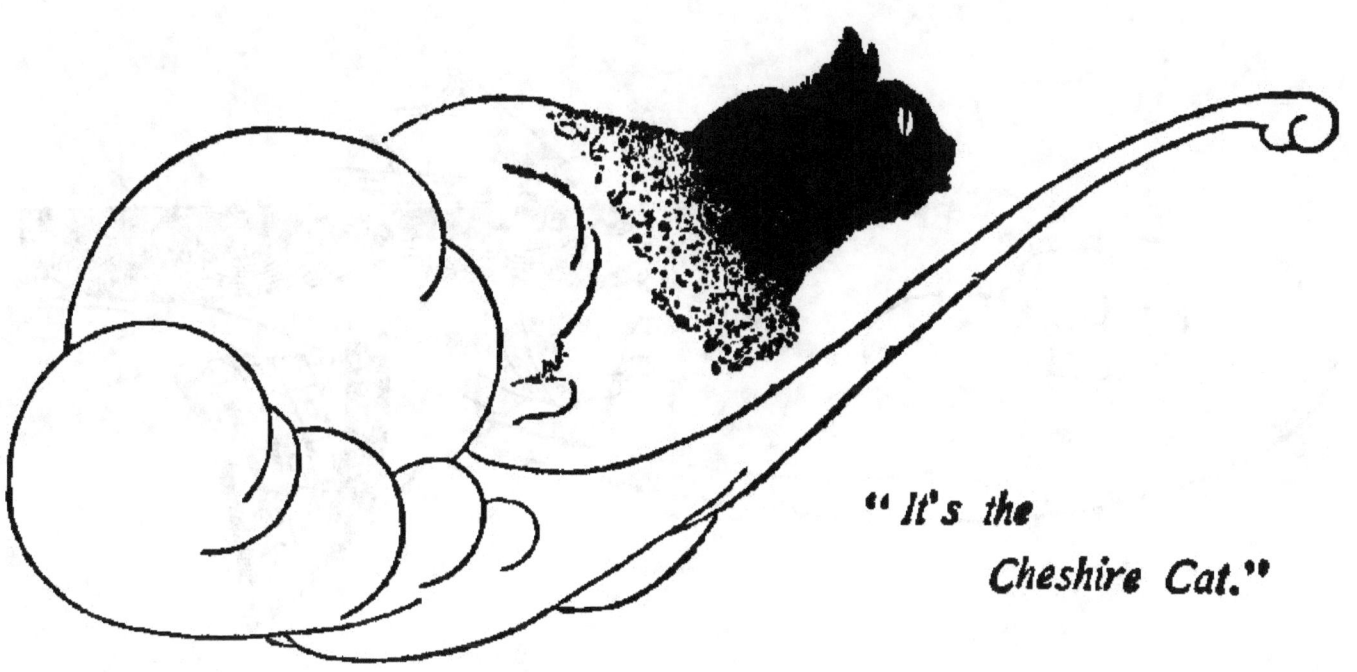

" It's the

Cheshire Cat."

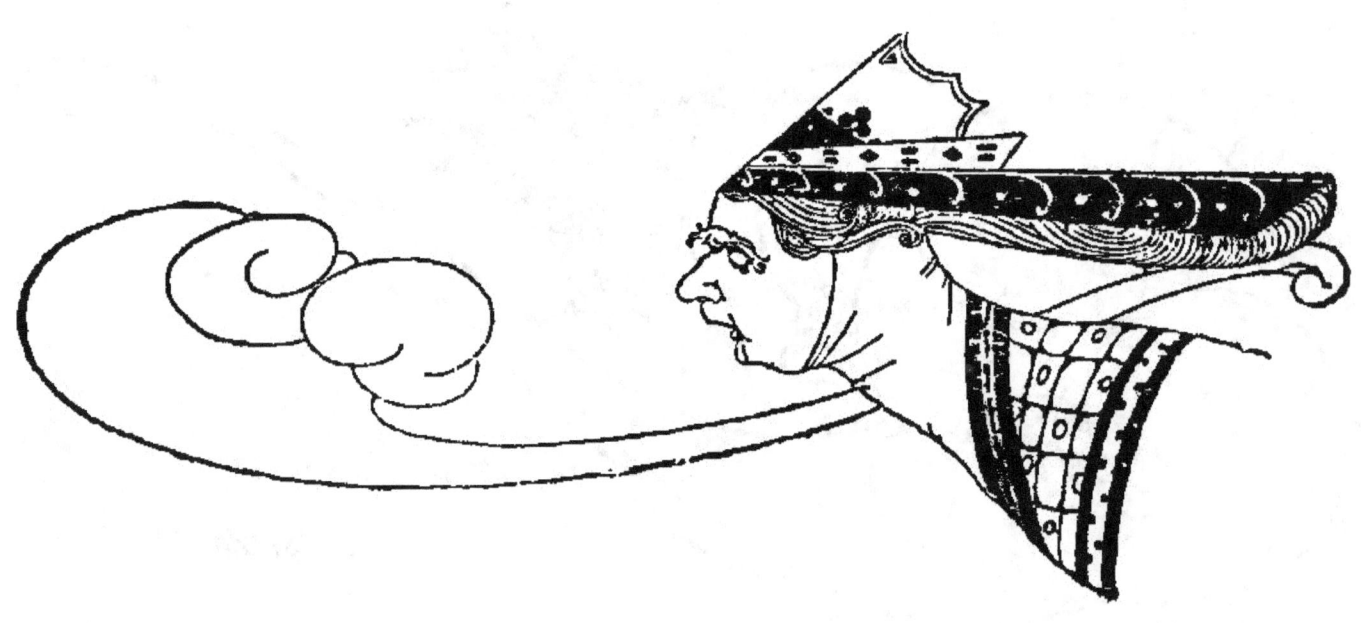

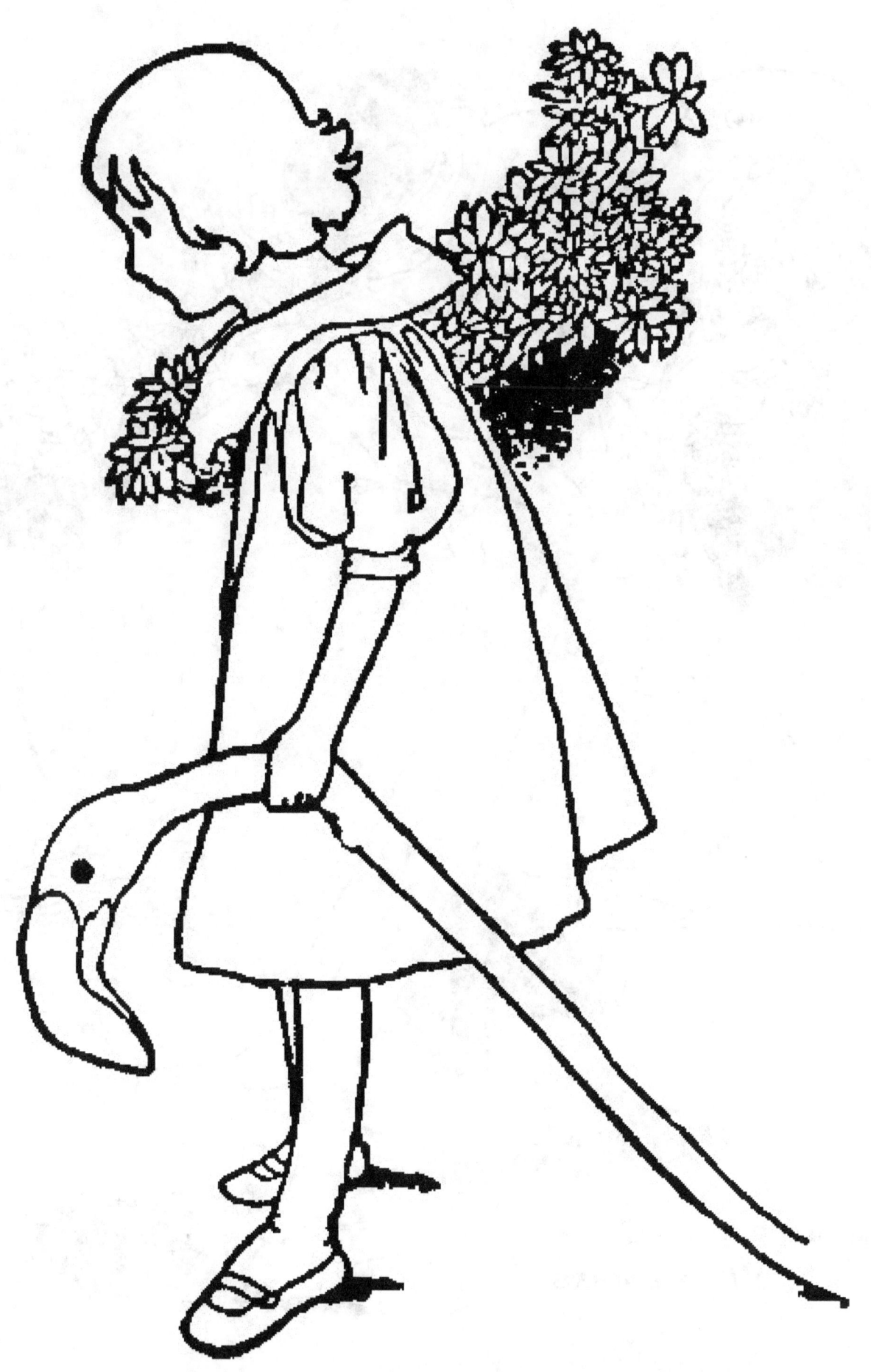

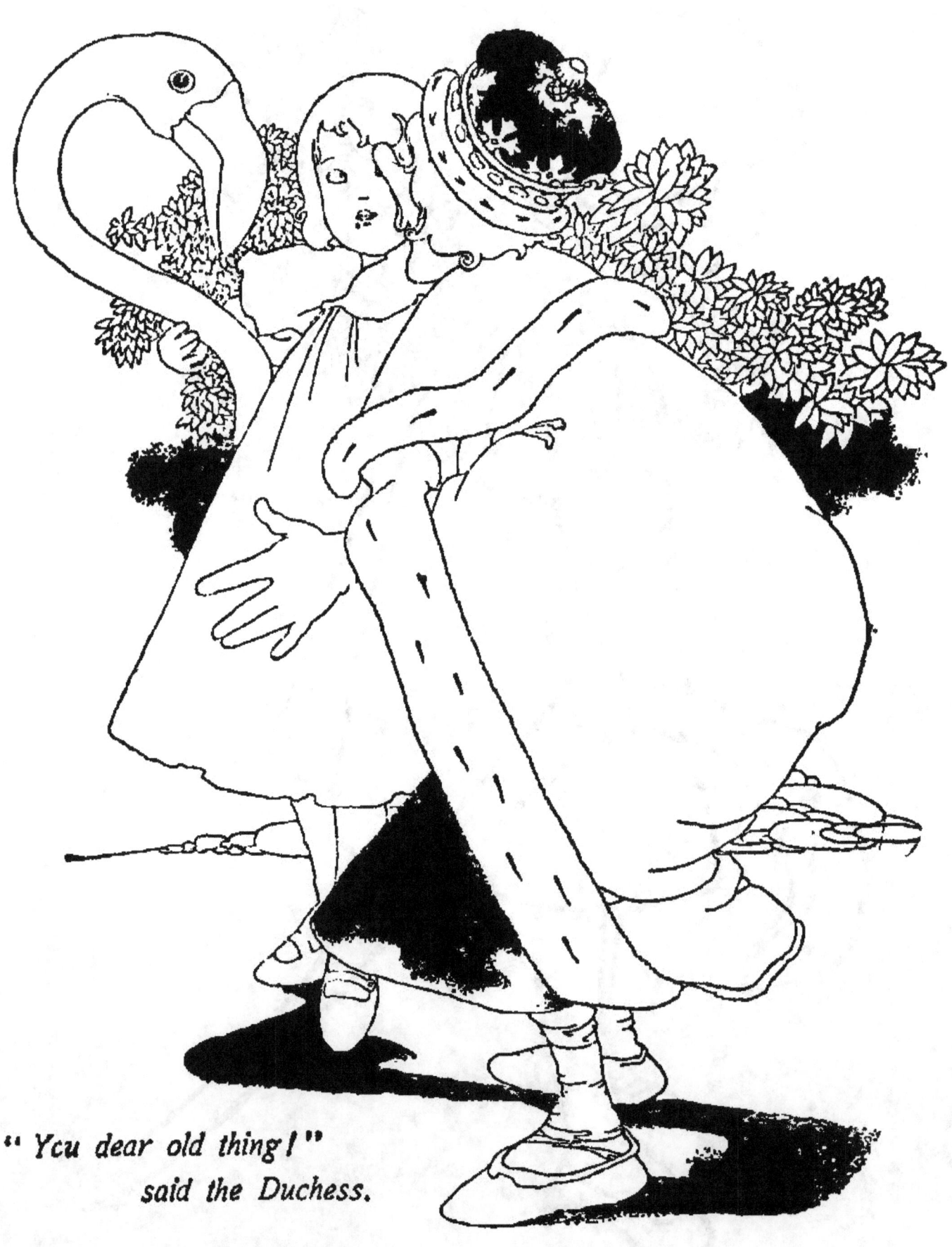

" You dear old thing!"
said the Duchess.

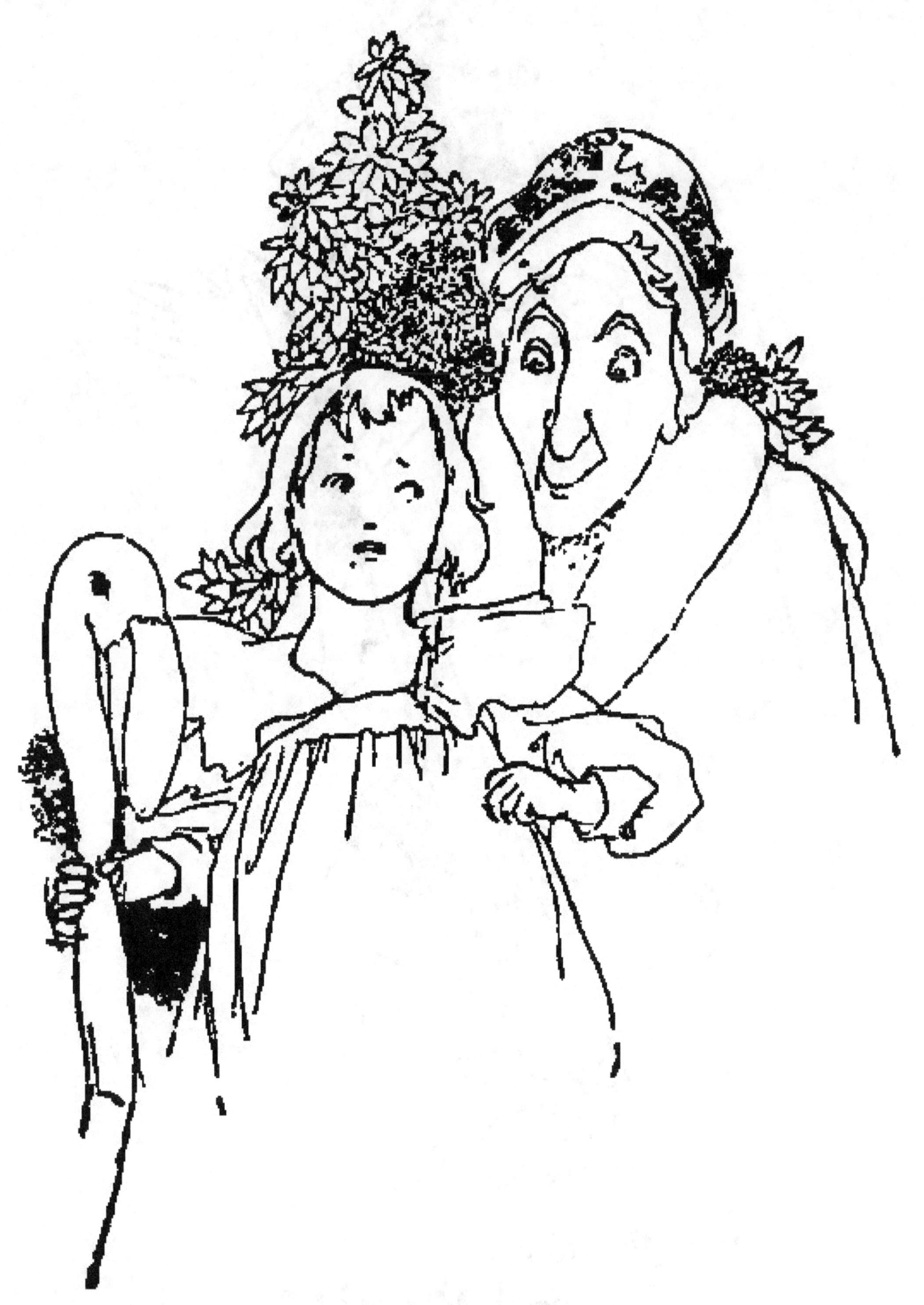

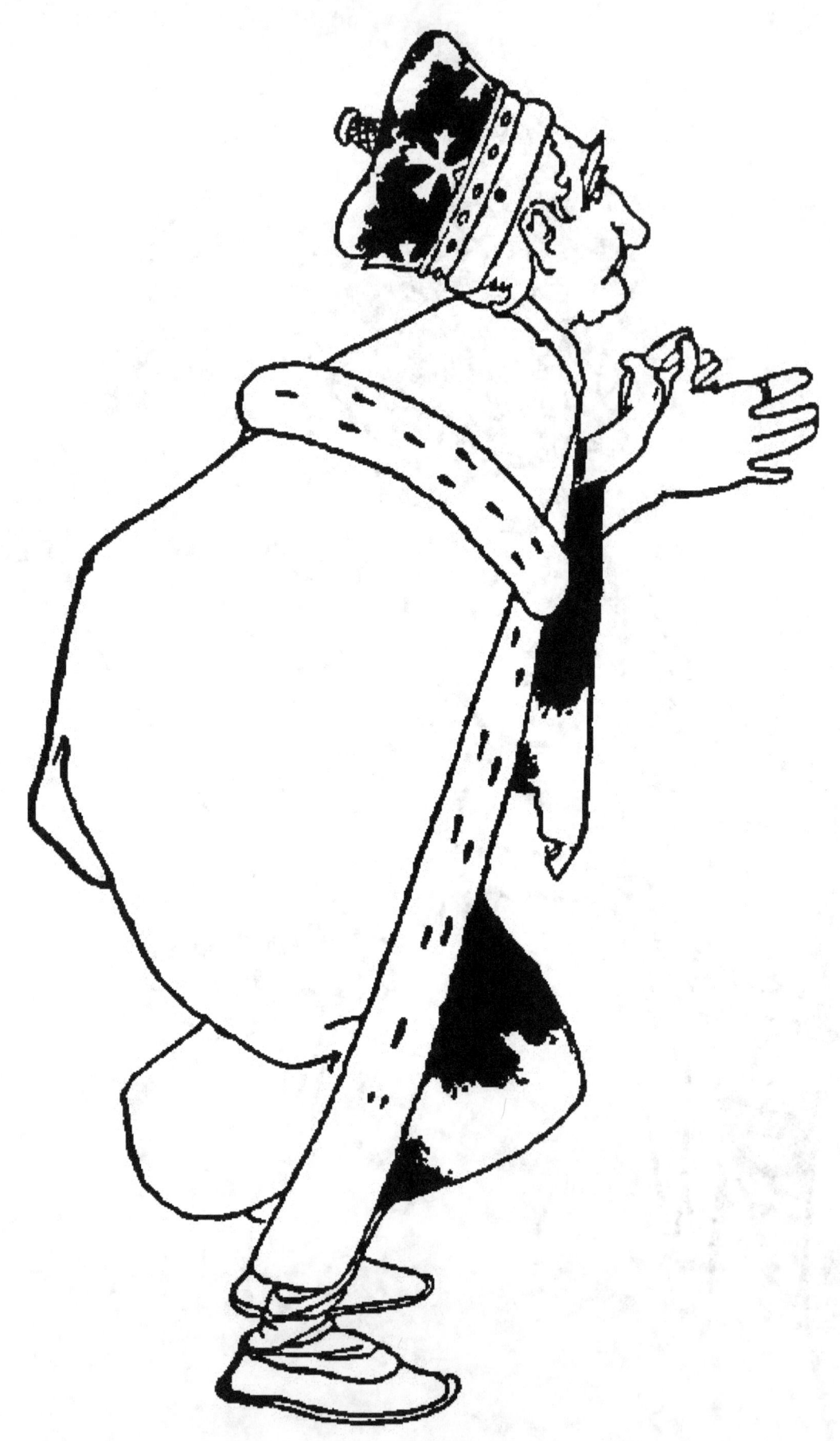

" A fine day,

your Majesty ! "

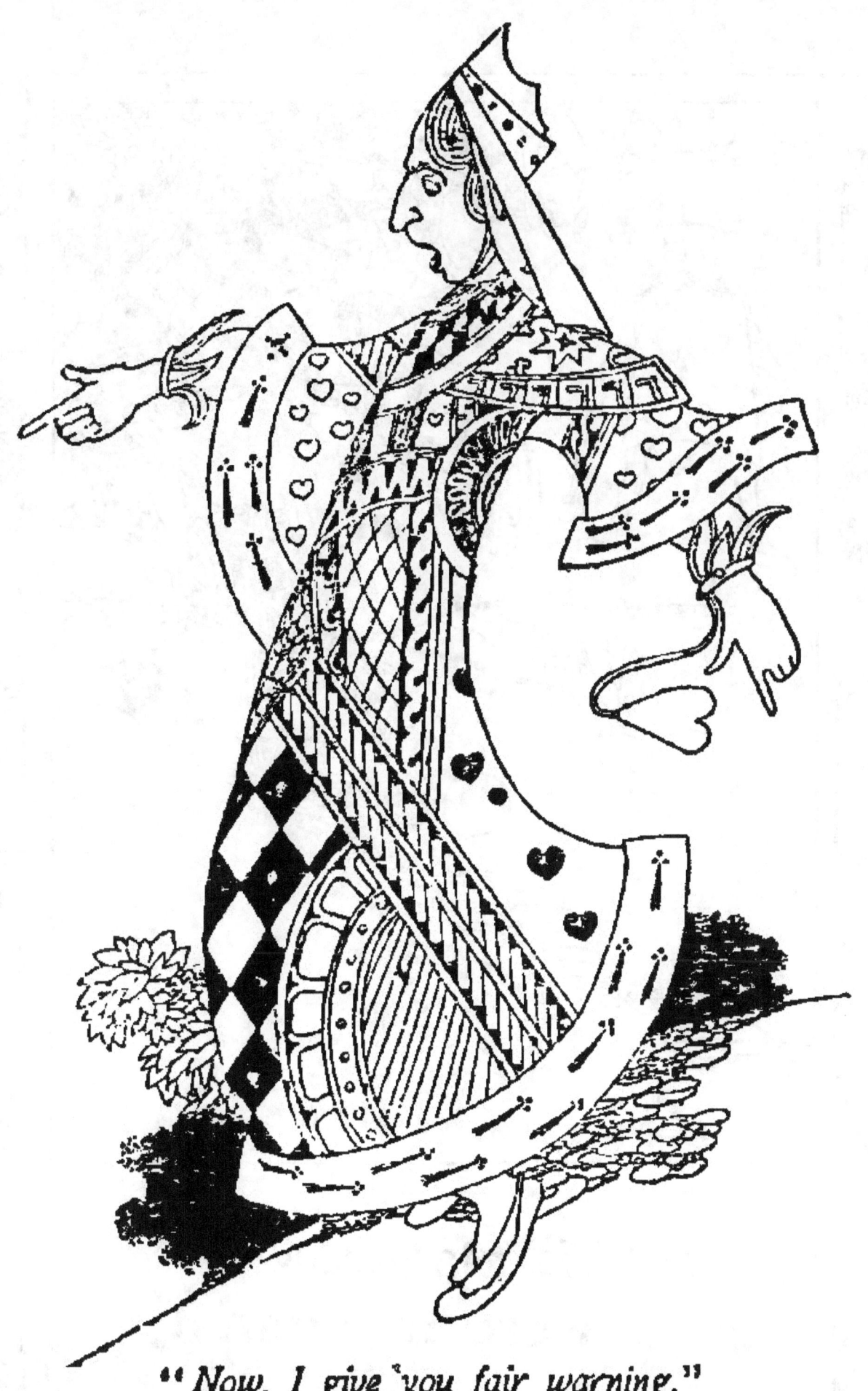

"*Now, I give you fair warning,*"
shouted the Queen.

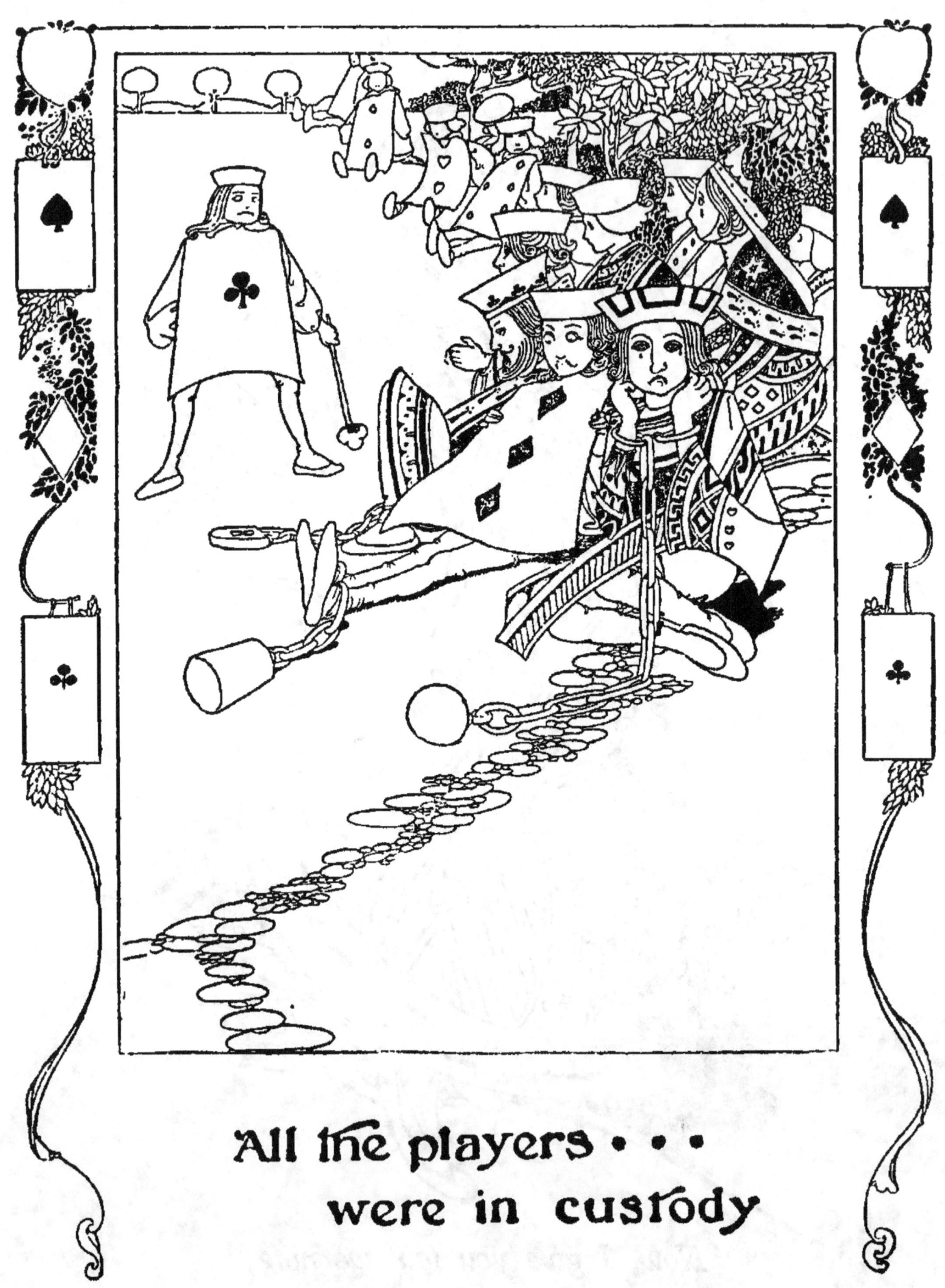

All the players . . .
were in custody

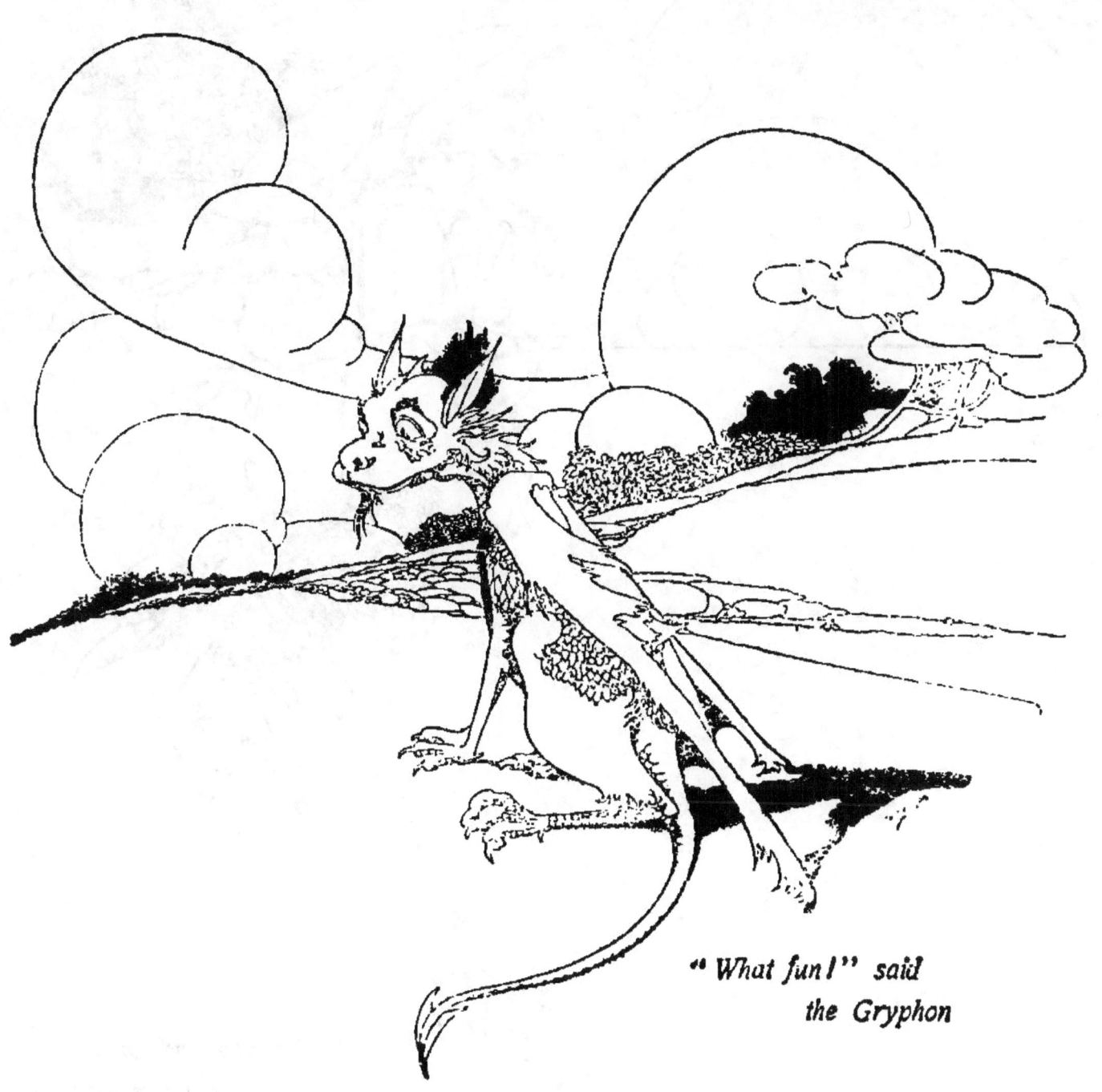

"What fun!" said
the Gryphon

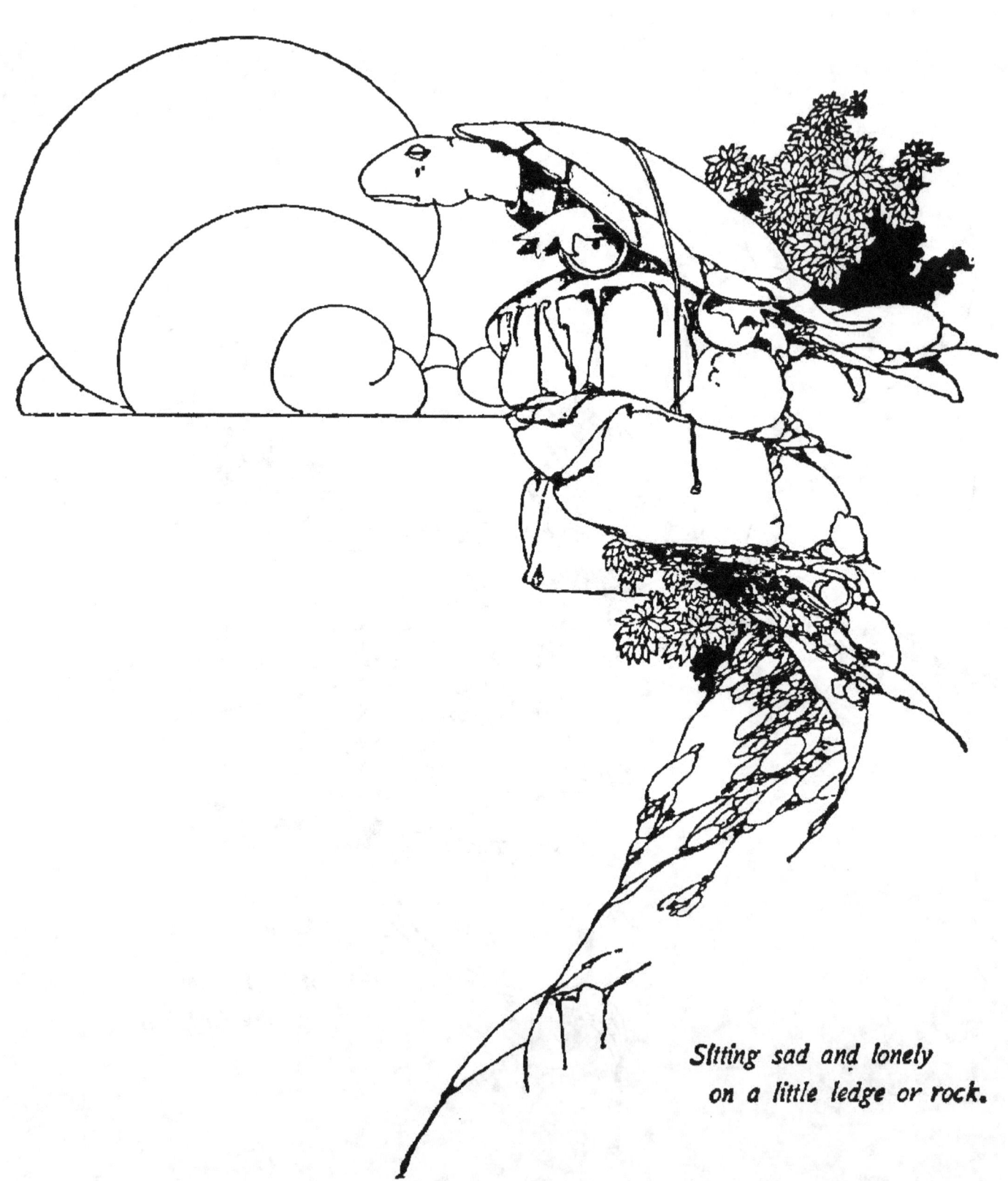

*Sitting sad and lonely
on a little ledge or rock.*

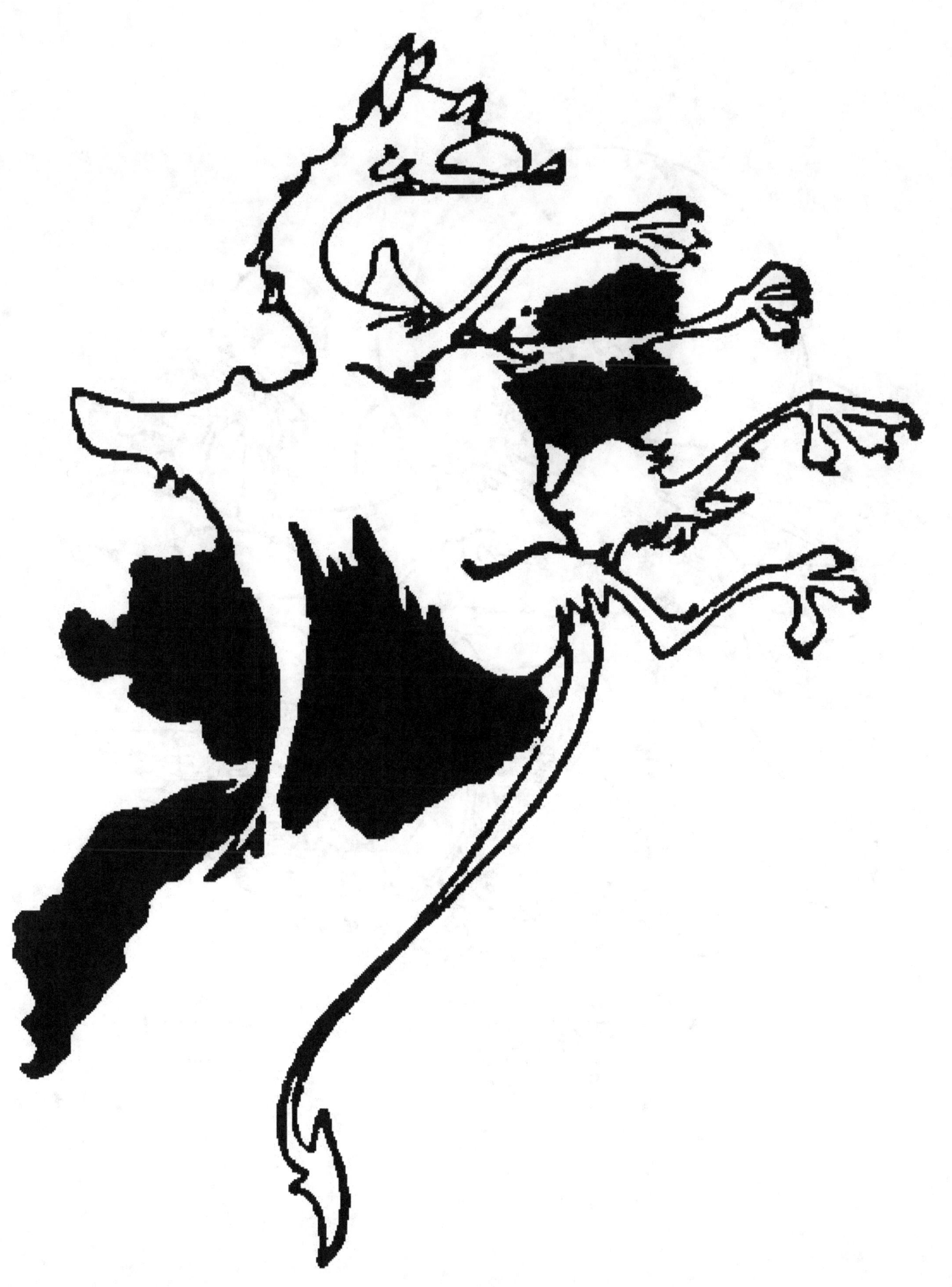

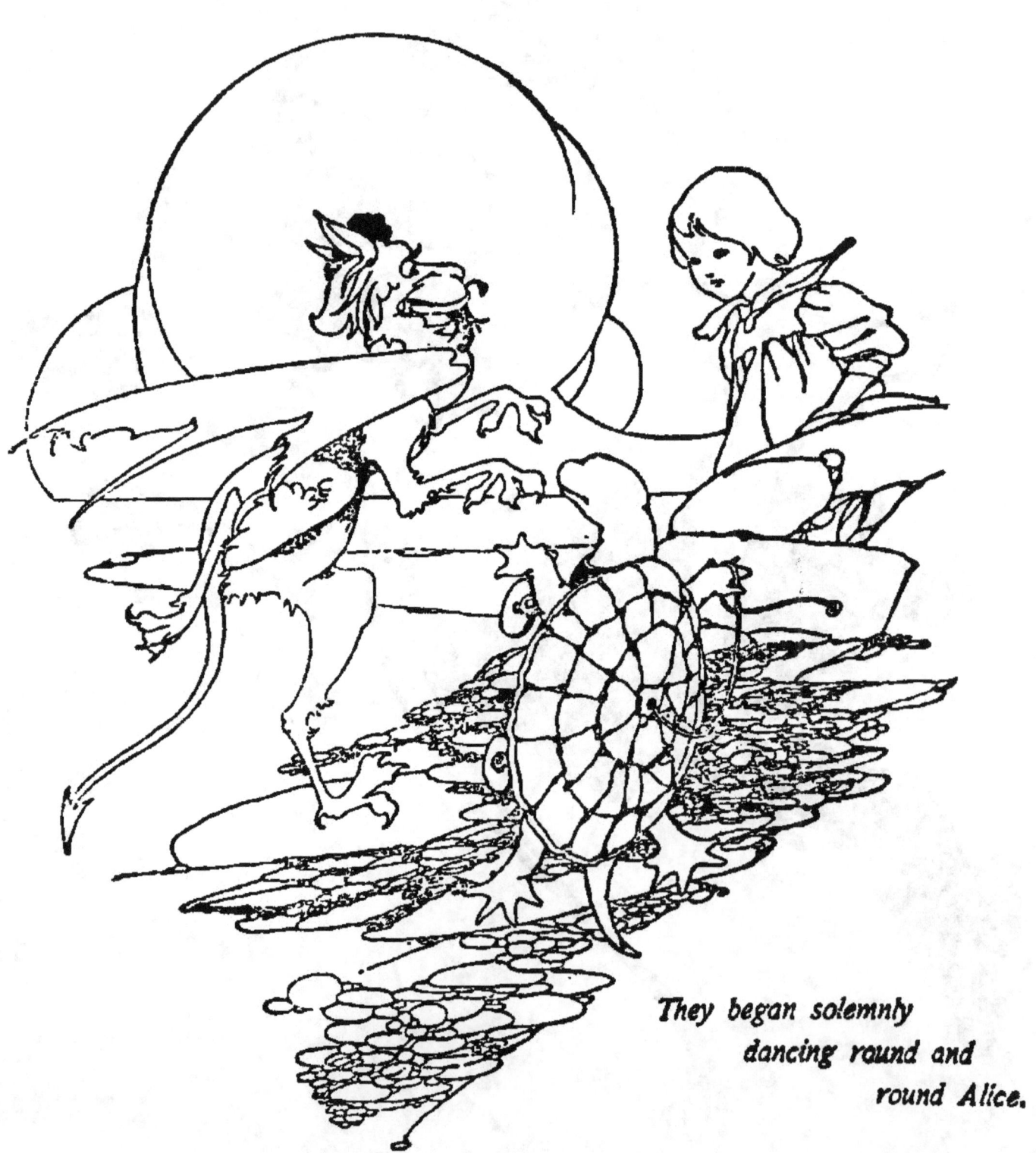

They began solemnly dancing round and round Alice.

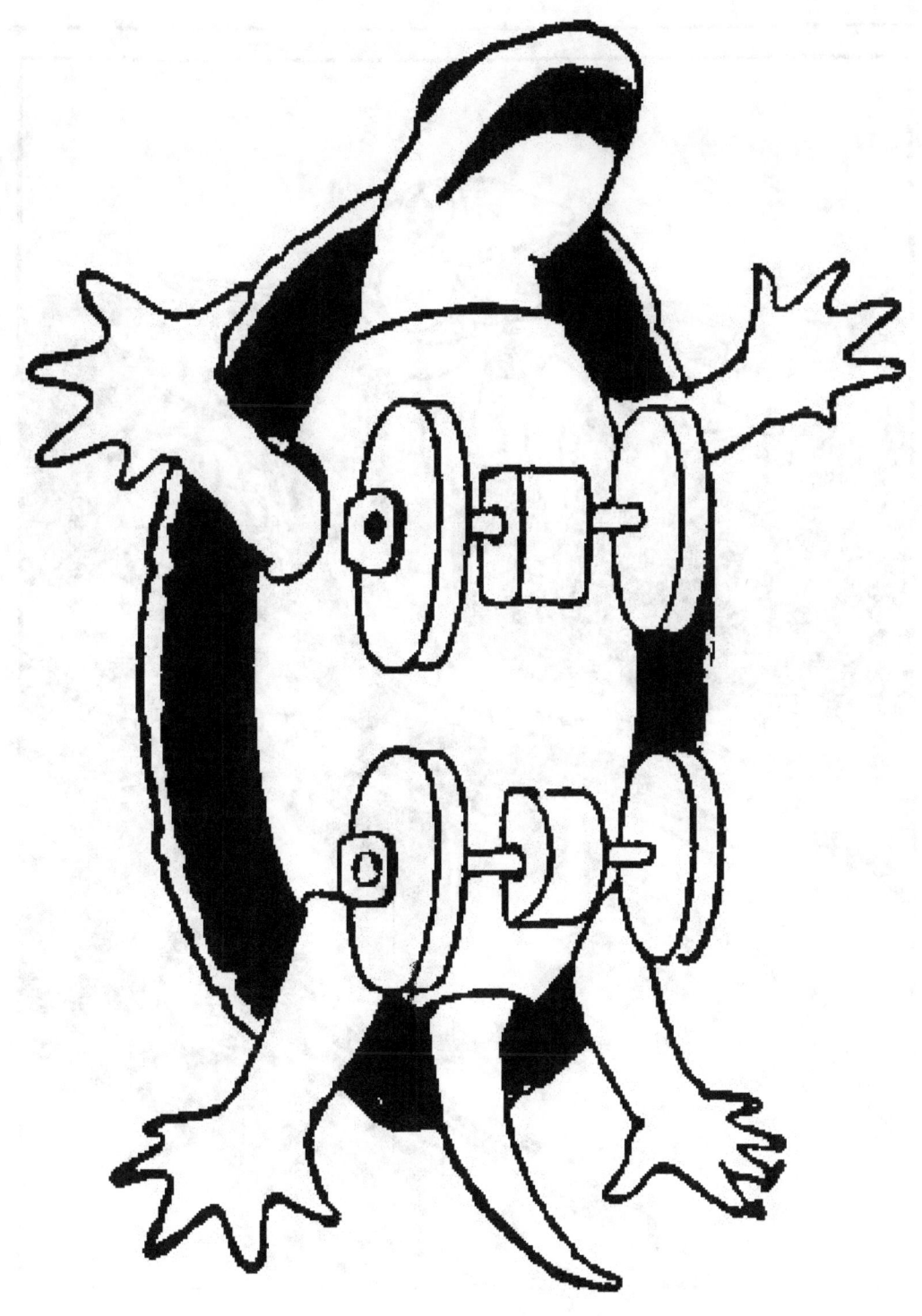

The Mock Turtle
sang . . . sadly.

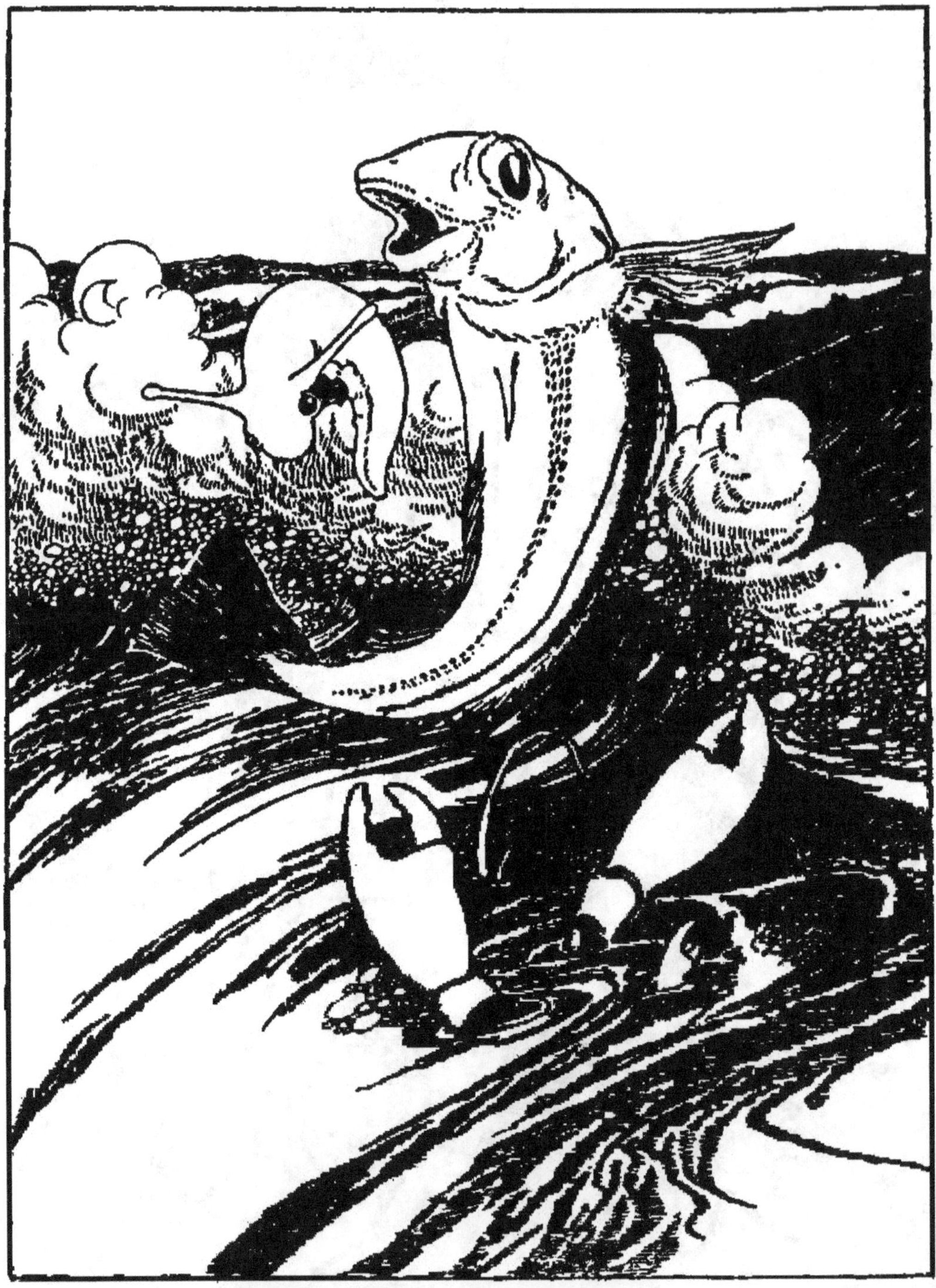

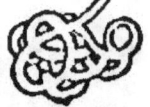

"When they take us up and throw us with the lobsters out to sea!"

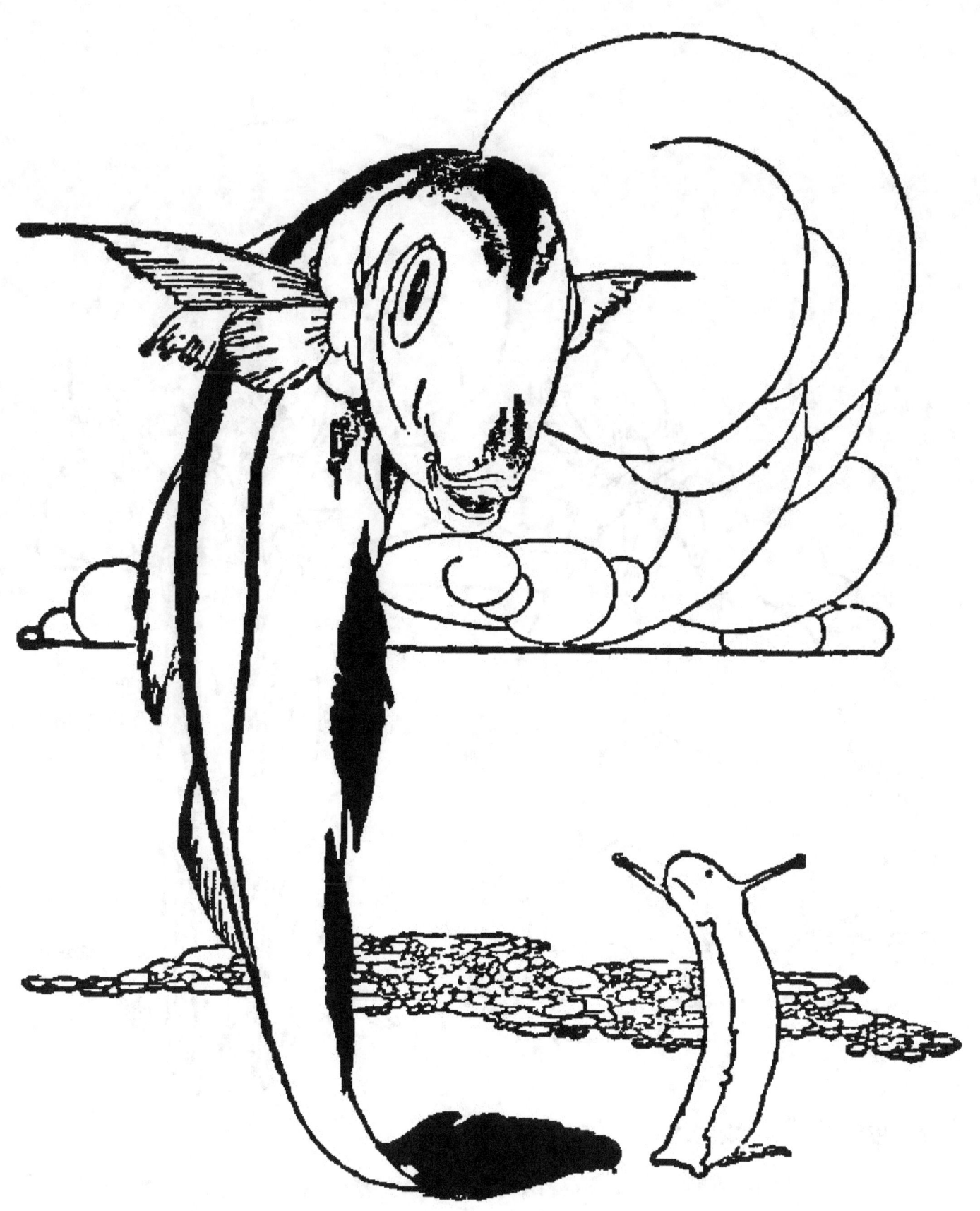

Said a whiting
    to a snail.

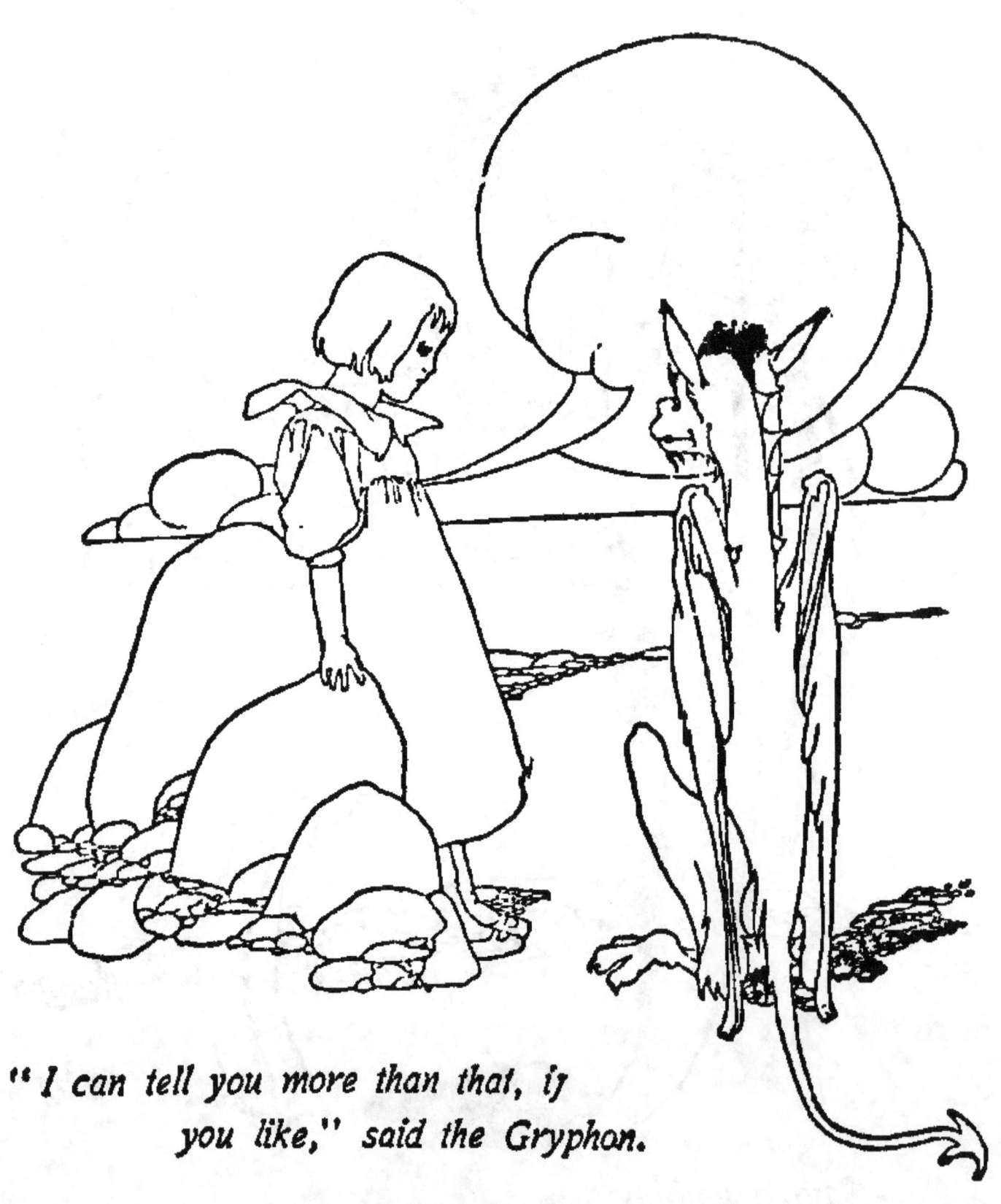

"I can tell you more than that, if you like," said the Gryphon.

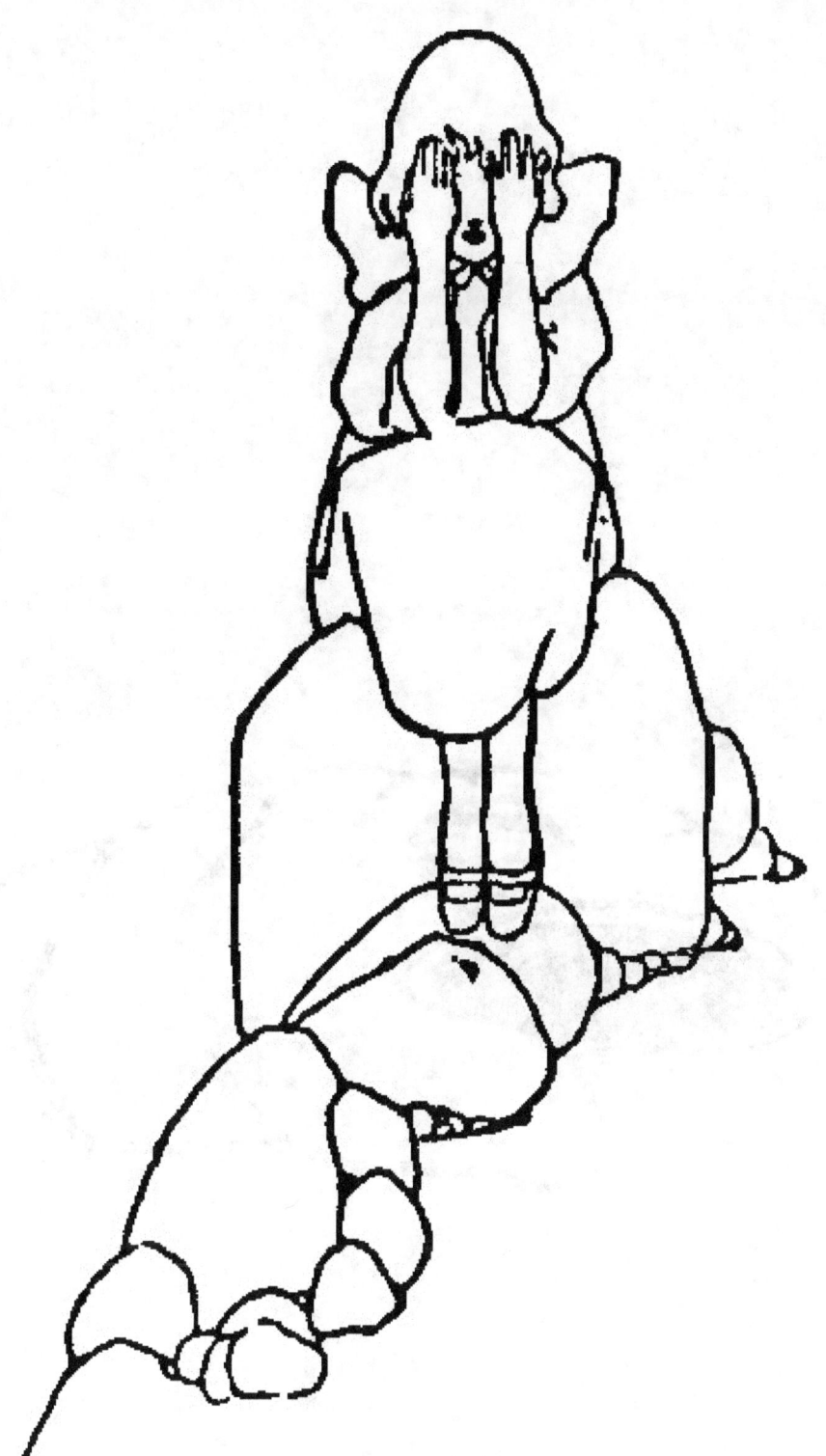

She had sat down with her face in her hands, wondering if anything would ever happen in a natural way again.

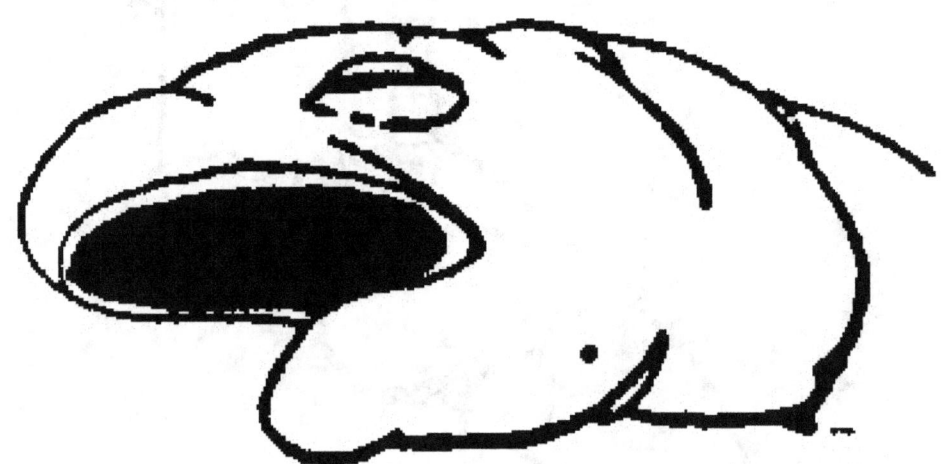

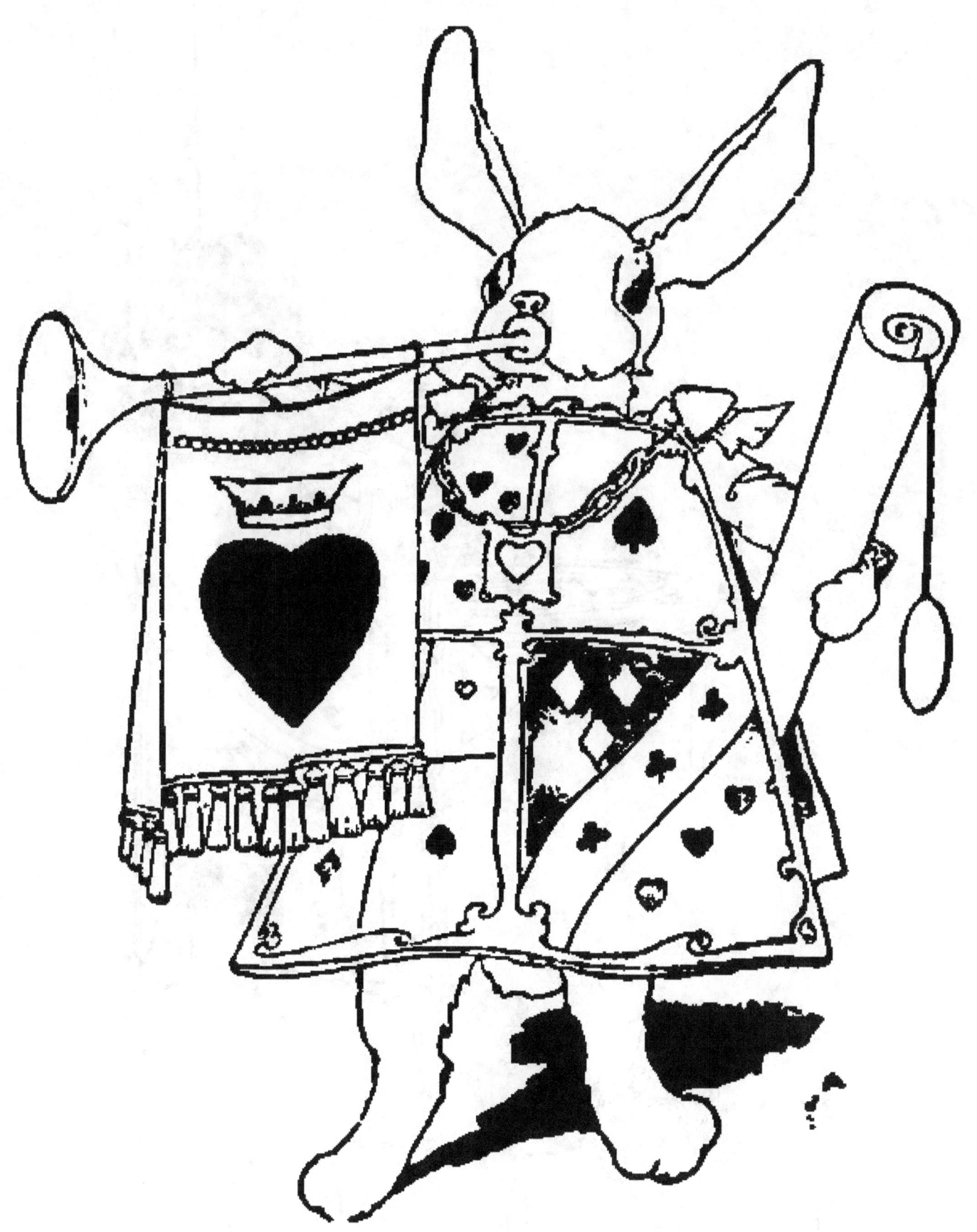

Near the King was the White Rabbit.

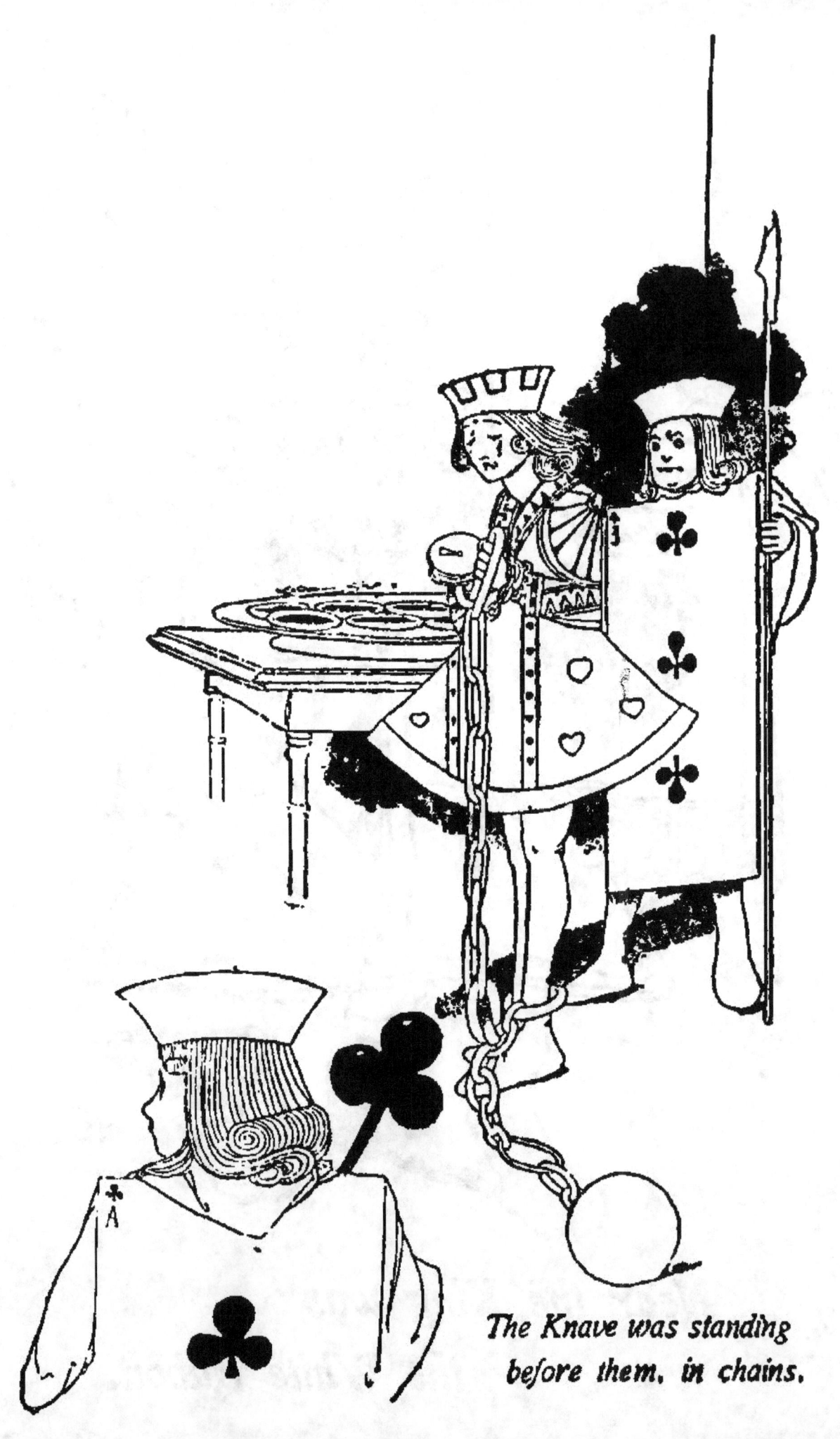

The Knave was standing before them, in chains.

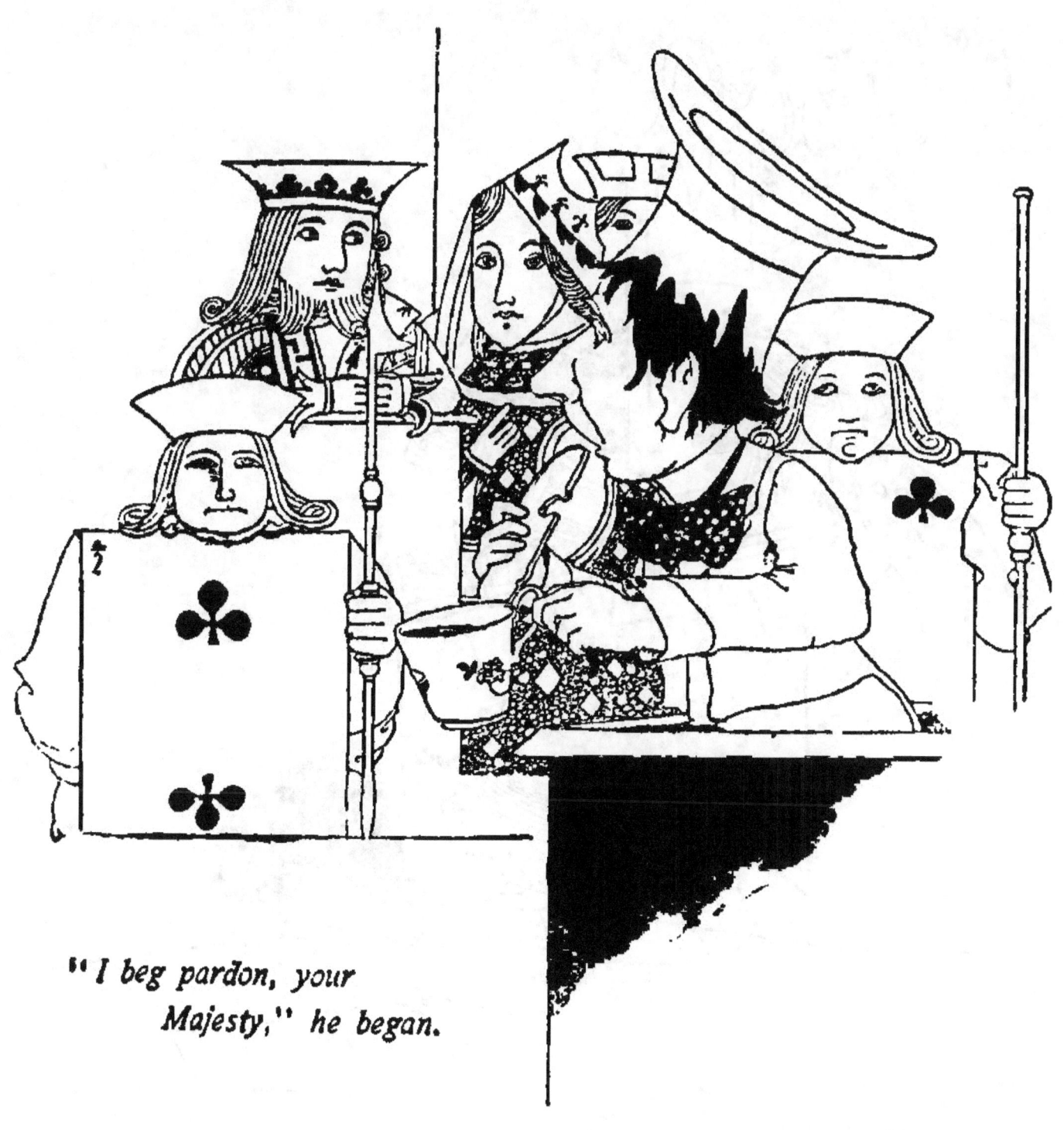

" *I beg pardon, your Majesty,*" *he began.*

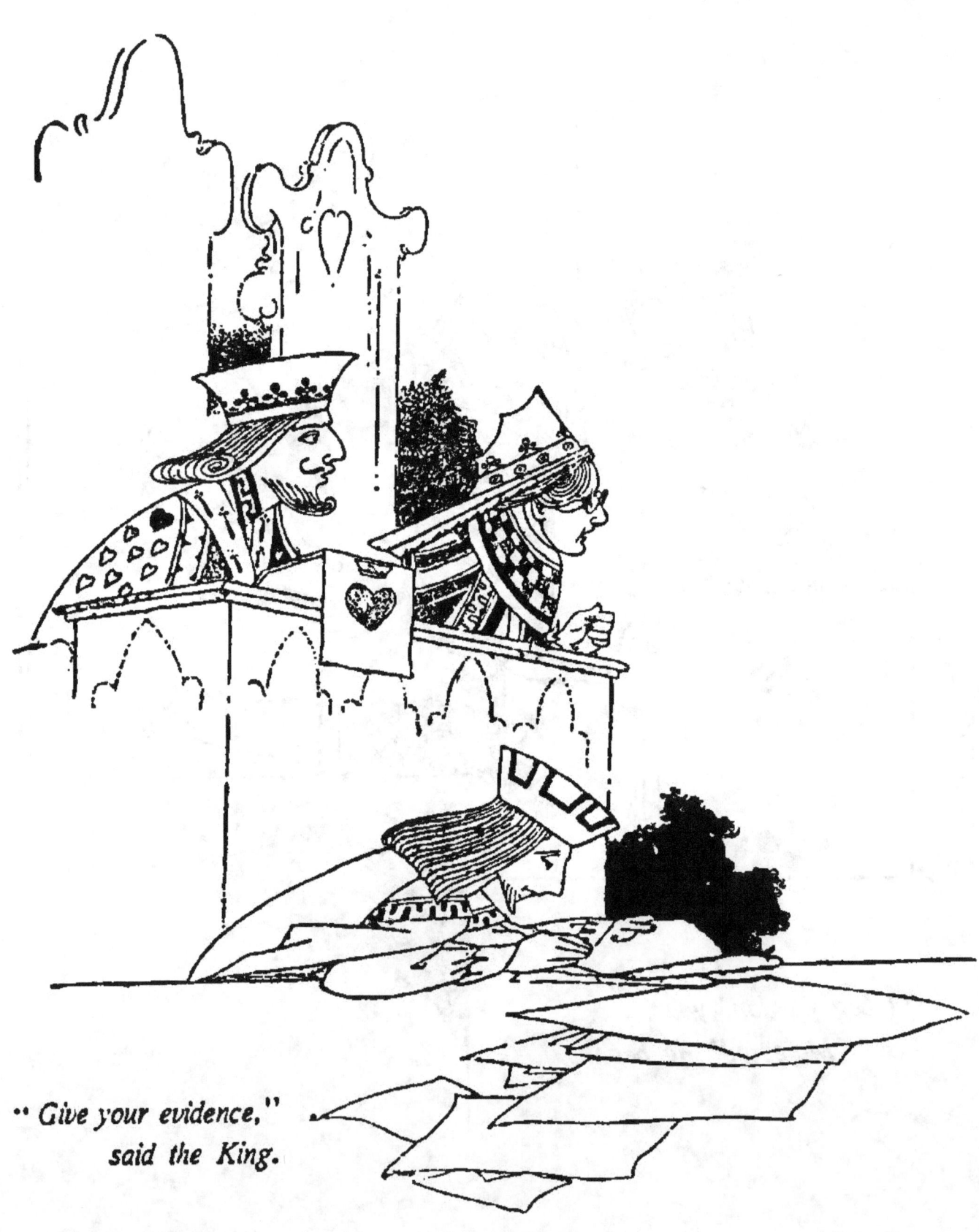

" *Give your evidence,*"
said *the King.*

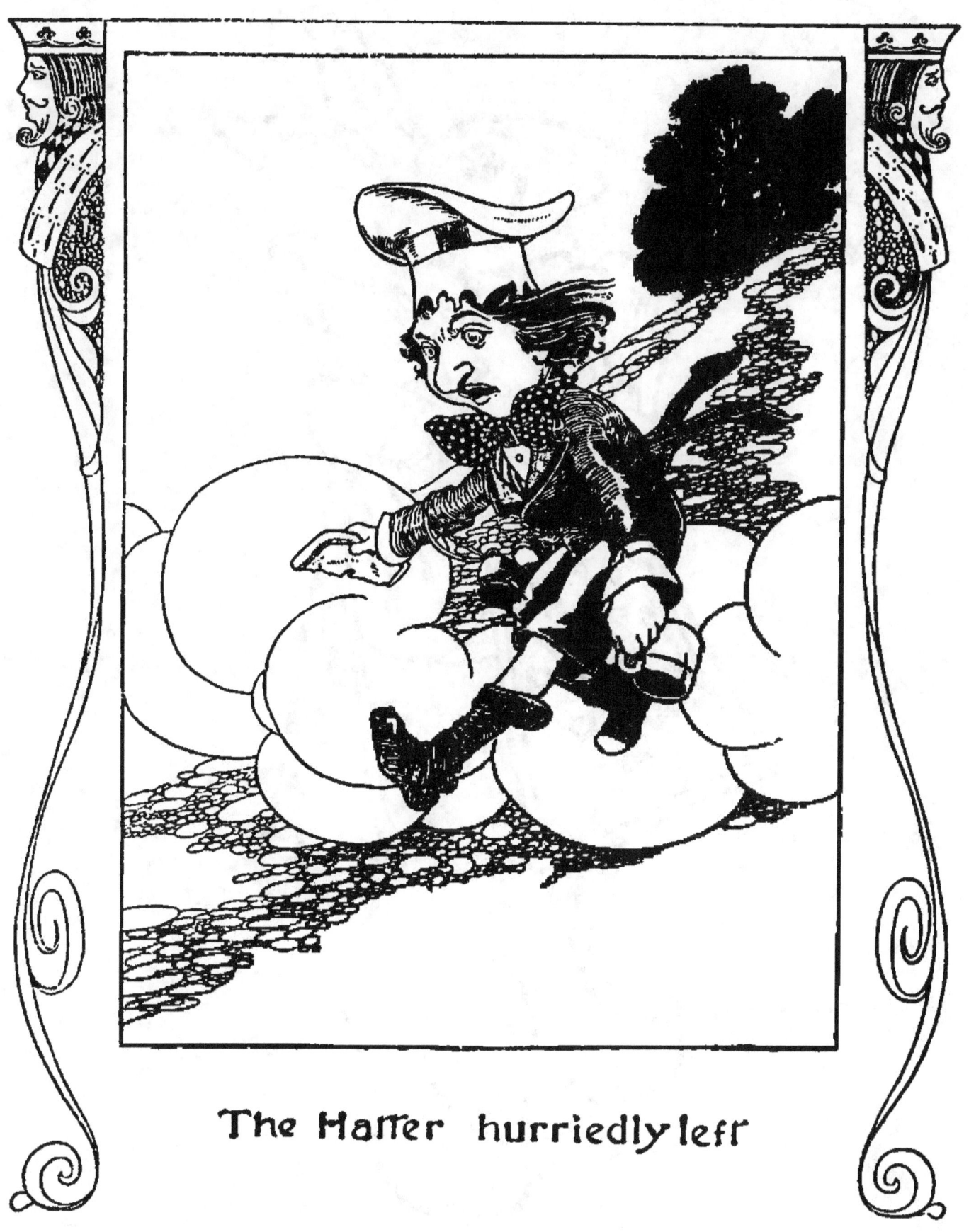

The Hatter hurriedly left

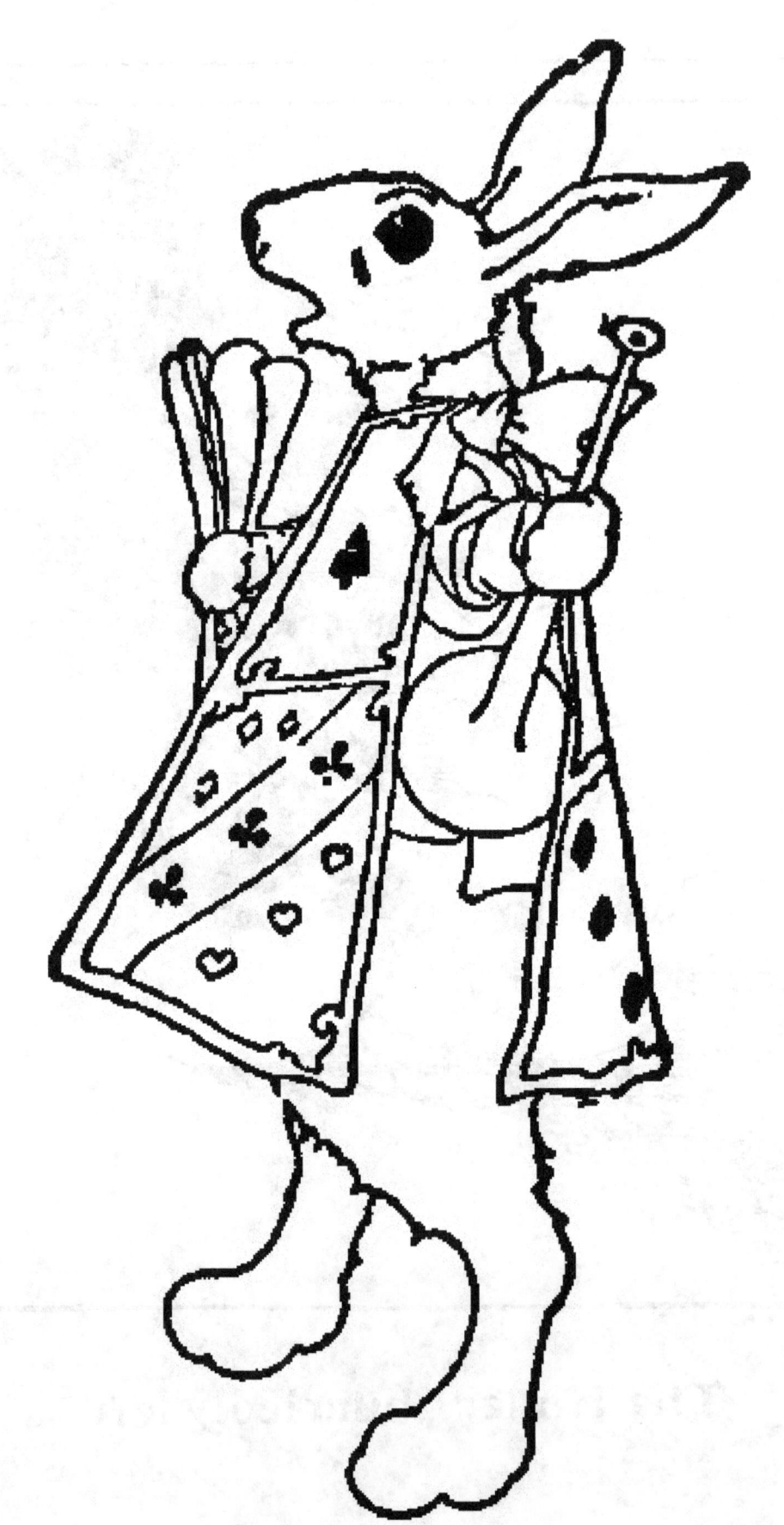

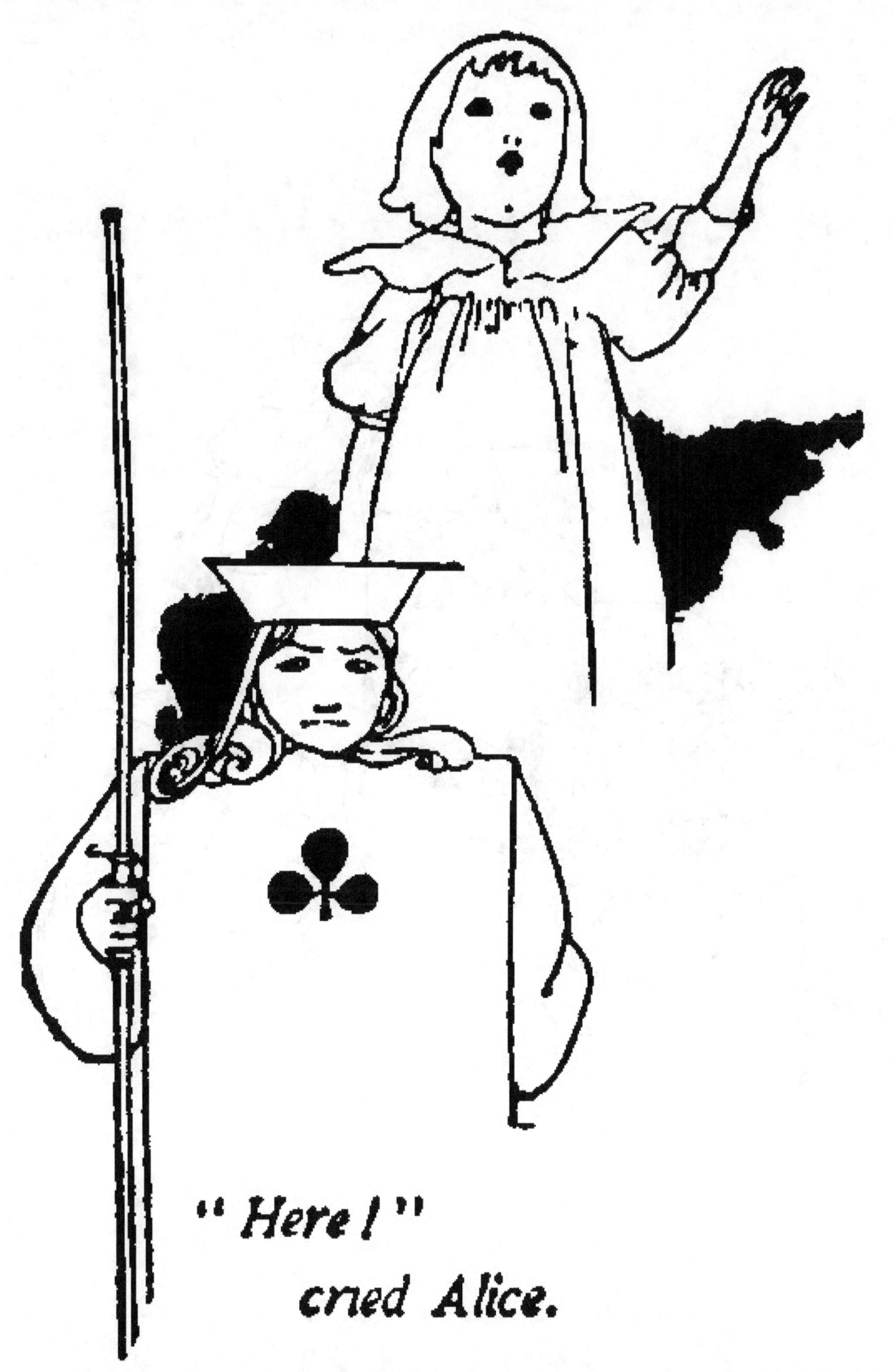

"Here!"
cried Alice.

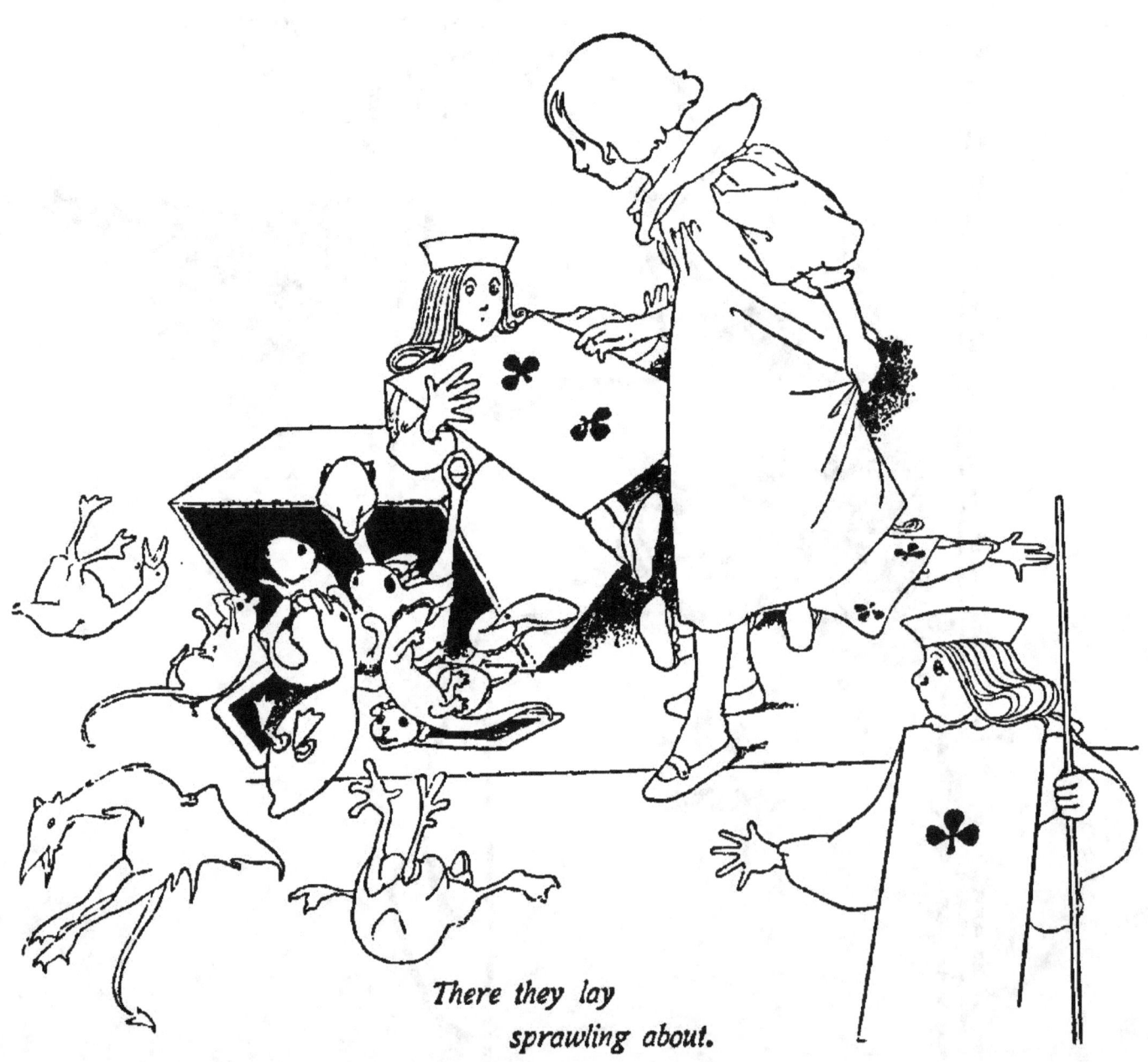

There they lay
sprawling about.

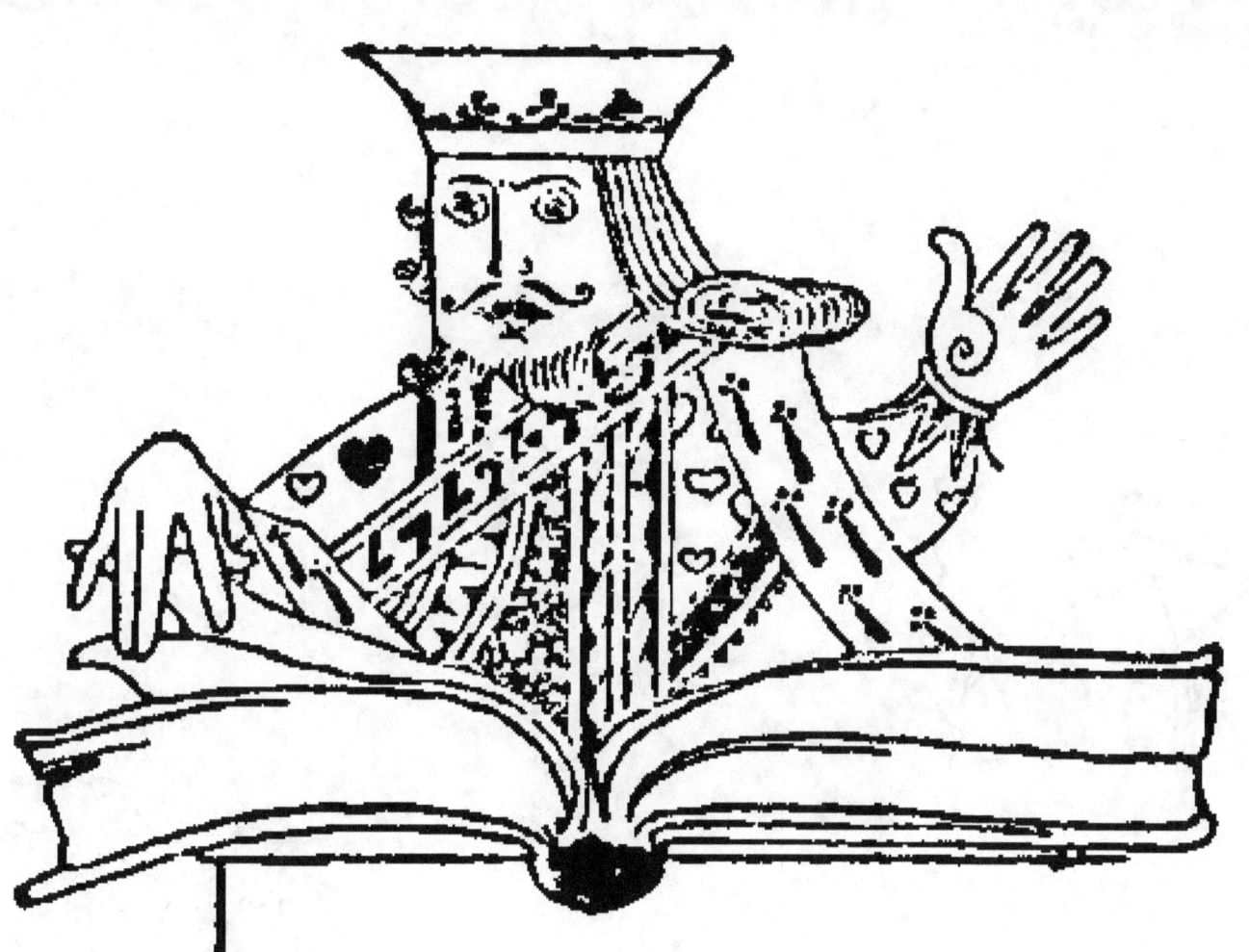

"Silence!" .. *"All persons more than a mile high to leave the court."*

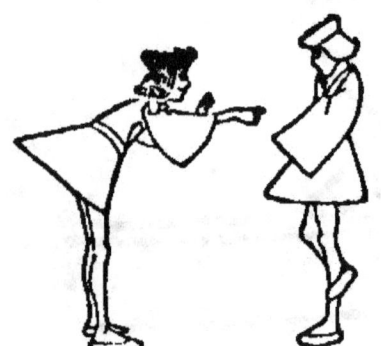

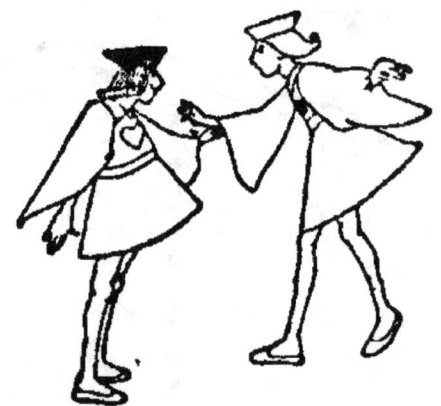

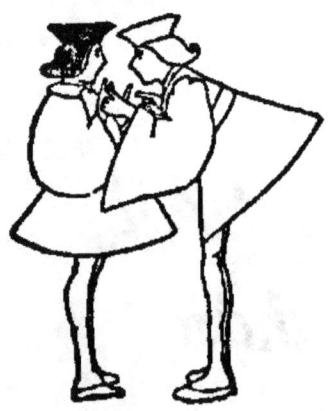

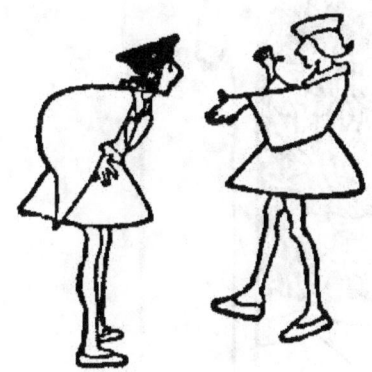

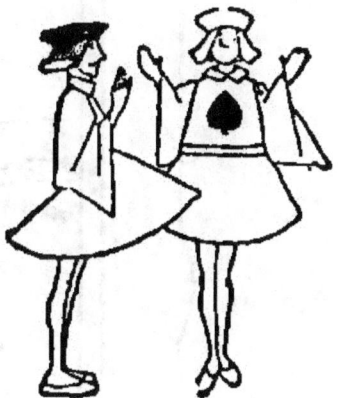

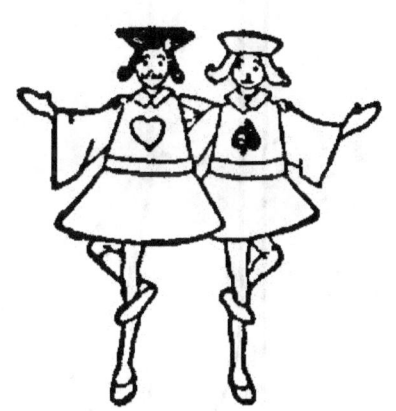

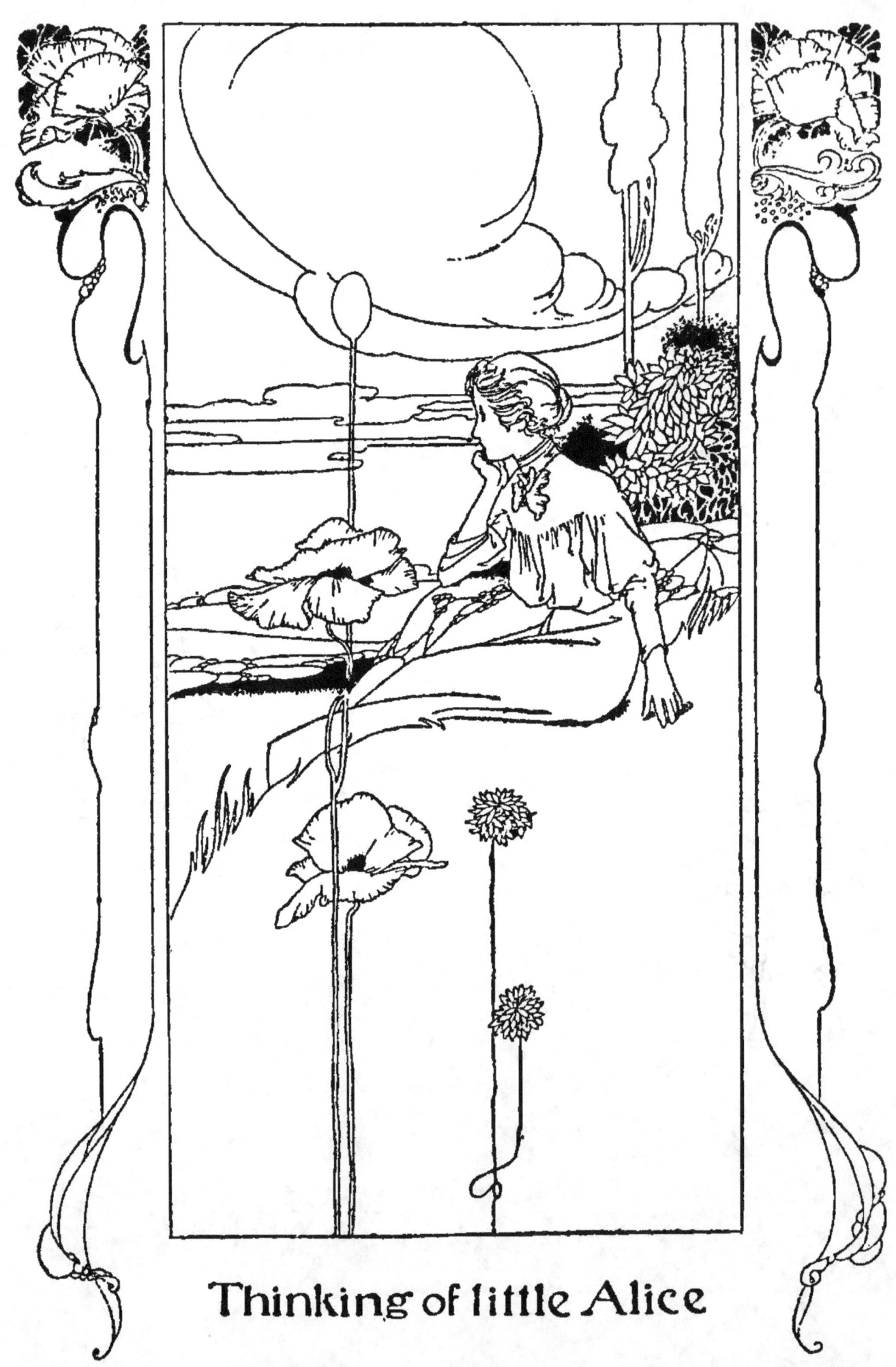

Thinking of little Alice

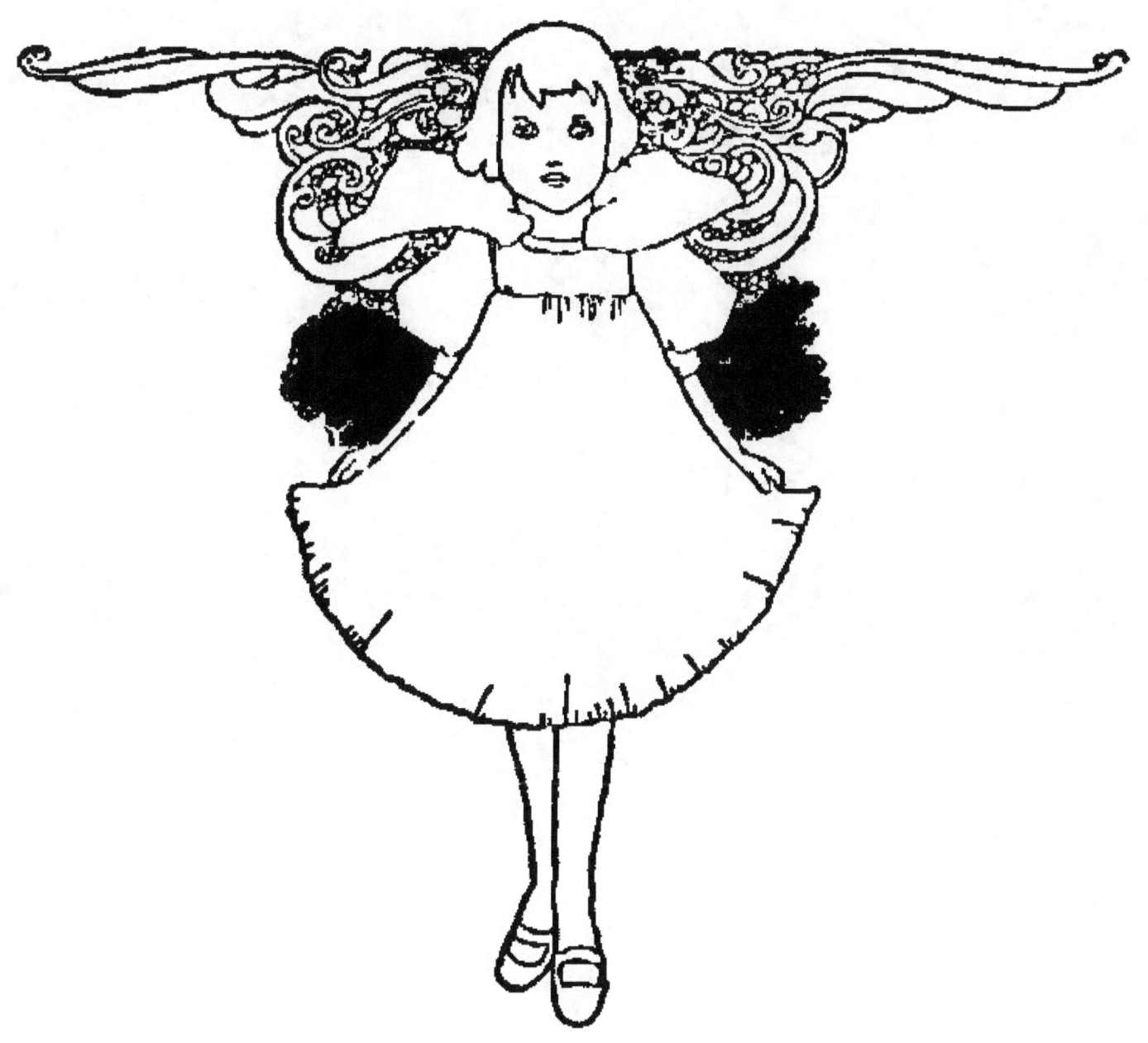